4UR Ranch

At Wagon Wheel Gap Hot Springs Resort

A History

SANDRA WAGNER

With contributions by Pete and Lindsey Leavell

THE History PRESS

Published by The History Press
Charleston, SC
www.historypress.com

First published 2020

Manufactured in the United States

ISBN 9781467144506

Library of Congress Control Number: 2020934337

Notice: The information in this book is true and complete to the best of our knowledge. It is offered without guarantee on the part of the authors or The History Press. The authors and The History Press disclaim all liability in connection with the use of this book.

CONTENTS

4UR RANCH

Evolution of owners and names of the 4UR

Henson, Godwin, Mead, Mullen	WWG Hot Springs Co. (Henson, et al	Wagon Wheel Gap Hot Springs Improvement Co. (Palmer, et al)	A.H. Jordan*	American Fluorspar Co. Collins, Hosselkus, et al	Ellwood Bergey	Arthur Sharp	Allan Phipps	Charles Leavell, Leavell Family
1872	1877	1881	1916	1918	1924	1943	1959	1972 to present

Liberty Hot Springs → Wagon Wheel Gap Hot Springs → Wagon Wheel Ranch, 4UR brand → 4UR Ranch at Wagon Wheel Gap →

*Mortgage that defaulted back to Palmer heirs

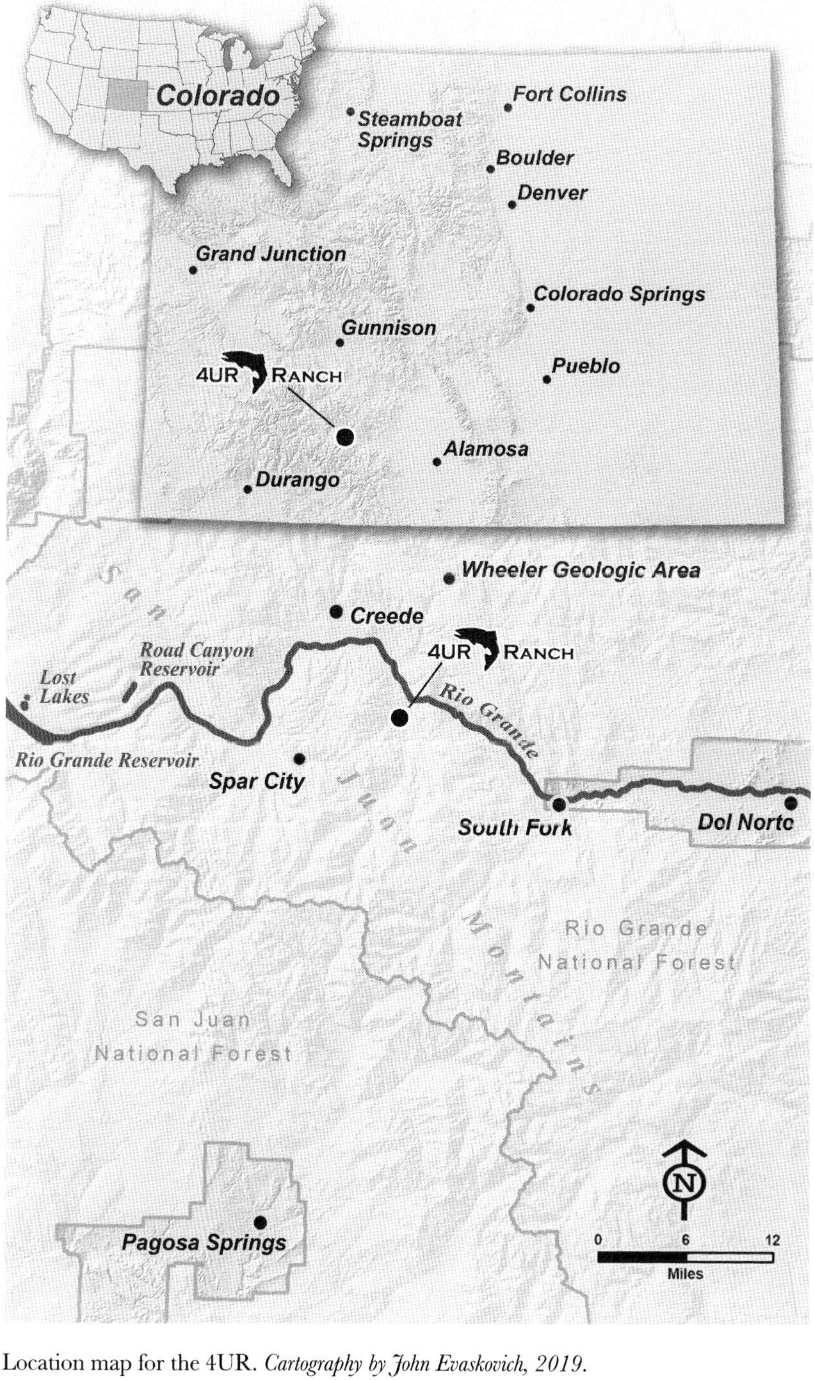

Location map for the 4UR. *Cartography by John Evaskovich, 2019.*

ACKNOWLEDGEMENTS

The person with the most significant input to the success of this book, a researcher and finder of all things obscure, is CJ Backus.

Frankie Colton, Alacrity House Publishing, provided wonderful editorial reviews and was instrumental in helping create a much more readable book.

Lesa Lanier, Jeff Lovett, Marty Jones, Janice Jacobs—alpha readers and disconnect finders.

Phoebe Waynick for her beta review.

John Evaskovich, cartographer extraordinaire.

Steve Baer for his contributions to the Lost Lakes discussion, and to Travis Smith for providing historic documents.

Robert Berguist for his technical input about the mill and donating his wonderful photographs—thank you!

Robert Kirkham for his contribution about the reclamation effort at the fluorspar mine, thanks.

Bill Dooley, Casey Adelman, Kenneth Wyley, Kim Wintz, Kate Myers, Howard Britain, Chad Cochran, Doug Davlin, Tom Wartman, Mary Mortimer Chapman, Ed Cook, William Getz, Graham Phipps and Tony Phipps all contributed interesting personal information for the book.

Ashley Bosa, who wrote the geology chapter for this book, is a recent graduate of Adams State University with a bachelor of science in geology and former student of Dr. Robert Benson. On her way to a doctoral program in geology, Ashley clearly has an amazing future ahead of her.

Acknowledgements

The Adams State University Library staff, especially Mary Walsh, Karen Melgares and Ronnie Medina; Jan Jacobs, Bob Seago and Allie Quiller of the Creede Historical Society; Grant Houston, *Silver World Newspaper* editor; Denver Public Library digital photo archive librarian Coi Drummond-Gehrig; History Colorado staff; the county clerk/recorder at Mineral, Erin Wintz; Rio Grande, Cindy Hill; and Hinsdale, Joan Roberts, provided input and support for the book.

There are numerous others who shared information, made suggestions or provided encouragement—thank you all.

PROLOGUE

The Goose Creek valley is a place of great beauty producing an almost spiritual effect on those who love it. When one faces south from the main 4UR compound, the mountains are gentle and emerge like two arms in a welcome embrace. Goose Creek comes out of the center, or the heart, and flows through the ranch property, joining the Rio Grande seven miles away. To the north lie massive volcanic cliffs. They appear unyielding, strong and protective. Under the ranch compound itself are two artesian hot springs that rise to the surface from deep in the earth.

Stewardship of this land is a privilege for our entire family. As of the writing of this book, we are in our third generation and fifth decade of ownership. During that time, we have all come to understand this ranch is far more than a guest resort but rather a place where history has been made by those who came before us and will live on in those who follow.

According to a Colorado historian, it is unusual for ranches to have the many layers of history found in this valley. It began with the explosion of a super volcano twenty-eight million years ago that created the La Garita Caldera. The valley has been home to Native Americans, followed by trappers, miners, health seekers and tourists answering the call to come west. The more we have learned about this, the more we have developed a relationship with that history.

On the east side of the property is an old fluorspar mine and mill that were begun in 1914. There are abandoned shacks and discarded equipment, some as large as automobiles, that were hauled up steep slopes to construct an aerial tramway for transporting ore from the upper reaches of the mine down to the mill. At the summit of this mine hill, the view to the north reaches past Wagon Wheel Gap, up the historic Rio Grande toward its headwaters. There are deep pits in the hills where men have dug into the earth looking for fluorspar, silver or gold.

In the fluorspar mill itself there is evidence of the miners and mill workers who, on the day the mill closed in 1950, hung up their overalls and walked away, never to return. Jackets are still hanging on hooks and gloves still lying on benches after almost seventy years. The giant pulleys, wheels, engines and boilers are all still in place and waiting for what comes next.

On the west side of the valley are ruins of the cabins of early homesteaders. There is the Elliott family cabin abandoned in 1919, then farther up the mountain, Swede's cabin, named for a logger from Sweden who built a structure halfway up the mountain at the turn of the twentieth century.

All these layers of history lend a powerful magnetism to the valley. It is something that can be felt as well as learned, and it is a history that needed to be recorded before it was lost.

We are grateful to Sandra Wagner for taking on this important work. We learned of her talents when we read her first book, *The Hidden History of the Upper Rio Grande*. We knew then that the three of us were linked together in the early history of this area and that she would be the perfect author for this book. We have so enjoyed our relationship with Sandra and are great admirers of her extraordinary talents. We have learned more than we could have originally imagined, and we're so pleased to share this history with you.

When reading this book, or visiting this valley, we hope you, too, will experience the magic and wonder of it all.

Pete Leavell
July 2019

1

4UR AND WAGON WHEEL GAP GEOLOGY

by Ashley Bosa

Eighteen major ash-flow tuff sheets were deposited and perhaps as many related calderas developed during emplacement of an underlying shallow batholith [large mass of intrusive igneous rock] *in late Oligocene* [about thirty-four to twenty-three million years ago] *time.*

—Calderas of the San Juan Volcanic Field, Southwestern Colorado, *by Thomas A. Steven and Peter W. Lipman, Geological Survey Professional paper 958, United States Geological Survey, 1976*

INTRODUCTION

Look down, and right underneath is evidence of one of the world's largest calderas and biggest volcanic explosions in geologic history. Echoing beneath one's toes is a geologic story of violent volcanic events, incredible outpourings of lava and layer upon layer of volcanic ash flows. Now look up, and all around, and admire the geologically beautiful and historically complex nature of one of the most unique places on Earth—the San Juan Mountains (SJM). These majestic towers of rock display nearly two billion years of Colorado's geologic story, from Precambrian to Cenozoic representations. Many people have traveled far and wide to seek solitude, inspiration, natural resources and scientific understanding in Colorado's purple mountain majesties to discover their abundant wealth. The San Juans are no exception, offering an epic story of fire, water, ice, wind and tectonic plates smashing into each other—all of which is preserved within the ancient rocks around the 4UR Ranch.

Remnants of the uplift of the Ancestral Rocky Mountains—which began about three hundred million years ago,[1] can be better seen in the Sangre de Cristo Range on the eastern side of the San Luis Valley. These rocks represent a time when the supercontinent Pangea was forming. The collision of the Gondwana and Laurasia landmasses that formed Pangea are responsible for the formation of the Appalachian Mountains in the eastern United States; however, the effects also translated through the North American Plate, causing the Ancestral Rocky Mountains to rise in what is now central and southwestern Colorado and parts of Utah.[2] Over time, much of the evidence of this mountain range has eroded, although some evidence can be found in select areas of southwestern Colorado.

Another uplift took place during the Cretaceous period, subsequent to the formation and erosion of the ancient Rockies. During this time, Colorado was underneath a vast inland seaway, which retreated as the present-day Rocky Mountains rose up between about eighty to thirty-six million years ago.[3] Volcanic activity in the area probably began between forty million years and thirty-five million years ago, when composite-type volcanoes started exploding, ejecting large volumes of hot ash, gas and likely some spectacular displays of lava fountains. Then came the calderas.

WHAT IS A CALDERA?

A caldera is a type of volcano that has formed when the surface has collapsed in on itself (sometimes called a depression) after the magma chamber below the surface has emptied. This generally happens during a cataclysmic volcanic eruption, where hundreds of cubic miles of ash, magma and volcanic rock are spewed from the vent, and the weight of the overlying surface is too much for the chamber to support. This type of event is hard to imagine in Colorado today, but is exactly what happened between thirty and twenty-five million years ago in the eastern San Juan Mountains.[4]

Apart from being a spectacular display of volcanism and terror, calderas also serve some economic purposes. They commonly host hydrothermal systems, which can form valuable minerals (silver, gold, copper, fluorite and

Figure 1: Location of San Juan Volcanic complex in southwestern Colorado. *Modified from Steven and Lipman,* Calderas of the San Juan Volcanic *Field, Southwestern Colorado.*

so on). The fracturing and faulting occurring from the caldera collapse act as conduits for the hydrothermal fluids to rise and deposit precious metals. The past volcanic activity and the presence of groundwater underlying much of the area throughout Mineral County may account for the dominant mining presence and history seen in and around the Creede area, as well as other historical mining towns throughout the San Juan Volcano Complex, shown in Figure 1. This includes the fluorspar mine developed at the 4UR ranch, which is discussed briefly here and in more detail in chapter 10.

The La Garita and Creede Calderas

There are at least fifteen known calderas in the San Juan complex.[5] The youngest of these calderas is the Creede Caldera, which erupted roughly 26.5 million years ago.[6] The caldera is named for the small mining town located on the north end of the depression, and is the most well-preserved caldera in the SJM Volcanic Complex—typifying this type of volcano to

Caldera Relations	Ash-Flow Sheets	Lavas and Related Rocks
Creede Caldera Cycle (26.8 Ma?)	Snowshoe Mountain Tuff*	Fisher Dacite*
	*Ancient Lake Creede formed between Snowshoe Mountain formation and the Fisher Dacite deposition.	
San Luis Caldera Complex (27.0-26.9 Ma?)	Nelson Mountain Tuff Cebolla Creek Tuff Rat Creek Tuff	Baldy Cinco Dacite Stewart Peak Volcanics Mineral Creek Dacite Premonitory (?) Lava Flows
South River Caldera Cycle (27.1 Ma)	Wason Park Tuff	South River Volcanics
Blue Creek Cycle (27.2 Ma)	Blue Creek Tuff	Lava flows of McClelland Mountain Volcanics of Beaver Creek
Bachelor Caldera Cycle (27.3 Ma)	Carpenter Ridge Tuff	-
Silverton Caldera (W. San Juan) (27.5 Ma)	Crystal Lake Tuff	-
La Garita Caldera Cycle (28.08 Ma)	Fish Canyon Tuff	Huerto Andesite Pagosa Peak Dacite
Platoro Caldera Complex (28.2 Ma)	Chiquito Peak Tuff	-
Masonic Park Cycle (28.3 Ma)	Masonic Park Tuff	Sheep Mountain Andesite
Western San Juan Calderas (28.0-28.4 Ma)	*Age relations with Chiquito Peak and Masonic Park Tuffs uncertain.*	Silverton Volcanics
Platoro Caldera Complex (SE San Juan) (28.5-29.5 Ma)	Treasure Mountain Group	Summitville Andesite
Rocks Predating Central Caldera Cluster	*Tuffs erupted from northeast sources; Cochetopa Park?*	Conejos Formation
	Prevolcanic deposits	

Figure 3: Conceptual stratigraphy column showing caldera occurrences and depositions. The oldest caldera collapse occurs at the bottom. Those highlighted in gray have been referenced throughout this chapter. *Modified from Lipman,* Geologic Map of the Central San Juan Caldera Cluster, Southwestern Colorado.

such an extent that it has been used extensively in geologic research. The caldera boasts an impressive resurgent dome (known as Snowshoe Mountain today)—an elevated mound formed after the collapse of the former caldera, as magma is still moving beneath the surface pushing upward on the crust. The dome resurgence created a moat with no outlet, and consequently, a lake once occupied and filled the area with layers of sediment.[7] Lake Creede, as it was known, suffused the valley floor southeast of the town of Creede[8] as part of the Creede Formation—seen in Figure 2 (color insert) around the resurgent dome in yellow.[9] The lake was no trivial puddle, as demonstrated by the striking thicknesses of lake sediments—some as thick as 3,900 feet,[10] which were deposited over 100,000 years. Figure 3 gives a broad overview of the caldera relations (in other words, the order in which they formed) and the geologic units that were deposited within them.

BIGGEST VOLCANIC EXPLOSION AND COLLAPSE

Underlying the Creede Caldera, and many other calderas in this region of the SJM volcanic complex, is evidence of the much larger and imposing La Garita Caldera. The La Garita Caldera is arguably one of the world's largest calderas. Its size is so immense that it took geologists nearly thirty years to figure out and map the extent of the caldera. Although much of the caldera's features are hard to discern due to subsequent caldera formation and erosion, it spans an impressive 30-by-50-mile stretch of the Eastern San Juan Mountains.[11] The La Garita Caldera also boasts one of the world's largest volcanic explosions. Around twenty-eight million years ago,[12] in less than a week, over 1,200 cubic miles of ash spewed from the La Garita Caldera collapse.[13] The dust and ash settled onto the surrounding landscape, casing the area in an ash layer formation known as the Fish Canyon Tuff. In some expanses, this imposing ash layer is as thick as 1,000 feet.[14] Imagine, a massive explosion followed by a dense cloud of ground-hugging hot ash and pumice racing down the flanks of a collapsing volcano, destroying and covering everything in its path.

In order to compare such explosions and to demonstrate the magnitude of such an event, volcanologists use the Volcanic Explosivity Index (VEI) to measure the volume of tephra—simply, the particles and material ejected from the volcano. In other words, the more tephra, the bigger the explosion. The volume of volcanic material ejected is measured and then given a numerical value between 0 and 8 based on quantitative measurements, as shown in Figure 4. Numerically, a zero (0) on the scale is considered a nonexplosive, "gentle" eruption (something you might generally see on the Hawaiian Islands), whereas an 8 is considered a large, "colossal" explosion indicating a violent, cataclysmic event. When Mount St. Helens in Washington erupted in 1980, it ejected a mere 0.06 cubic miles of tephra and was categorized as a VEI 4.

In order for an eruption to be classified as a VEI 8, it must eject more than 240 cubic miles of volcanic material. The Yellowstone Caldera, which

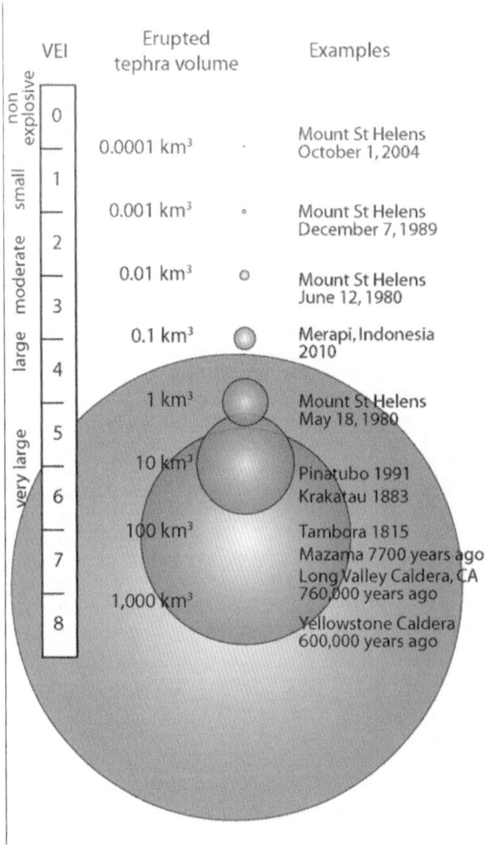

Figure 4: Volcanic Explosivity Index (VEI). Each increase in a number indicates an increase in explosivity by a factor of ten. *Modified from U.S. Geological Survey, Volcanic Hazards Program VEI.*

erupted approximately 600,000 years ago, spewed a remarkable 480 cubic miles; the even bigger explosion of Toba (now present-day Toba Lake in Sumatra, Indonesia) expelled 670 cubic miles. Let this sink in for a minute. The numbers candidly presented here *pale* in comparison to the La Garita Caldera. Toba ejected roughly *half* the violently destructive material of La Garita, which hurled 1,200 cubic miles of tephra—enough to bury the entire state of California in 35 feet of hot volcanic ash and gas.[15] This type of volcano is commonly denoted as a "supervolcano," but the true scientific label for this type of event is "mega-colossal." An event that size is unfathomable today, but evidence of the La Garita Caldera explosion and subsequent collapse can still be seen today; the 4UR Ranch rests on a small portion of this geologic wonder.

WHAT HAPPENED TO ALL THE VOLCANIC ACTIVITY?

Obviously, Colorado has an exciting geologic history. The question that arises, however, is where has all of this volcanic activity gone? The volcanic activity hasn't disappeared altogether, and remnants of it exist today that are still very much active. The hot springs on the 4UR are one example, and the role of volcanism in their development is discussed later in the chapter, but there is an even more discernable event occurring now. During the later stages of the San Juan volcanism (late Oligocene, early Miocene epochs), the Rio Grande Rift became active in the San Luis Valley—essentially tearing the Colorado Plateau apart from the Great Plains—producing more of the basalt-type geology that is seen east of the San Juan Mountains.[16] The rift is still actively pulling the San Luis Valley apart at an astonishing rate of two millimeters per year. A little facetious, of course, but the fact remains that volcanic-related activity still exists in the region. Rifting occurs when bulges of magma push upward on the crust, thinning the crust enough for magma to break through the surface and spew lava flows across the region. The lava displays have abated, but rifting continues. While the effusive eruptions that once accompanied the rifting are no longer seen, small seismic activity can be felt every so often from the fault slips—especially along the eastern edge of the valley. The Colorado Geological Survey monitors the earthquake activity due to rifting with the use of seismograph stations, including one located on the 4UR.

GENERAL GEOLOGY

Just west of the entrance to the 4UR ranch, on Highway 149, is the Wagon Wheel Gap—a geologic wonder that dominates the landscape. Along the highway from South Fork to Creede, the canyon walls describe a history carved out and exposed by the Rio Grande. The Gap, itself, is a narrow passageway, created by the erosive power of the Rio Grande through relatively resistant igneous rock. This large towering geologic feature is composed of welded tuffs, which can be seen on either side of the road.

Much of the volcanic geology in the Wagon Wheel Gap area displays dacitic lava flows and breccia, which were deposited subsequent to the La Garita Caldera, as shown in Figures 2 and 3. Many of the ensuing caldera eruptions (Creede, Bachelor and others) have camouflaged the existence

Image 1: The "Gap," circa 1874. *Denver Public Library, Western History Collection, WHJ-1185. Photo by William Henry Jackson.*

of La Garita Caldera around the ranch, but there are still observable remnants of the episodic eruptions that occurred millions of years ago. Of note, features of the San Juan Volcanic complex are ash-flow tuffs and flow breccias, both of which are visible in the northern part of the 4UR ranch property—essentially from Highway 149 south.[17]

Along the south side of the Rio Grande, the imposing walls of the Wagon Wheel Gap tower overhead. Here, evidence of brecciated faults can be seen, as outlined in Image 2 (color insert). There is a stark difference in textures along the fault. Look closely, and a texture known as schlieren, see Image 3 (color insert), displays itself. The small, tabular bodies (which look like streaks across the rock) are due to shearing or compressional forces created by the faulting. On the other side of the fault, the texture is more solid, like a densely welded ash-tuff. As material was ejected from the volcano as superheated, turbulent mixtures of gas and ash composed of glass shards, dust, pumice and other fragments, it cooled and welded together, forming many of the tuff layers observable in the area today.

The welded tuffs on the north side of the Wagon Wheel Gap exhibit undulating layers of dacitic ash-tuff as shown in Image 4. These layers demonstrate a kind of ebb and flow of volcanic activity, like waves lapping up against the shoreline. It's a beautiful demonstration of the pulsating flows of a time of cataclysmic destruction—of clouds of hot ash and heat relentlessly flowing over the land. These layers are of post-caldera flow, the Fisher Dacite, that erupted after the resurgent uplift of the Creede caldera.[18] Columnar jointing is also a dominant feature of the Wagon Wheel Gap—which formed as the volcanic rock cooled and contracted, shaping the volcanic dacite into an array of polygonal columns. To locals, these geological structures on the north side of the river are known as the "Palisades."

The Fish Canyon Tuff, a product of the La Garita explosion, is hardly noted in and around the ranch itself, except in parts around the Wagon Wheel Gap and the upper northwest section of the ranch property. The Fish Canyon Tuff hides within other layers of subsequent caldera deposits around the 4UR and may be hard to find. The best area to view the Fish Canyon Tuff is near Penitente Canyon north of the town of Del Norte, Colorado.

More conspicuous on the 4UR are the Masonic Park Tuff formations seen in the southeastern portion of the Goose Creek valley. The Masonic Park Tuff origins are not well known but may be from an eruption preceding the formation of the La Garita Caldera.[19] The greenish-gray Masonic tuff soars above the south end of the valley. The area also showcases volcanic hoodoos and spires. Over time, water, ice and wind have carved out less-resistant

Image 4: Undulating layers of ash flows, likely Fisher Dacite, which were created after the resurgence of the Creede Caldera. The surrounding rock cliffs containing columnar jointing are locally referred to as "The Palisades" and can be better viewed just west of Wagon Wheel Gap. *Photo by Scott Hizny, 2019.*

layers mainly composed of poorly welded tuffs, which lack a strong cohesion between the grains and therefore erode more rapidly than surrounding deposits, creating these structures.

On the western side of Goose Creek valley, diverse depositions are observed. An abundance of green-colored rocks with layering is visible, as seen in Image 7 (color insert). These rocks are igneous in nature and contain crystals such as black quartz and feldspars. Their presence is likely a result of the hydrothermal activity related to mineral depositions containing copper, chlorite, epidote or any number of minerals that can produce the greenish hues seen in the outcrops. More specifically, these green depositions could be due to something called *deuteric* alteration—which describes changes that transpire in the rock due to reactions between different water-rich solutions as they separate from the magma body as it begins to cool and solidify.

In other areas on the western end of the Goose Creek valley, the trees disappear and looking up the hillsides an obvious transition of different depositions is displayed, as shown in Image 7. Erosion has revealed layered ash-tuff near the bottom, which transitions into a more orange-reddish discoloration toward the top of the hill. Just as the greenish hues occur from hydrothermal alteration, the orange-red appearance along these hills may have also occurred through a specific hydrothermal alteration known as greisen. Greisen refers to hydrothermally altered granitic rock that consists of, among other things, fluorine (related to the fluorite mined out of the area) and iron oxides. As iron reacts with oxygen in the air, it forms "rust" (oxidation) that produces the orange-red discoloration in the rocks and surrounding soils.

The most interesting perspective to note at this point is the complexity of studying such igneous events. Imagine the excitement, but also the frustration, of geologists who have studied the SJM Volcano Complex extensively. Definitive evidence is somewhat hard to come by due to the intricacy and sabotage of the volcanic history by subsequent caldera events or overlying sediments and vegetation. Processes such as oxidation of the rocks and the complexity of the layering of millions of years of volcanic deposits only compound the problem. In short, some of the relationships remain elusive, despite the extensive and immensely detailed mapping done by field geologists.

HOT SPRINGS

The various hot springs dotted around southwestern Colorado's landscape, including those on the 4UR, and the deposits of ore minerals are all indicative of fracture-and-faults systems—many of which were emplaced by the collapse of the calderas. These fractures and faults in the ground provide conduits of flow for the deeper and hotter groundwater fluids that circulate up to the surface. Both fractures and pores in welded and non-welded tuffs facilitate water transport owing to the high porosity and permeability of such rock types. Disruption of the geologic layers due to chaotic volcanic activity (such as caldera collapse) and a variety of fault zones and intrusions that cut across the landscape, create a perfect channel by which subsurface waters can rise to the surface. The SJM aquifer lies below much of the San Juan Volcanic Complex, and the topography of the San Juan Mountains provides a natural capture zone for the precipitation (mainly snowmelt), which infiltrates and filters through the sedimentary and more porous and permeable volcanic layers to recharge the aquifer.[20] Eventually, these geothermally heated subsurface waters are pushed back up through fractures and other conduits to create those natural bubbling hot mineral springs.

THE FLUORSPAR MINE

The fluorspar mine is an echo of a Colorado past, where pioneers came from far and wide to stake their claim on the fortunes and riches this bountiful state has to offer. Dotted around the hills that create a charming backdrop to the wooden structure, the abandoned mine workings wind through the earth like arteries and continue in various directions without end or imposition of sunlight. Walking around the mine gives a sense of touring through the hollow bones of Mother Earth. It's a reminder of a time when men adventurously burrowed into the hills and whittled away at the valuable treasures the earth has been hiding for millions of years.

Ample fluorite in old tailings can be found scattered around the mine. In some cases, the fluorite has a milky and dull luster to it—a product of bleaching due to fluorite naturally consuming silica —although more commonly, specimens in the area are more vitreous (glassy). The Mohs Hardness Scale, developed in 1812 by the mineralogist Friedrich Mohs, is a measurement of the hardness of minerals from 1–10 based on their resistance to scratching. Fluorite ranks as a 4 on this scale. The hardness of the mineral is an important, distinct feature, as it is one way in which geologists determine a mineral like fluorite from similar-looking minerals, such as amethyst, which ranks as a 7. There are a few ways to determine the hardness of minerals, but for fluorite, in particular, a steel nail will do the trick. The nail will scratch fluorite but won't scratch amethyst (a mineral that is slightly harder than the nail). Why early miners didn't use this technique to determine that their newfound vein contained fluorite, rather than amethyst, is anyone's guess. Perhaps it was easier to assume it was amethyst, since the vein was a relatively short distance away from other mines and veins in Mineral County that were rampant with amethyst ores.[21]

Fluorite crystals are not always large in size, so a keen eye is needed to discern some of the physical properties of the specimen. If one looks closely, cubic crystals, which are characteristic of fluorspar, can often be seen. Fluorspar may not always form these cubical structures. It comes down to a sort of "Goldilocks" zone—where conditions of pressure and temperature have to be *just right* to create such beautiful specimens. Nevertheless, whether the crystals are cubical, octahedral or some other complex arrangement, fluorspar is an alluring mineral to behold. Fluorite is sensitive to elemental impurities, giving this mineral a spectacular array of colors. In a comprehensive study of fluorite in Colorado done in 1920, it was noted that the Wagon Wheel Gap deposits displayed the greatest variation in color, demonstrating "perhaps every color in which the mineral has been found."[22]

The 4UR Ranch mine was best known for the purple variety of fluorite, which perhaps is another reason it might have been mistaken for a purple variety of quartz known as amethyst, which is abundant in the Creede Mining District, a mere eight miles away. Early prospectors erroneously identified fluorite as amethyst, hopelessly mining minerals not associated with the highly sought-after Creede ore deposits that contained gold and silver.[23] In fact, the mineralization near the 4UR likely occurred several million years later—accounting for the difference in deposits.[24]

The main source of the fluorite deposits around the 4UR occurred through hydrothermal veins. The very nature of the presence of fluorite depends on a variety of factors, including temperature, the fluid's composition (e.g., pH, salinity and so on), and the microstructure (e.g., grain size, fracturing in rock and so forth) in the host rock. Water that contained hydrofluoric acid and other fluorine compounds utilized fractures and faults created by the collapse of the calderas, depositing fluorite under ideal hydrothermal conditions around the 4UR Ranch, subsequently leading to the discovery and successful mining operation millions of years later.

The Wagon Wheel Gap fluorspar deposits are relatively unique in that they are one of the few mines in Colorado that produced *nearly* pure fluorspar—which accounts for its once highly sought-after economic value. It's important to note *nearly* here, as these deposits are often incorporated with rhomboid barite, as shown in Image 9 (color insert). Fluorspar is mined for a variety of purposes, most importantly to eliminate impurities in steel production. When the process by which steel is made changed, fluorspar mining ceased and the mine was shut down in 1950. Many of the mines in this area and around Colorado have been shut down due to changing market prices and demand. For an eerie example of the fate of mining, take a tour of the mines around Creede. This once booming town now hosts a small community of residents and operational mines (which are currently closed) and affirms that just as geology is always changing, nothing truly lasts forever.

2
NAMES

What a name, and for Why…An interesting and beautiful place.

—Rocky Mountain News, *October 19, 1877*

The story, or in some cases, stories, of how places were named, is often interesting and sometimes confusing. The origin of the names of places near Wagon Wheel Gap, and of course its name, too, is both simple and perplexing.

GOOSE CREEK

Some early references to this tributary to the Rio Grande referred to it as Hot Spring Creek, since it passed by and received water from the hot springs. The name that endures to this day is Goose Creek. The story goes that George Howard, a prospector, left Cimarron, New Mexico, in April 1872 with burros, several firearms and a goodly amount of supplies, heading north along the Rio Grande into the San Juan Mining District. Howard tells the story in a journal entry, referring to the small creek that flows into the Rio Grande:

> *My camp is a beautiful one…on the bank of the river in a fine little park surrounded on all sides by high mountains…grand and majestic.…This*

place is called by some the "Wagon Wheel Gap." Goose eggs are no bad thing to take, so I found today a dinner. The two old geese flew by camp in the evening, I turned the old shot gun loose on them, and broke the wings of one of them, but it fell in the river and escaped me.[25]

THE 4UR

Arthur Sharp expanded the operation of the Wagon Wheel Ranch into cattle ranching. Running range cattle requires a way to identify ownership of each animal, so Sharp needed his own unique brand. In November 1945, he registered the 4UR brand, created by using four Us from the Ws in Wagon Wheel plus R for Ranch, resulting in the 4UR brand that is still registered to the owners of the 4UR. Sharp called his operation the Wagon Wheel Ranch, but after Allan Phipps purchased the property and found there was another ranch by the same name, he renamed the place the 4UR Ranch at Wagon Wheel Gap, or the 4UR for short.

PIERCE, CALDWELL AND ELLIOTT CREEKS

These creeks were named after homesteaders. Fidelia E. Pierce homesteaded 83 acres along what came to be known as Pierce Creek in about 1875, patent granted December 30, 1880. Henry C. Caldwell homesteaded 40 acres, patent granted October 21, 1900, and 120 acres, patent granted on December 27, 1905, along a creek named after him farther north. Thaddeus Ezra Elliott homesteaded 160 acres on the upper end of Lime Creek, in the Seven Parks area, along what is now known as Elliott Creek, granted January 11, 1904.[26]

WAGON WHEEL GAP

"Wagon Wheel Gap is a point at the upper, west end, about four hundred feet wide, with perpendicular cliffs on either side, between which the river dashes along for two or three hundred yards and then suddenly opens out

Wagon Wheel Gap and the palisades on the Rio Grande River, circa 1874. *Department of the Interior, United States Geological Survey Denver Library Photographic Collection, jwh01088. Photograph by William Henry Jackson.*

into a broader scope of country."[27] The narrow gap through the cliffs, barely wide enough for the waters of the Rio Grande, created the only practical path for travelers from the San Luis Valley to make their entry into the rugged San Juan Mountains.

The origin of the Wagon Wheel Gap name is a puzzle for modern historians. The Utes referred to the Wagon Wheel Gap hot springs as "Little Medicine" and to those at Pagosa Springs as "Big Medicine."[28] The Wheeler expedition of 1874 called them the Liberty Hot Springs, a name that persisted for several years and may be found in publications of the time. However, the owners of the hot springs called them the Wagon Wheel Gap Hot Springs, which became the common usage.

All stories agree that the name Wagon Wheel Gap resulted from someone meeting with an accident in that narrow mountain gap, moving on and leaving the running gear and wheels of a wagon behind. Traveling along primitive paths hacked out of rough terrain using heavily loaded wooden-wheeled wagons, with limited suspension (if any), was a tough journey. It was not uncommon to find pieces of broken wagons and damaged goods discarded beside the rough trail along the length of the Rio Grande. Travelers, mostly miners, following the Rio Grande route into the San Juans referred to the distinctive narrow defile as the Gap, associating the abandoned wagon wheels with it, resulting in the name "Wagon Wheel Gap."

The someone who left those wagon wheels has spawned a variety of far-fetched stories. Early visitors to Wagon Wheel Gap typically inquired about the origin of the name—as they do to this day. Old-timers of the area, eager to appear wise and all-knowing, told gullible visitors an assortment of fanciful tales, some containing a grain of truth, others fantastical, containing information that is simply untrue. Newspaper accounts, published books and local legend all contributed to the bizarre mix of fact and fiction.

The first of these stories is a romantic tale of two young lovers who left their home in Kentucky to escape the Civil War and, in pursuit of the gold and silver reputed to be in the San Juans, ended up in Del Norte. Finding the fishing and hunting good, they continued with their wagon following the placid valley of the Rio Grande up to the hot springs near Wagon Wheel Gap. There they settled among the friendly Utes under the leadership of Chief Bonito. In 1861–62, recovered from their trip, having been eating well and enjoying the hot springs, they could not resist the lure of riches in the San Juans farther west. Although there was no road, the travelers headed west, along the rocky and treacherous paths. The wagon soon broke down, and the young husband, attempting to either prevent the accident or repair the wagon, was crushed beneath a wheel. The Utes helped the despairing wife care for him, but the wounds were grievous and he shortly died. The Utes buried the man on a rocky bluff overlooking the river and helped the wife return to Pueblo; she returned home to Kentucky. This story is at least plausible, although the only place it appears is in a single article in the *Denver Times*'s *Friday Magazine* in August 1905. The Utes were a friendly tribe and likely would have provided assistance. Burial was not their custom, although they may have been sensitive to the wishes of the wife. No grave has ever been found in the area.

A local legend about the name still staunchly defended in parts of Southern Colorado is that the wheels came from wagons of the ill-fated fourth John C. Frémont expedition of the winter of 1848–49.[29] Attempting to find a route through the San Juans into California, the group became mired in heavy snow just west of Del Norte, and progress halted. Frémont's fourth has been referred to by some as the Wagon Wheel Gap disaster. Of course, this name was applied sometime after the event. Several of the Frémont parties left their snowbound winter camp at different times, taking different routes; some survived and others did not. The exact route that Frémont took out of the snowbound winter camp is not known, and he most likely never went through the Gap.[30]

Even if Frémont and his few men came back through the Gap, they certainly had no wagons with them. There never were any wagons, and the pack mules that started the trip with the expedition had all died or been killed for food for the men.[31] The Frémont story, perpetuated by old-timers during the early days at the Wagon Wheel Gap Stage Station, was picked up and repeated in newspapers around the country for many years. The school at Wagon Wheel Gap was named the Fremont School in honor of the explorer. While the story of Frémont coming through Wagon Wheel Gap with his wagons is totally fictitious, it made for great press.

> *It was related that when the first modern settlers came, they found strewn along the river banks, in this gorge, a number of wagon wheel and various other fragments of wagons, and that they formed a part of Colonel John C. Fremont's expedition which passed that way in 1848. These explorers, as the story runs, were attacked by Indians at this point and compelled to abandon some of their wagons; that the Indians secreted themselves among the cliffs and built rifle pits of loose stone from which they fired down up on the intruders, etc., etc. Now all of this except the single fact that Fremont attempted to cross the mountains through this gap in pure fiction. He had no wagons at all, but pack mules, nor was he attacked by Indians.*[32]

Yet another legend, published as fact, is related to the western San Juan prospecting parties of 1860 and 1861, commonly referred to as the Baker Expeditions. A detailed account of the so-called Baker expedition of 1860 relates that Captain Charles Baker, at the head of a pack string with a prospecting party of twenty-one miners, first approached the San Juans from the north, coming up the Lake Fork of the Gunnison and over what is today known as Cinnamon Pass, settling in an area known as Baker's City (or Park) at the mouth of Cunningham Gulch, near modern-day Silverton. Arriving during the summer of 1860, the prospectors were not prepared for the hardships of the coming winter, when almost all of the stock perished and most miners departed, half-starved and despondent. They departed from the San Juans "driven from the merciless mountains by snow, cold, disillusionment, comprehension of how awfully far from civilization they were, curiosity about the conflicts between the Union and the blossoming Confederacy, and perhaps a thousand more reasons no one ever heard."[33]

Although the 1860 effort was generally a disaster, the lure of riches was too strong to deter a larger group from attempting another expedition the next year. Early in 1861, a large group of settlers and prospectors, as part of the Pollock-Kellogg party, traveled into the San Juans by a southern route, leaving Denver in December 1860, and arrived in the Animas River Valley in the early spring. The wagon train stopped at a point that became known as Camp Pleasant, about fifteen miles north of Animas City, still some fifteen miles south of Baker City. No wagons went as far north as the original Baker City site at the mouth of Cunningham Gulch during the 1861 expedition.[34]

The party that arrived in the early spring of 1861 comprised not only miners and prospectors but also families: women and children who were not used to the harshness of mountain life and living with Indians. During their trip from Denver to the Animas River Valley, states were seceding from the Union, culminating with the start of the Civil War in April 1861. The increasing hostility of the Indians, the lack of gold and the start of the Civil War led to the departure of all the prospectors and settlers from the Animas River Valley. Wagons headed south along the route they had taken in. Other parties headed north along the Cinnamon Pass route on foot and with pack animals. Still others decided to attempt a route directly east, leaving from Baker City, up Cunningham Gulch, over Stony Pass and down the Rio Grande. By July 1861—as incredible as it seems—virtually everyone was gone.[35]

The Rio Grande Route over Stony Pass appealed to some of the Baker group for two reasons—it was shorter and it was devoid of Navajos, who were known to be more hostile to the settlers than the Utes. This route was little traveled, limited to Native American and game trails. Survivors' stories of this trek were of starvation and hardship. Traveling on foot, one of a party of eight managed to make it to Fort Garland, and soldiers were dispatched to find the survivors of the party near present-day Del Norte. Others avoided the San Luis Valley and stayed north through Saguache, then on to Fort Garland.[36] During the mining frenzy that developed during the early 1870s, the pack trail route over Stony Pass served as the route into the Silverton Mining District from the San Luis Valley until 1879, when a wagon road was finally completed.[37] As modern travelers will attest, the Stony Pass route is steep, treacherous and not for the faint of heart.

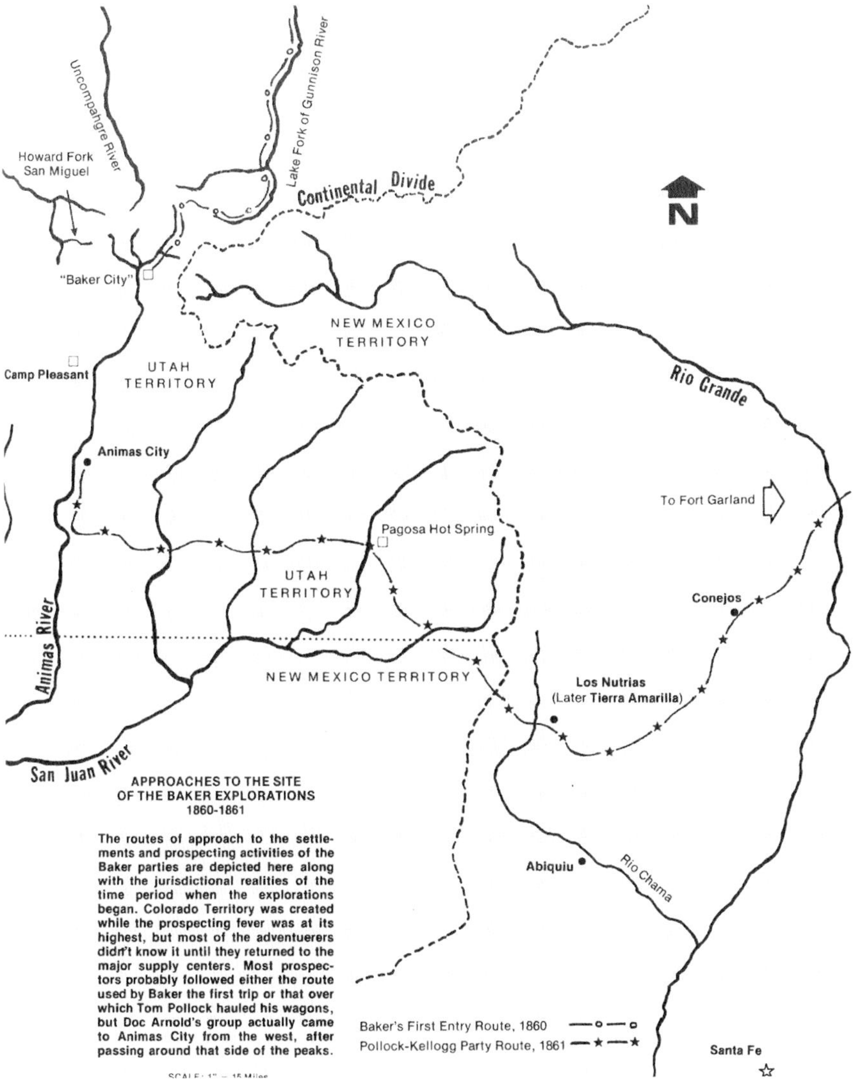

Approaches to the site of the Baker explorations, 1860–1861. *From* Many More Mountains, Volume 1: Silverton's Roots, *Allen Nossaman, 1989, page 59.*

Another locally popular, but wholly unbelievable, legend about a massacre of white men was written over a century after the alleged event.

Wagon Wheel Gap[38]

White men were driving through a mountain gap
When warring Utes got them in a trap,
The battle was bloody and lasted days
So, a man went down the river a ways,
To deliver a tale of much import
To the men down at the nearest fort.
When help arrived, hundreds of men were dead
And the cool, clear water had turned red.
The Indians had hung a wagon's wheel
Across the narrow gap. They'd hung a wheel-
The Indian symbol of victory
To tell other tribes of their victory.
From that day hence, the narrow mountain gap
Has been known as and called Wagon Wheel Gap.

While poets are allowed a significant amount of literary license, the errors in this verse are egregious and obvious to any student of the history of these times. First, there is no date mentioned in the verse. In Lieutenant Ruffner's diary of his 1873 expedition up the Rio Grande, he mentions Wagon Wheel Gap by name numerous times. Therefore, the name must have been in common use by that time. Additionally, Ruffner states that he left his wagons at Camp La Loma (near modern-day Del Norte) about twenty-five miles east of Wagon Wheel Gap. With thirteen pack mules and a mounted escort, he proceeded up the Rio Grande. The reason for leaving the wagons was that there was not a passable wagon road along the Rio Grande beyond Camp Loma. "Camp Loma was, when we passed up, the end of wagon transportation."[39] Therefore, what large group of white men would be "driving" through a mountain gap, if there was no road upon which to drive?

The 1873–74 Wheeler expedition also found no road into the San Juans: "The train consisted of more than a score of fine mules, heavily laden with provisions and company utensils."[40] During their expedition, an effort was made to identify a path for a future road into the San Juans and over the mountains. By special request of Superintendent Wheeler, the surveyors were tasked to be on the lookout for feasible passes in the mountains for the transportation of army supplies across the main range.

If two credible sources such as Ruffner and Wheeler both refer to the place as Wagon Wheel Gap, the name was obviously in common usage prior to there being any roads into the San Juans. Therefore, the basis for the massacre story is fundamentally flawed and cannot be considered credible—not to mention the fabrications contained in the individual verses.

"The battle was bloody and lasted for days." The white men would have had to have a significant amount of ammunition and supplies to engage in a battle for days, which, unless they were there on purpose to fight Indians, they would not have had. An earlier story was published about a large Indian battle between two warring tribes up the river, which may have led some to confuse that battle with the fictitious attack of a nonexistent wagon train. However, this story about the inter-tribal battle was published almost twenty years after the alleged event and should also be considered with a jaundiced eye.

> *William's Creek, beautiful trout stream four or five miles above the Gap, flowing into the Rio Grande from the northeast, is where in 1857, a desperate encounter took place between a large body of Apache warriors on the one side and a formidable band of Utes on the other. The Apaches were encamped in a narrow gorge among the rocks about a mile up the stream, when the Utes came down in battle array and left none to tell the tale. The fight was desperate, long and bloody, but the little northern Indians* [Utes] *were too much for the wily sons of the south* [Apaches]. *Old pioneers estimate the number of ponies killed on the occasion at one hundred, and there are human bones with other evidences of the battle to be seen at the present time. It is said there were four or five hundred warriors on a side, and the contest lasted three days, during which time about half their number were slain.*[41]

Ruffner's report mentions that there appeared to be evidence of intertribal battles near the Gap, although that was speculation, and an in-depth evaluation was not part of his mission. "The only place of special interest on the way was Wagon Wheel Gap, where the river passes for a few hundred yards between two high bluffs about 300 feet apart. This point has evidently been, in times past, a great battle ground between the Utes and their enemies of the plains, the Cheyennes, Arapahoes, etc. Many little heaps of rocks on the south side of the bluff seem to have done service as rifle pits."[42]

"A man went down the river a ways to deliver a tale of much import to the men at the nearest fort." The only forts in the area down the river were Fort Massachusetts (1852–1858) at the base of Mount Blanca, some seventy miles away from Wagon Wheel Gap, or Fort Garland (1858–1883), about eighty-five miles away.[43]

"When help arrived, hundreds of men were dead, and the cool clear water had turned red." The death of "hundreds of [white] men" would certainly have made the newspapers of the time, but there is nothing documenting this massacre.

"The Indians had hung a wagon's wheel across the narrow gap. They'd hung a wheel—the Indian symbol of victory—to tell other tribes of their victory." The narrowest portion of the Gap is about three hundred feet, which would require a significant amount of rope that the Indians most likely would not have had. The Native Americans never had a wheel, only a circle, as in the Medicine Wheel, which is sacred and spiritual, not a sign of victory or violence.

Another variation of this story says that the Indians hung the scalps across the Gap, weighing the whole mess down with a wagon wheel. Again, the issues of the width of the Gap and source of the rope contradict this story.

Pieces of earlier factual events may have been combined at a later date into this fanciful story. The inclusion of the large massacre between the Indian tribes leaving hundreds of dead bodies and horses, and the Baker Expedition story of one survivor making it to Fort Garland for help seems like more than coincidence.

The three most prominent legends of the origin of the wagon wheels at the Gap have been shown not to be credible. But someone did indeed leave a wagon wheel, or parts of such, sometime after the end of the Civil War in 1865 and prior to 1873. With the existence of a military fort on the eastern side of the San Luis Valley from 1852 to 1883, plus the growth of permanent settlements increasing the population of the San Luis Valley,[44] it is likely that someone unknown and forever forgotten, hearing the siren song of those alluring mountains, developed a serious case of wanderlust and made an attempt to explore them by way of the "seemingly gentle valleys of the Rio Grande."[45] The lack of a road, rocky terrain and difficulties of wagon travel caused the wanderer to leave pieces and parts along the route. Ruffner stated that "the amount of wreckage strewed along the trail followed by us was sufficient evidence of the difficulties encountered by pioneer teamsters of this region."[46]

3

TRAILS INTO THE SAN JUANS

To get to this paradise [Wagon Wheel Gap] *of the trout fisherman, it is only necessary to take a ticket to Denver, thence by rail to Canyon City, thence one-hundred and forty-three miles over one of the finest mountain roads in* [fourteen-passenger] *Concord coaches to Del Norte. Here, saddle horses or mule wagons can be obtained at reasonable prices for the remaining thirty miles of the trip.*

—Colorado Daily Chieftain, *September 7, 1875*

FIRST FOOTPRINTS

Native American Paleo-Indian cultures, beginning with the Clovis and Folsom Complexes (eleven thousand years ago) were the first known inhabitants of the Upper Rio Grande region. The Ute, primarily the Capote band, lived by hunting, fishing and gathering native plants found in the San Luis Valley and northern New Mexico. The Navajo, Apache and Comanche Indians came to trade, hunt and raid. The Weminuche band of the Utes lived in the San Juan basin but hunted on both sides of the San Juans. The Tabaguache Utes lived in the Uncompahgre and Gunnison drainages. The Utes lived in the high country seasonally as members of the ecosystem, following the migration of wildlife for their sustenance.[47]

Evidence of Indian occupation in the Wagon Wheel Gap area was documented in the Hayden Survey in 1874, which reported finding apparent fortifications and arrowheads or fragments of material that were not local, especially obsidian, which would have come from farther south. Stone structures with circular or curved walls, dry-laid masonry on high points and small corner-notched projectile points, which are usually an indication of Utes, were reported.[48] The land around the 4UR has been private since 1874, and no other published on-site investigations have been performed.

The original Ute lands and hunting grounds encompassed the vast majority of what would become the state of Colorado and a good part of eastern Utah. The Utes established trails throughout the mighty San Juans as they drifted and hunted. Spanish explorers came from Mexico in the 1600s. The Utes acquired horses from them and were able to travel the mountain trails both on foot and on horseback.[49] As the Spanish continued their explorations of southwestern Colorado, they took advantage of the many Ute trails, sometimes peacefully and other times not.

The vast San Luis Valley was once a northern frontier of the Spanish Empire, which claimed all of the Rio Grande, although no colonies were founded. During the seventeenth and eighteenth centuries, occasional exploration parties, traders and military groups came from Santa Fe to the Valley and surrounding mountains. One of the earliest expeditions, that of Governor General Don Diego de Vargas in 1694, passed through the southern part of the area. Almost a century later, in the summer of 1779, Juan Bautista de Anza explored the entire Rio Grande basin of the San Luis Valley. On his way north, Anza apparently crossed the Rio Grande near present-day Del Norte, having an easy ford there.[50] Records and maps of the Spanish explorations in the upper Rio Grande region remain largely unpublished in the archives of Mexico. Because of this lack of available information, American and European historians have stressed later non-Spanish explorations in the upper Rio Grande area, such as those of Americans Zebulon Pike in 1807, Jacob Fowler in 1822 and John C. Frémont in 1848–49. The area was part of the Spanish empire until the liberation of Mexico from Spain in 1821.[51]

There were undoubtedly many Anglo traders and trappers prior to the documented travels of well-known expeditions. For example, Frémont depended on the guidance and advice of mountain man Bill Williams (or maybe not enough, according to some interpretations) to go into the San Juans. These parties utilized the well-traveled trails of the Utes following the Rio Grande.

Wildlife played an important role in the early explorations of the West, as European fashion created a market for beaver top hats. By the 1820s, the beaver had been trapped out of many eastern rivers, but they were abundant in western rivers. Having successfully traded with the Spanish for horses and firearms as early as the 1600s, the Utes took the opportunity to trade their hides and furs with Anglo trappers such as Kit Carson, Jim Bridger and Otto Mears. In the early 1820s, there were about one hundred trappers working along the Rio Grande and almost as many on the Western Slope of Colorado.[52]

One of these early trappers, Jacob Fowler, came to the Upper Rio Grande west of present-day Del Norte in the winter of 1821–22. Jacob was born in 1765 to a wealthy family in New York and moved to Kentucky as western migration gripped the country. He was an officer in the U.S. Army and performed surveying work. His early experience with the western wilderness in Kentucky, coupled with his surveying expertise, translated into a lifelong curiosity about what might be beyond the next horizon. When the rush for beaver pelts in the rivers of Colorado arose in 1820, Jacob was keen to go. Well-educated and married to a lady of society, he nevertheless decided to record his writings in the vernacular of the day, spelling words as they were pronounced, possibly to add flavor to the journal, which his children published after his death.[53]

Departing on September 6, 1821, from Fort Smith, a frontier military outpost on the Arkansas River, the Fowler party of about twenty men headed west, traveling through the San Luis Valley to the Rio Grande, where they started trapping and moving slowly west into the mountains. On March 12, 1822, Fowler describes a nearby hot spring, known today as the 4UR Hot Springs at Wagon Wheel Gap:

> *Robert and myself Set out early to hunt and having been Informed* [likely by Spanish explorers] *that a Hot Springs had been found up the Crick Which put into the River from the West (south) side a little above our Cam(p)—We went to the Spring about one and a Half miles up the Crick—But the smoke appeered like that of a Salt furnis as soon as We Came in view of it—the Snow Was now about Six Inches deep over the valley of the Crick But the Hot Watter Head kept the ground Cleane for a few Rods* [one rod is 16.5 feet] *Round the Spring—but what appeered to be Straing to look at Was to see Ice Exstended about three feet from the Shore over the Watter—tho a boiling up In the middle of the Pon(d) Which was about three rods a Cross and nearly Round the Spert of Watter Rose up some distance above the leavel of the Watter in the Pon and Was about the Size of a flour Barrel—now the questions Was How can Ice*

> *existe on Hot Watter. I Caught hold of the Ice as I soposed—and was not only Scalded with the Watter, but was burned with the ice, it being nearly as Hot as the Watter—bout on a further Examination I found it was a mineral Substance that Had Congeled on the Watter of Which there Ware vast quantitys laying below the Spring In the Crick Which Runs from it—We then Went up the mountain till the Snow got So deep We Ware obliged to Return—killed nothing.*[54]

The Wagon Wheel Gap hot springs contain dissolved silicates and carbonates, which in crystalline form resemble ice. As the water on the edges of the pool evaporated, the concentration of minerals became enough that it crystallized out of the solution where it floated, or was littered around the edge of the pool, creating Fowler's "Ice." The Fowler party then turned their feet eastward and reached Fort Osage (also called Fort Clark) on the Missouri River, July 6, 1822. In response to questions about the dangers of exploring in the Wild West, Fowler commented, "We Ware treeted Heare [Fort Clark] with more Coolness than amongst any Indeans or Spanierds We meet With."[55]

The land along the Rio Grande, owned by Mexico, eventually became a source of conflict with the United States as the United States continued to expand westward, culminating with the Mexican-American War from 1846 to 1848. The Treaty of Guadalupe Hidalgo resulted in a significant amount of land being ceded from Mexico to the United States, creating the current border along the Rio Grande.[56]

Upon finalization of the Treaty of Guadalupe Hidalgo, western expansion went into high gear. John C. Frémont's five western explorations were conducted starting in 1842, the last being conducted shortly before the Civil War in 1853. In 1848, Frémont embarked on his fourth, ill-fated expedition into the southern Colorado mountains along the Rio Grande. It was a hard winter, and they were not able to find a safe and reliable trail to penetrate the mighty San Juans. The party lost all of their animals, and twelve of the thirty-three men who started with the expedition did not return.[57]

With the difficulty of getting into the San Juans following the Rio Grande so tragically demonstrated by the Frémont disaster, Charles Baker's foray in 1860 came in from the north. Baker went up the Lake Fork of the Gunnison River, over Cinnamon Pass and down into the Animas River Valley. This was not a trapping expedition, but the first major effort to get into the silver and gold country of the San Juans on the west side on the Continental Divide.[58]

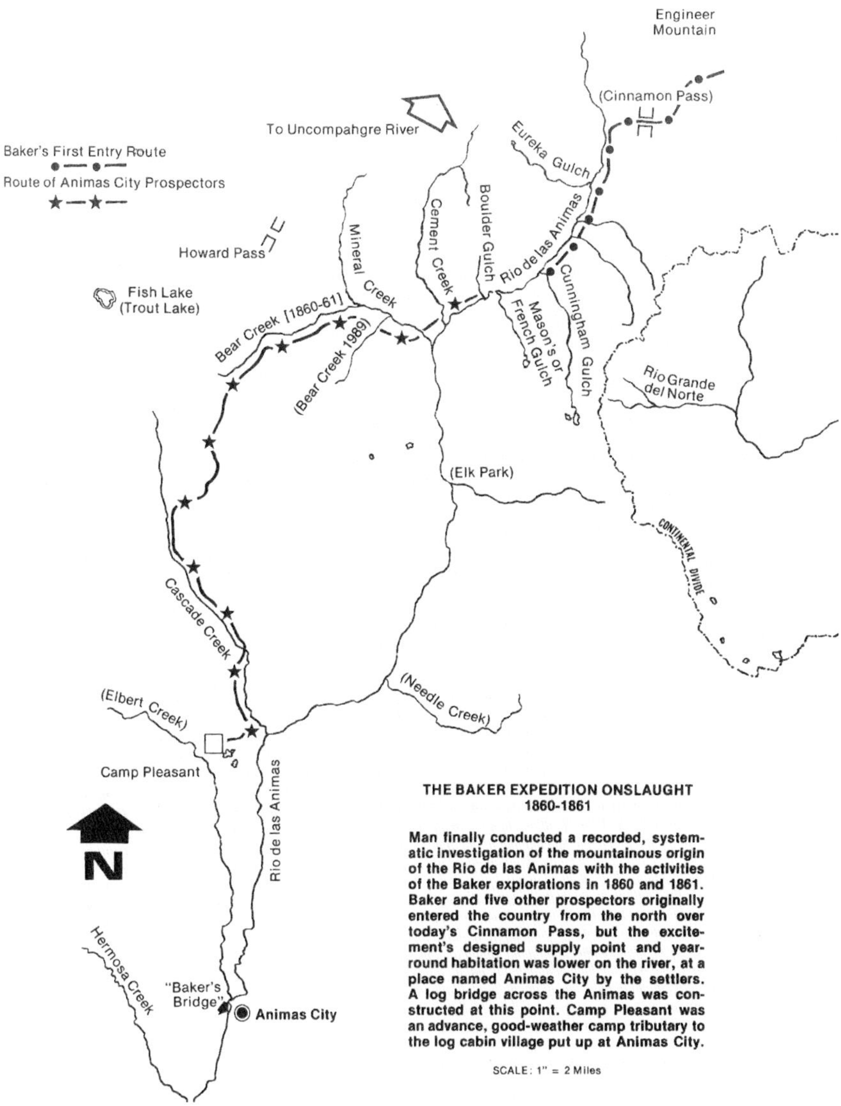

The Baker expedition onslaught, 1860–61. *From* Many More Mountains, Volume 1: Silverton's Roots, *Allen Nossaman, 1989, page 55.*

The Baker party was not limited to miners but included many adventurers and potential settlers. Their efforts were cut short by the outbreak of the Civil War in the spring of 1861, and the little settlement was abandoned almost overnight. The focus of the entire country for the next few years was on the war, but when the conflict was over in 1865, the all-consuming desire for gold and silver to be found in the San Juans reignited.

The incursion of Anglo-American explorers and settlers into Ute lands resulted in significant conflicts with the Native Americans. Since the discovery of gold and silver in the San Juan Mountains in the early 1860s, white prospectors, including Baker, had been trespassing on Ute lands on the west side of the San Luis Valley. The U.S. government had negotiated a series of treaties with Ouray, who became chief of the Uncompahgre band of the Ute tribe at the age of twenty-seven in 1860. Raised and educated by a Spanish family in Taos, New Mexico, the multilingual Ouray sought reconciliation between peoples, with the belief that war with the whites likely meant the demise of the Ute tribe. He willingly negotiated treaties to ensure the safety of his people, but there were still numerous minor conflicts with settlers and miners. In the 1860s, the U.S. government was fully occupied with the bloody and devastating Civil War, with little attention paid to the Indian conflicts out west.[59]

Over the next few years, incredible stories of mineral wealth in the San Juans were told by trespassing miners. The Ute, a tribe encouraged to be peaceful by the great Chief Ouray, allowed the miners more freedom of illegal access than they might have had with other tribes. Kit Carson is credited to have told prospectors that "the Utes are not to be feared if not molested, but look out for the Navajo."[60] Of course, Carson had earned enmity from the Navajo for his brutality toward them, most notably during the Long Walk.[61]

Indian agents, proposed treaties and increased U.S. military presence culminated in a ratified treaty between the Utes and the U.S. government in 1868. The treaty created a reservation for the Utes consisting of approximately the western third of what would become the state of Colorado. Ouray was selected as principal chief over the Tabeguache, Mouache, Caputa and Weminuche tribes.[62]

The treaty of 1868 served to reduce the tensions in the settlements of the San Luis Valley and on the eastern side of the San Juans but did nothing to allow the miners (legally) into the mineral-rich area of the Upper Rio Grande and over to the western San Juans into what is now Silverton and Lake City. The lure of riches was too much for many miners, and they surreptitiously found their way into the San Juans through the Ute reservation, sometimes without conflict. One prominent example of the miners that violated the Ute lands were the discoverers of the Ute-Ulay mine at what is now Lake City in 1871: Albert Mead, Joel Mullen, Charles Godwin and Henry Henson, who was part of the 1860–61 Baker expedition.[63]

Because of the irresistible mining discoveries, the early 1870s saw a significant increase in the Ute/miner conflicts. The reconnaissance expedition along the Rio Grande into the San Juans, led by Lieutenant E.H. Ruffner, U.S. Army Corps of Engineers, in 1873, was for the express purpose of determining a good eastern boundary for the Ute reservation that would allow the gold and silver mines in the San Juans to be developed.[64] As a result of the information gleaned from Ruffner's expedition, the Brunot Agreement was negotiated in 1873 and finalized in early 1874, creating a pathway for miners to have access along the Upper Rio Grande into the San Juan Mountains. The "spring flood" of miners, entrepreneurs and materials surged into the mineral-rich San Juans. Their destinations were the mines and mining opportunities in the areas known today as Lake City and Silverton.[65]

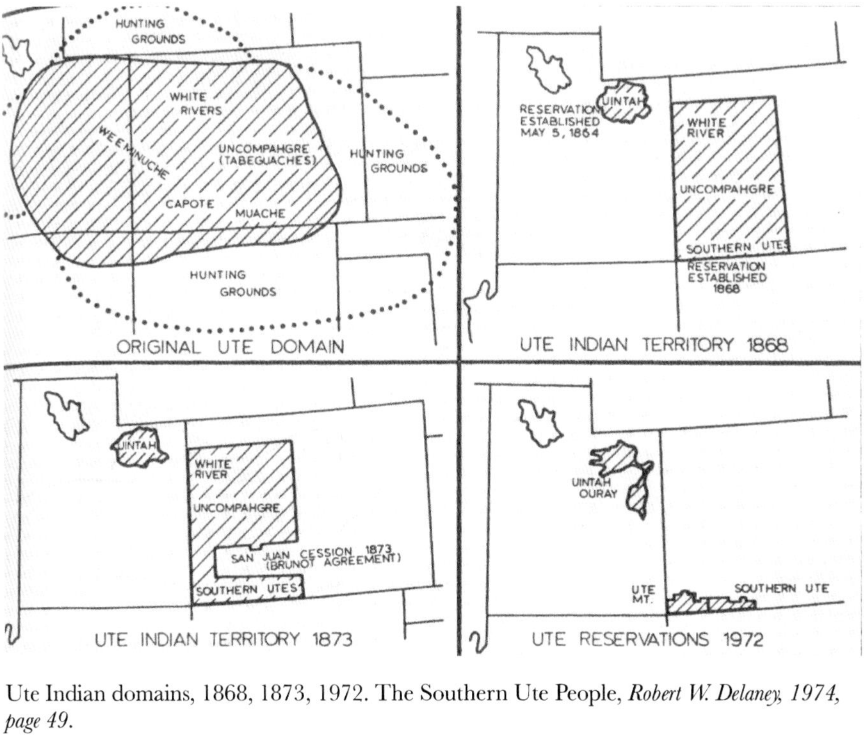

Ute Indian domains, 1868, 1873, 1972. The Southern Ute People, *Robert W. Delaney, 1974, page 49.*

TRAILS TO ROADS

After the Mexican-American War, permanent settlements were established along the Rio Grande in Colorado. The first, known as San Luis de la Culebra, was established in 1851 on the Rio Culebra River on the Sangre de Cristo Grant. To protect the early settlers, Fort Massachusetts was established about six miles north of the present-day town of Fort Garland, Colorado, on the eastern edge of the San Luis Valley, in 1852. La Loma de San Jose, west of present-day Del Norte, was first inhabited by Hispanic families from the Santa Fe area in 1859. Irrigation ditches were constructed and farms developed.[66]

Another Loma, or La Loma, was a purely speculative enterprise, having articles of incorporation filed on April 28, 1873. This settlement was on the north side of the river across from the town of Del Norte. La Loma was laid out with ninety-six full blocks and sixteen partial blocks. The names of those purchasing the lots were all Anglo, so this was not a Spanish or Mexican settlement.[67]

As the little towns of Loma and Del Norte were struggling to meet travelers' needs on both sides of the river, it became increasingly apparent to the locals that a road was needed for wagons to travel to the mines and back. With the land west of Del Norte belonging to the Utes, there was not a reasonable way to make a road, but expansion was coming. As early as 1872, enterprising gentlemen of the town were extolling the opportunities of the area, as documented in one of the Pueblo newspapers. "Major Cary French [president of the town board of Del Norte], and his good friend James Phillips [key founder of the town of Del Norte, and owner of the *Del Norte Prospector* newspaper], two well-known and enterprising citizens arrived in Pueblo yesterday, and paid us a pleasant call last evening. The Major is enthusiastic over the beauties and resources of that country, and gave us considerable valuable information."[68]

DEL NORTE AND ANTELOPE PARK TOLL ROAD COMPANY, MARCH 1874

The route into the San Juans was along an existing Indian/Spanish trail that followed the Rio Grande until it reached Antelope Springs (modern-day Broken Arrow), where it divided between the route southwest over Stony

Pass into Silverton and west over Spring Creek and Slumgullion passes into Lake City.[69] Because it was a trail, not even the roughest sort of road, travel into the mining areas was by foot or horseback, including large pack trains of oxen, burros and mules carrying materials and supplies. "Thousands of men, boys, tens of thousands of oxen, mules and burros are packing in milling machinery and freight to the three mining districts: Summit, Silverton and Lake City. Del Norte and Saguache are departure points."[70]

The Brunot Agreement was accepted by the Utes in October 1873, and Congress approved it on April 24, 1874.[71] Anticipating the resultant flood of miners into the San Juans, a few energetic capitalists formed the Del Norte and Antelope Park Toll Road Company to build part of the road into that country: James Phillips, Major French, William M. Van Liew (successful Del Norte Attorney and businessman) and others. During the winter of 1873–74, James Phillips visited his family in Illinois and met up with an old friend named Alonzo Hubbard, whom he had known in the California gold fields in 1850–52. James persuaded his friend to come to Colorado. In the spring of 1874, James Philips and Alonzo Hubbard contracted to build a road from the South Fork of the Rio Grande (there was no town there in those days) past Wagon Wheel Gap to the Franklin-Galloway Ranch (present-day San Juan Ranch) at the head of Antelope Park. The name of the company they formed was the Del Norte and Antelope Park Toll Road.[72]

The road was an expansion of the existing trail with boulders and trees removed, and possibly some leveling, but without the heavy equipment available today, everything was done by human hands using draft horses and mules. Water bars were put in place to drain the road and keep it from becoming full of bog holes. The most important thing that the road provided was the ability to travel in a stage, as opposed to having to travel by horseback.[73]

> *We left Del Norte just as the shades of night were falling over the Rio Grande. The moon shone brightly, and the evening was just cool enough to make an outside seat* [on the stagecoach] *desirable. I rode that way until we reached the Southfork, then took an inside seat until we reached Wagon Wheel Gap.*[74]

The toll road crossed the river twice near Wagon Wheel Gap. The first bridge was made to cross the Rio Grande from the south side of the river to the north side to avoid a boggy place where Goose Creek flows into the Rio Grande, creating a large delta that would not support wagon travel.

Looking upriver west toward the Gap. Second (westernmost) bridge that crossed the Rio Grande near Wagon Wheel Gap, circa 1874. The road to the hot springs was on the south side of the river, left in photo. *History Colorado, CHS J3846. Photo by William Henry Jackson.*

That bridge was on the downstream side of present-day Cottonwood Cove. A tollgate was erected on the north side of the river, just past where the first bridge crossed the river. The tollgate was operated by Alonzo Hubbard and his family, who were also responsible for maintenance of the road. Toll roads in the early west were an economical way to get roads constructed with private money, recouping the construction costs and those of ongoing maintenance by charging a toll to all and sundry who used the road.[75]

During the late winter/early spring of 1876, the year Colorado became a state, Alonzo Hubbard and his son built the Toll House at Wagon Wheel Gap. The family moved to the Toll House in the spring of 1876. Hubbard remained until the spring of 1882, buying up toll road stock until he owned practically all the stock.[76]

The road re-crossed from the north side of the river to the south because of a large cliff and squeezed between the south wall of Wagon Wheel Gap and the Rio Grande. "There is just room for the stage road beside the stream."[77] The second bridge is near where the railroad bridge is today. Traffic going up to the hot springs had to cross the second bridge from the north to the south and double back to the east a bit before joining up with the road south along Goose Creek to the Hot Springs.

Loma Wagon Wheel Gap and Antelope Park Toll Wagon Road Company, December 28, 1874

The fact that there was no bridge across the mighty and often dangerous Rio Grande between Del Norte and La Loma resulted in both settlements growing, prospering and competing—at least for a time. Traffic came up along the river on both sides, and most crossings were done farther upriver at the South Fork or Wagon Wheel Gap, where the fords were wider and safer. The competition between the two towns resulted in an interesting official race to build two roads to Wagon Wheel Gap and eventually on to Silverton. La Loma would build on the north side and Del Norte on the south side of the river—the loser having to move to the winner's town. This was a serious deal, and both sides competed fiercely.[78]

The north road was built, but La Loma, having less money than the Del Norte toll road folks, lost the race. The north road was completed just a few miles west of the South Fork toward Wagon Wheel Gap but was really never developed by the founding company. The section from Del Norte to South Fork is referred to today as the North River Road, and it is a gravel, county-maintained road used primarily by locals. Loma lost, and businesses moved to the south side of the river into Del Norte. This was no small task, moving about four hundred homes, a flour mill, a sawmill and many other buildings, of which there is no trace now.[79] Today, Rio Grande County uses the old La Loma site for a highway gravel pit.[80]

The southern road became the highway between Del Norte and South Fork. After just a couple of years of heavy use, the southern road from the South Fork west was having problems. In the summer of 1876, the Del Norte and Antelope Park Toll Road Company folks recognized that the north road was probably better for travel past South Fork to Wagon Wheel Gap, and they decided to purchase the Loma Wagon Wheel Gap Toll Road Company. The owners were extolled as liberal-minded men "who would improve the road for travel and build necessary bridges across the river [Rio Grande]. Last season a gang of men were sent over the road to clear out the stones, and Mr. Hubbard [manager of the Toll Gate at Wagon Wheel Gap] is doing the same work this year. And doing it well."[81]

By the summer of 1877, from the South Fork west, a toll road had been established on each side of the river, both owned by the Del Norte and Antelope Park Toll Road Company. The one on the north side had a "water grade" the entire distance, meaning it had water bars, slopes and cuts to ensure that mud puddles did not become bog holes. "The road people are of the opinion that there will be no difficulty in keeping this open at all seasons and in good traveling condition."[82] The Del Norte Antelope Park Toll Road carried all sorts of freight and people. From the *Colorado Springs Gazette* of March 3, 1877: "The traffic was incredibly heavy on the road. Messrs. Hermann Schiffer & Co. of Del Norte, estimate that the amount of freight sent into the San Juan country in 1876, including mining machinery, amounted to 4 million pounds."

Shortly, the eastern portion of the road on the south side of the river from South Fork to Wagon Wheel Gap proved to be too difficult to maintain and was moved to the north side for about half the distance to Wagon Wheel Gap. The road re-crossed to the south at the current American Park bridge. Today's road, with the aid of heavy equipment, was changed to run completely on the north side of the river, even blasting out part of the confining cliff just west of Wagon Wheel Gap. If one looks carefully, the old stage roadbed is still visible on the south side of the river, as is the backtrack into Wagon Wheel Gap from the western bridge.

THE DENVER AND RIO GRANDE (D&RG) RAILROAD

The D&RG Railroad was organized by General W.J. Palmer in 1870. The first portion of the rail line, from Denver through Colorado Springs to Pueblo, was completed in 1872. A branch line from Pueblo west to Cuchara and La Veta was completed in 1876. From there, it was continued over La Veta Pass west into the town of Alamosa on July 4, 1878, and Del Norte in July 1881.[83]

The abandoned toll road roadbed between South Fork and Wagon Wheel Gap on the eastern end was on the south side of the river and was planned to be used for that section of the rail line spur. The rail line had to cross to the north side of the river about midway to the Gap, again following the abandoned roadbed. Then, of course, it had to cross to the south just past Wagon Wheel Gap.

After much dickering, the D&RG purchased the toll right-of-way, the toll house and 160 acres of land around Wagon Wheel Gap from the Del Norte and Antelope Park Toll Road Company, which was mostly owned by Hubbard, in 1881.[84] Once the property was acquired, the process of making a rail line up to South Fork and on to Wagon Wheel Gap was implemented, requiring two years to complete.

> *The railroad was completed to Wagon Wheel Gap this morning* [July 13, 1883]. *The road has been running for some time to South Fork, fifteen miles from this place, and was graded this far last year. The track laying has been going on for the past few days, and the completion of the road is regarded an auspicious event. It runs along the valley of the Rio Grande for miles, opening up one of the most beautiful bits of scenery in the Rocky Mountains.*[85]

The rail line was extended westward to South Fork in 1882 and in July 1883 as far as Wagon Wheel Gap, where it terminated. The railroad had been extended westward as far as Wagon Wheel Gap, with the intention of reaching the Creede Mining District. However, the railroad found itself financially overextended due to the rapid expansion during the early 1880s and decided to postpone further construction.[86] Therefore, materials and passengers bound for destinations farther west than Wagon Wheel Gap had to be transferred to stages and freight wagons for the remainder of their trip.

With no flood control on the Rio Grande, many times, bridges washed away and had to be repaired or replaced.

> *The Rio Grande was overflowing the tracks in the Wagon Wheel Gap canyon, and a washout has occurred that is estimated to be fully one hundred fifty feet in length and approximately fifteen feet deep; the bridges just above and below the Gap depot are said to be practically impassable; the freight train was not able to get over the wrecked bridge and was stalled on this side.*[87]

For the next few years, the railroad spur from South Fork to Wagon Wheel Gap was difficult to maintain and was closed during the winter months, opened only after the spring runoff had subsided, usually mid- to late June—depending on the snow and high water—and closed before the snows got too deep, usually in October. Round-trip ticket prices were sixteen dollars from Colorado Springs to Wagon Wheel Gap, with daily trains running.[88]

Wagon Wheel Gap Depot, circa 2009. *Denver Public Library, Western History Collection, AUR-811.*

During the early spring of 1889, rail operations were cut back to Del Norte because of little to no traffic and heavy snow on the west end of the line, thus suspending rail service to Wagon Wheel Gap for the next three years.

The last passenger train ran past Wagon Wheel Gap on its final trip between Alamosa and Creede on June 18, 1932. The railroad tracks remain, and the segment between Creede and South Fork, including Wagon Wheel Gap, was formally abandoned in 1999.[89] Thankfully, the depot building was saved the fate of demolition that so many structures of the early railroad era met. The depot building was listed in the National Register of Historic Places in 1976, when the property was owned by Allan Phipps. The depot remains as a surviving reminder of a booming time when the future lay there at the station, the hub of Wagon Wheel Gap.[90]

4

TAKING THE WATERS

The hot spring of the Wagon-wheel is a bowl of ten or twelve feet in diameter, sunken in a rich meadow whose dark, heavy grass grows down to the edges of the heated water. The water of this spring is strongly sulphur—the temperature 115–120° Fahrenheit. Only a few feet from this central bowl of still hot water, there is another spring, very cold, and still another of hot sparkling soda, which the residents have learned to sip like coffee or hot punch. They allege the water to be very pleasant, but the taste must evidently be acquired. Bathing places are arranged for both the hot sulphur spring and the hot soda.

—Rocky Mountain Presbyterian, *October 1, 1877, page 1*

People have used geothermal water and mineral waters for bathing and to remedy health issues for thousands of years. Based on archaeological finds in Asia, we know that mineral water has been used for bathing for about five thousand years. In 1326, Collin le Loup, an iron master, "discovered" the chalybeate (iron-bearing) springs of Spa, Belgium, as a cure for his illness. Around these springs, a famous health resort eventually grew, and the term *spa* came to refer to any health resort located near natural springs.[91]

> *Centuries of experience have demonstrated that in certain disorders, the intelligent use of mineral waters is a more potent curative agency than drugs. The term "mineral waters" is applied to those waters which are used in the treatment of disease, either by internal administration or by*

> *external applications, and which owe their virtue to their solid or gaseous constituents or to their elevated temperatures.*[92]

Evidence for tuberculosis has been found in skeletons dated to 5000 Before Common Era (BCE) and is commonly found in the preserved remains of Egyptian mummies. As people spread throughout the world, they brought along the disease. The first evidence of tuberculosis in England appeared at the same time that the Romans invaded. By the mid-seventeenth century, one in five deaths in London was due to tuberculosis. From the seventeenth to the nineteenth century, in Europe, the epidemic of tuberculosis was called the White Plague. There is significant evidence that Columbus did not bring tuberculosis to America; it was here long before he arrived. About the turn of the nineteenth century, the death rate worldwide was estimated at seven million people a year, another fifty million openly infected, with London and New York being the two most affected cities in the developed world.[93]

Although the bacterium can infect any part of a body, the most common was pulmonary tuberculosis, an infection of the lungs resulting from inhalation of the bacterium. The person so infected would develop shortness of breath, cough up blood and have limited lung function, commonly described as "consumption." In other words, the person would just wither away, the infection literally consuming the body. Once contracted, it was most often fatal in a short time. The name *tuberculosis* was coined from the observation of small cheesy-looking boils that clustered together in infected lung tissue, which resembled a group of potatoes—tubers—hence tubercules in the lungs, or tuberculosis.[94]

In 1859, the first sanatorium was developed in Germany to remove the ill to a place with clear air, opportunity for exercise, better nutrition and separation from the unhealthy and stressful conditions they had been living in. Without the benefit of any trials to determine effectiveness, but with no other options, sanatoriums sprang up around the world. Treatments varied widely; some were hideously cruel and none truly effective. The death sentence from consumption lasted into the 1950s, when, thankfully, modern diagnostics and treatments were able to actually cure tuberculosis. Up until that time, tuberculosis sufferers depended on sanatoriums.[95]

Although not equipped with the tools of modern medicine, the physicians of the nineteenth and twentieth centuries were tireless in their efforts to provide palliative, but rarely curative, relief for the millions suffering from consumption. The Germans believed, as theorized by Dr.

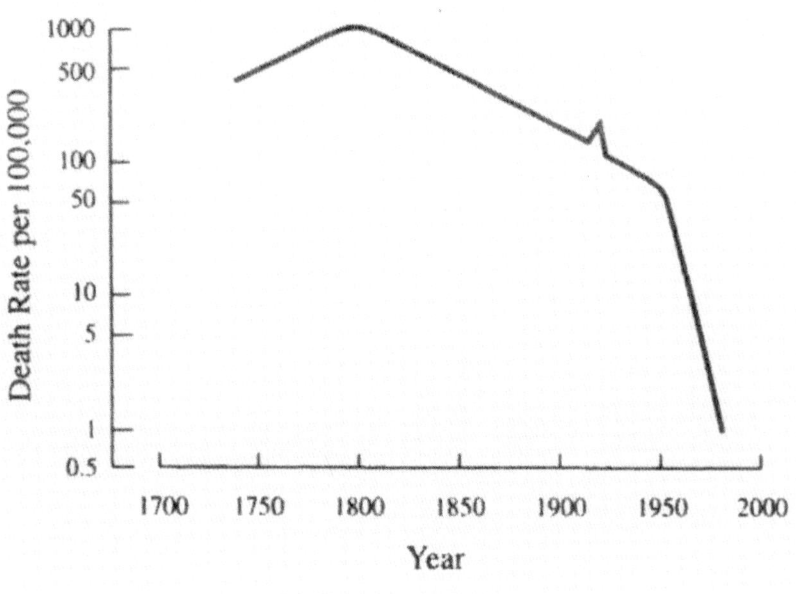

Annual mortality rates from pulmonary tuberculosis in England and Wales, 1850–1960. *Wayne LaMorte, MD, PhD, MPH.*

Felix von Niemeyer in 1868, that "the use of the alkaline muriatic [sodium carbonate, sodium chloride and carbonic acid] springs has, in many patients, a really curative influence."[96]

American medicine, based primarily on the more advanced work in Europe, followed suit. Mineral water sanatoriums were developed across the eastern states, notably the Virginia Hot Springs and the celebrated Arkansas Hot Springs. As expansion moved the United States' population westward, hot springs were a much sought-after source of possible cures. With the geologically recent volcanic activity in the Rocky Mountains, the state of Colorado was found to have numerous hot springs bubbling out of ravines, hillsides and valleys. "There are few, if any, regions in America richer in mineral springs than Colorado."[97]

Rheumatic fever was another bacterially caused disease relatively common during these times. While not always fatal, rheumatic fever usually led to a lifetime of dealing with the debilitating effects of "rheumatism." The damage from rheumatic fever often resulted in inflammation in the heart, joints, skin or central nervous system, causing long-term health problems, including rheumatic heart disease. A bout of rheumatism caused the patient extreme pain and loss of functionality, sometimes even death. Rheumatic fever is now treatable with antibiotics when diagnosed properly. However, at the time, it was basically untreatable, and these patients were also looking for some sort of relief from their suffering.[98]

The hot springs at Wagon Wheel Gap were well known among Native Americans, who apparently referred to them as "Little Medicine." The Pagosa Hot Springs on the western side of the San Juans were known as "Big Medicine."[99] The springs themselves were actually too hot for immersion bathing, so a mud bath was taken in the warm, damp mire surrounding the springs. The Wagon Wheel Gap hot springs were made known to the general public by the reports of a number of government expeditions into this area in 1873–74. The Wheeler report, specifically, contained detailed descriptions of the area and also chemical analyses of the various springs.

> *The Lt. George M. Wheeler expedition was organized for explorations and surveys west of the 100th Meridian, conducted in 1873/1874. As the party left Pueblo, Colorado, heading west for the southwestern Colorado mountains in the late summer, the local papers included a summary description of the party. The expedition, which numbers over seventy men, is divided into nine parties under competent officers of the engineer corps, and of the line, assisted by civilians of reputation in science, the objects heretofore being a thorough exploration and accurate information, geographical and geological, and in the various branches of natural history, and the work will include a careful survey of the mining regions in the Sierra La Plata and San Juan regions. The outfit is very complete and promises results of more than usual importance. The men are well armed but expect no trouble with the Indians and no adventures except those which come legitimately to an expedition, whose objects are definite, in regions almost wholly unknown and undescribed.*[100]

One of the civilians with a "reputation in science" who accompanied the expedition was Dr. Oscar Loew, a chemist of some renown. He conducted numerous chemical analyses on a variety of sample types and matrices collected during the expedition. In a letter dated May 20, 1874, Dr. Oscar Loew wrote to Lieutenant George M. Wheeler, Corps of Engineers, in charge of the U.S. Engineer Office, Geographical and Geological Explorations and Services West of the 100th Meridian, Washington, D.C., about "the composition of mineral waters that were found throughout the extent of the survey area."[101] Many samples from mineral springs were collected and analyzed, including those from the hot springs at Wagon Wheel Gap, at the time and for several years also known as Liberty Hot Springs.[102] An excerpt from the Wheeler report follows. Note: historically, the element known today as sulfur was spelled in the European style, sulphur; similarly, the modern sulfide was sulphide. Quotes taken from older sources are verbatim and include the original spelling of sulphur or sulphide. However, the text will use the modern spelling of sulfur or sulfide.

> *No.1 has a temperature of about 150°F, is bubbling continually, and is about 8 feet wide and 12 feet long.* [This is today called the Hot Sulfur Spring.]
> *No. 2 is a small bubbling spring, cold, of about 1 foot in diameter, and gives out a strong odor of sulphureted hydrogen.* [hydrogen sulfide, H_2S. This is today called the Cold Spring.]
> *No. 3 is situated some distance from Nos. 1 and 2, on the foot of a hill; it bubbles constantly and is of a temperature of 140°F. This spring is about 3 feet wide and nearly the same length.* [This is today called the Hot Soda Spring.][103]

Indians, miners and locals used the Liberty Hot Springs at Wagon Wheel Gap for some years together, although prior to 1874 the land was officially part of the Ute lands recognized by the United States. Following the ratification of the Brunot Agreement in early 1874, which removed the Utes from the Wagon Wheel Gap area, afflicted Americans began to flock to the hot springs to seek a cure for a variety of ailments. Newspapers carried stories of miraculous cures effected by the healing waters. They also provide an excellent description of conditions in the early days of the hot springs. The attractions of climate, scenery and hope of healing drew many throughout the United States and even from Europe, all searching for a permanent cure but willing to accept temporary relief from their afflictions. The process was to immerse oneself into water as hot as one can take, then, upon emerging, wrap oneself in blankets and sweat out the impurities.[104]

> *The springs are about one mile from Henson's ranch, at the mouth of Wagon Wheel Gap, immediately on the creek known as Goose Creek, due south from the* [Rio] *Grande. We were prepared to see something unusual, of course, but nothing very unusual. We have been surprised—greatly surprised. There are four springs of size and peculiarity which deserve special mention. The first, situated about 20 yards from the "Pilgrim*

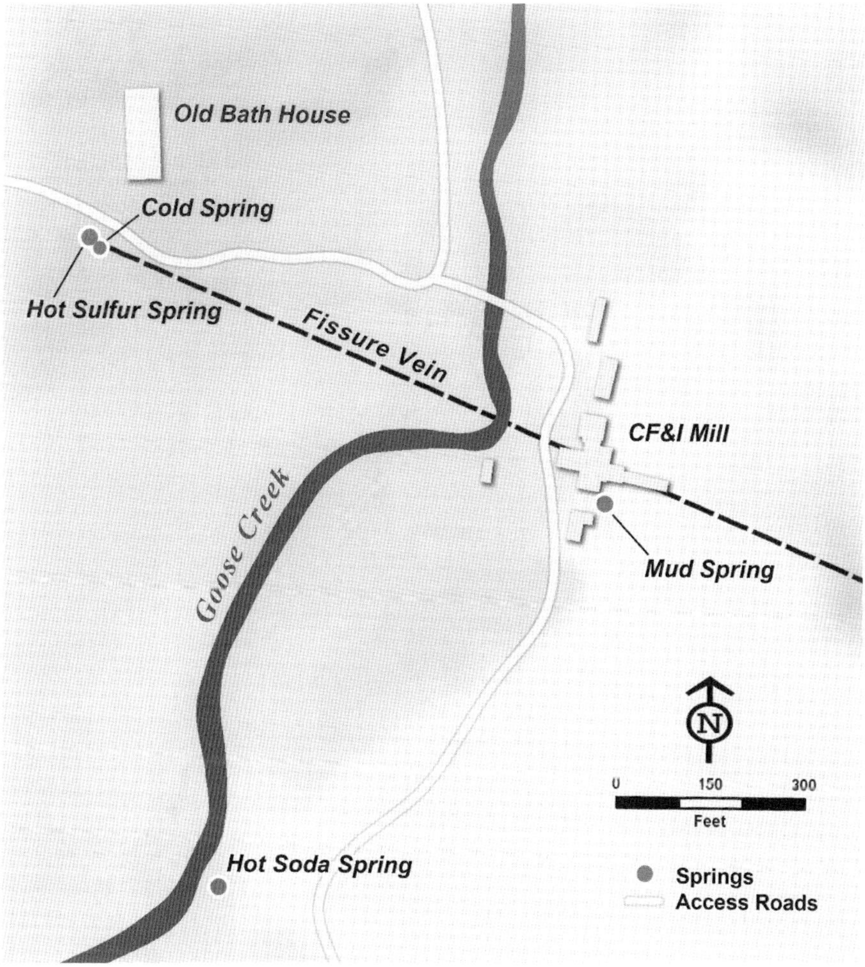

Location of Wagon Wheel Gap major springs. Note: The Mud Spring was not identified until later. *Cartography by John Evaskovich, 2019.*

House" and bath rooms, is very hot; has scores of bubbling, boiling, rushing "feeders" that never halt or tire in their work of throwing up boiling water, impregnated with mineral and possessed of healing powers that seem almost a fable. These waters have been turned into a pipe and directly through a house containing six neat, clean and comfortable bathing rooms, in which, by turning a cork, a bath is ready in five minutes, so hot that one cannot keep the hand in the water. Of course, any temperature can be secured by waiting a time for the waters to cool. The effects of these baths are wonderful, and one of our party, who came here sick, is as frisky as any

> *boy of 10. Adjoining the bath room is a comfortable house, where nothing is needed to add to the pleasure of the place. Within four feet of this great boiling spring is another about as large as a flour barrel. And singular as it may seem, its waters are as cold as ice water, and taste much like the waters of the celebrated Virginia Springs.*[105]

Not all were fans of the extremely hot springs, however. Temperatures ranged from 135 to 150°F (excluding the cold one). To put the spring temperatures in context, a home hot water heater set at 150°F will give users a third-degree burn within seconds. Recommendations are to set home hot water heaters to no more than 120°F, which will still provide a third-degree burn in five minutes.[106]

The following newspaper item discusses the relatively cooler springs in nearby Antelope Park, which were to be developed as competition for the hotter springs at Wagon Wheel Gap. The successful stage stop at Alden's Junction (today's Broken Arrow) was where the stage route to Lake City split off directly to the west, while the route to Silverton continued south and then west.[107] Developing the springs would be a boon to Alden's operation, and he proceeded to make pools and a bathing house. The major problem with these springs was that while significantly warmer than the nearly freezing river water, they were well below body temperature of 98°F and soon drained a body of heat. A backyard hot tub is usually kept between 100 and 104°F, so a lounging pool below 90°F would feel quite cold very quickly. In an anonymous quote, a long-term area resident who grew up learning to swim in the Antelope Springs pools said, "They were gosh-darn cold!" The cooler springs did not become much of a draw for the bathing public.

> *To-morrow I leave for the hot springs, at Wagon Wheel Gap. These springs, in my opinion, have been largely over-estimated. They contain too much caloric, and the transition from the cool surroundings of a mountainous region to the boiling temperature of a scalding bath, is too violent—at least for my physique. Mr. Alden, at Antelope Springs, has made arrangements to open next season a more enjoyable bath, with the confident knowledge of possessing more healthful chemical properties in the water. The temperature of these springs does not exceed 90 degrees Fahrenheit, and their effect upon the invalid is said to be marvelous. By the time travel sets in next season he will have prepared commodious bathing houses where invalids can stop off the stage and rejuvenate without loss of time or convenience.*[108]

THE CHEMISTRY OF THE SPRINGS

What are the properties of the mineral springs that were believed to be of such beneficial value? First, they are usually hot water. When people soak in hot springs, the heat vasodilates a lot of the blood vessels, which enhances health benefits with regards to circulation through the body. Vasodilation allows the body to absorb some of the alkaline minerals (such as calcium, magnesium, potassium, sodium and lithium), and the theory is that these minerals neutralize the acids the body produces in times of stress or injury. Is this factual? Many people believe that soaking in Epsom salt (magnesium sulfate) is beneficial, and that contains one of the alkaline minerals.[109]

Beyond the thermal effects, the variety of minerals found in the mineral springs, and their concentration, determines the type of disease for which the waters are most efficacious. In the late nineteenth century, there were numerous studies and reports on the large number of mineral springs across the world, including the United States, utilizing a scientific system of classification based on chemical composition. The waters at Wagon Wheel Gap were classified as: thermal, radioactive, saline, lithic and sodio-calcic-magnetic.[110]

WAGON WHEEL GAP HOT SULFUR SPRING

Also known as Spring No. 1, the Main Spring and the 4UR Ranch Spring, this is considered a purgative spring because it contains sulfated water, consisting of sodium sulfate and also sodium chloride and alkaline (sodium, calcium and magnesium) carbonates in active amounts. The most important of this group of waters is that of Glauber's salt, after the Dutch/German chemist and apothecary Johann Rudolph Glauber who discovered it in 1625 in Austrian spring water. He named it *sal mirabilis* (miraculous salt) because of its medicinal properties: the crystals were used as a general-purpose laxative until more sophisticated alternatives came about in the 1900s. The chemical is sodium sulfate decahydrate, $Na_2SO_4 \cdot 10H_2O$, and it occurs as white or colorless monoclinic crystals, highly soluble in water.[111] The Hot Sulfur Spring is used for bathing and has a trace of hydrogen sulfide odor. These bathing waters were reported to be the best for rheumatism.

> *Administered warm or hot, they at first increase, but later diminish intestinal peristalsis* [involuntary movements of the muscles in the digestive tract]. *These waters also stimulate biliary secretion and excite gastric and duodenal peristalsis. The secondary effects are seen in the improvement of the appetite and of the general metabolic interchange. Their continued use causes a diminution in body weight.*[112]

In addition to the metals and salts in the water, there are two isotopes of naturally occurring radioactive elements in the springs, which are found in almost all groundwaters in Colorado. The first is an isotope of radium, Ra-226, which is a radioactive decay product of uranium-238 found occurring naturally in the soil, especially on the Colorado Plateau. The other isotope found in these waters is radon, Rn-222, which is a radioactive decay product of Ra-226 and is a gas—also naturally occurring. The levels of the two isotopes found in the Hot Sulfur spring are Rn-22 at 72 picocuries per liter (pCi/L) and Ra-226 at 3.6 pCi/L.[113]

To put those values in context, the Environmental Protection Agency (EPA) and various states have recommended standards for radon in drinking water ranging from 300 to 10,000 pCi/L, but no standard currently exists. The EPA Safe Drinking Water Act limit for all isotopes of radium combined is 5 pCi/L. Therefore, neither of the radioactive isotopes found in the Wagon Wheel Gap waters are of any negative health concern. However, low levels of radioactivity are credited with positive results, known as the "hormesis effect," as demonstrated through observation of exposure to low levels of naturally occurring radioactivity.[114]

Scientists lacked the ability to detect radiation until 1903, when J.J. Thompson was able to detect radioactivity in well water. This led to the discovery by others that the waters in the majority of the world's most famous health springs were also radioactive. This radioactivity is almost always due to radon and radium that is present in the soil through which the waters flow. In the 1920s, water containing high levels of radium was sold as Radithor, believed to be responsible for many curative properties.[115]

Who could doubt that it must be the radioactivity that was responsible for the curative properties of the health springs? Certainly not Surgeon General Dr. George H. Torney, who wrote (circa 1910), "Relief may be reasonably expected at the Hot Springs in…various forms of gout and rheumatism, neuralgia; metallic or malarial poisoning, chronic Brights disease, gastric dyspepsia, chronic diarrhea, chronic skin lesions, etc." Further details were provided by Dr. C.G. Davis, who noted in the

American Journal of Clinical Medicine, "Radioactivity prevents insanity, rouses noble emotions, retards old age, and creates a splendid, youthful, joyous life."[116]

Professor Bertram Boltwood of Yale explained the scientific basis for the cures in the following way: The radioactivity was "carrying electrical energy into the depths of the body and there subjecting the juices, protoplasm, and nuclei of the cells to an immediate bombardment by explosions of electrical atoms." It stimulated "cell activity, arousing all secretory and excretory organs…causing the system to throw off waste products" and was "an agent for the destruction of bacteria." Radon was believed to be so important to water that it was considered its life element. Without it, water was dead. Radon was to water what oxygen was to air.[117]

Now that turn-of-the-century science, in 1900, had an explanation for the curative properties of the springs, the health spas and resorts associated with them began to do a booming business. Names were changed to include the magic terms *radioactive* or *radium*. Visitors came from near and far to soak in the waters and inhale the air. Marble palaces (still open for business) were built over the springs in Joachimstal in what is now the Czech Republic, and luxurious spas sprouted like weeds around hot springs worldwide.[118]

Many countries around the world and European states offer a chance to be healed by the radioactive hot springs through their official medical plans. European studies speak of the function of radiation in the healing process. Unfortunately, the Cold War–based fear of radiation has made this branch of medicine disappear in North America. Across the United States, the composition of these healing waters has not changed, but at most of them, the signs and advertising no longer proclaim the presence of radioactivity in their hot springs.[119]

The first bathhouse known to be erected by the Henson group is reported to have been there as early as 1872, even though the lands were still part of the Ute reservation. The spring was walled with rock and the water transported into the bathhouse, along with a source of cold water to allow temperature control for bathing purposes. The early Wheeler data give the water temperature of the main spring at 150°F, with a flow rate of "several barrels per minute." The current temperature is about 138°F, with a flow of forty-five gallons per minute.

> *It boils up in a sparkling fountain at the upper end of an oval being seven or eight feet wide by, perhaps, twenty-five feet long that has been walled up*

> *with stone and cement. It is about five feet deep and too hot for bathing. The water is conducted thence through wooden troughs to the bath houses, which contain six private rooms with a tub in each, and two large plunge baths. The latter are about four feet deep, and ten by twenty in size, floored and walled with plank.*[120]

From the original bathhouse, which served for almost thirty years, "Extensive improvements are being made at Wagon Wheel Gap hot springs by General Palmer, who owns the property. The old bath-house will be replaced by a modern structure and the hotel greatly improved."[121] And as with all things done by General Palmer, the new bathhouse was upscale, similar to the famous baths of Europe and the eastern United States. It had

Earliest bathhouse at the Hot Sulfur Spring, owned by Henson and Goodwin and others, circa mid-1870s. *From the Charles A. Harbert collection.*

Remodeled bathhouse with re-walled spring at the Hot Sulfur Spring, owned by Henson and Goodwin, circa late-1870s. *From the Charles A. Harbert collection.*

separate bathing rooms for men and women and also "sick rooms" for those invalids who came to the springs in hopes of a cure.

As part of the Palmer renovation, the earlier rock-walled pool was reworked and lined with concrete, with a railing around it. The water from Hot Sulfur Spring was piped into the pools inside the large bathhouse and is also the source of water for the main bathing pool now.

Used for many years, the Palmer Grand bathhouse was decommissioned by Allan Phipps in the early 1960s and replaced by an open-air ground-level pool. The large modern inside hot tub and heated outdoor pool were constructed by Pete and Lindsey Leavell in 2012. Restoration of the Palmer bathhouse was in process during the tenure of Charles Leavell, but upon his

Wagon Wheel Gap Hot Sulphur Spring and bathhouse built in 1902, circa 1910. *Colorado Springs Pioneers Museum, accession # 42147, File Location, oversize 24, Folder Wagon Wheel Gap.*

death in 2000, work was suspended. For the 4UR hot springs outdoor pool, well water is used that is heated through a heat-exchange system with the hot water from the Hot Sulfur Spring. The 4UR hot springs indoor pool uses water that is piped in from the Hot Sulfur Spring and cooled appropriately.

WAGON WHEEL GAP COLD SPRING

There were early reports of a very small, very cold spring with a strong sulfur odor and significant hydrogen sulfide content located just a few feet away from the Hot Sulfur Spring. An early engraving from 1885 clearly shows the cold spring adjacent to the hot sulfur spring.[122] "One of them, the largest, is eight feet wide and 12 feet long, and the water comes out of the ground at 150 degrees Fahrenheit. The second spring is a small, bubbling, cold, about a foot in diameter, that gives out a strong smell of sulphureted hydrogen [hydrogen sulfide].[123]

HOT SULPHUR SPRINGS, WAGON WHEEL GAP.

Woodblock print of Wagon Wheel Gap Hot Sulfur Spring with adjacent Cold Spring, people depicted drinking from both. Two-story hotel in the background, with bathhouse and cottages. *From* Crofutt's Grip-sack Guide of Colorado, *page 154.*

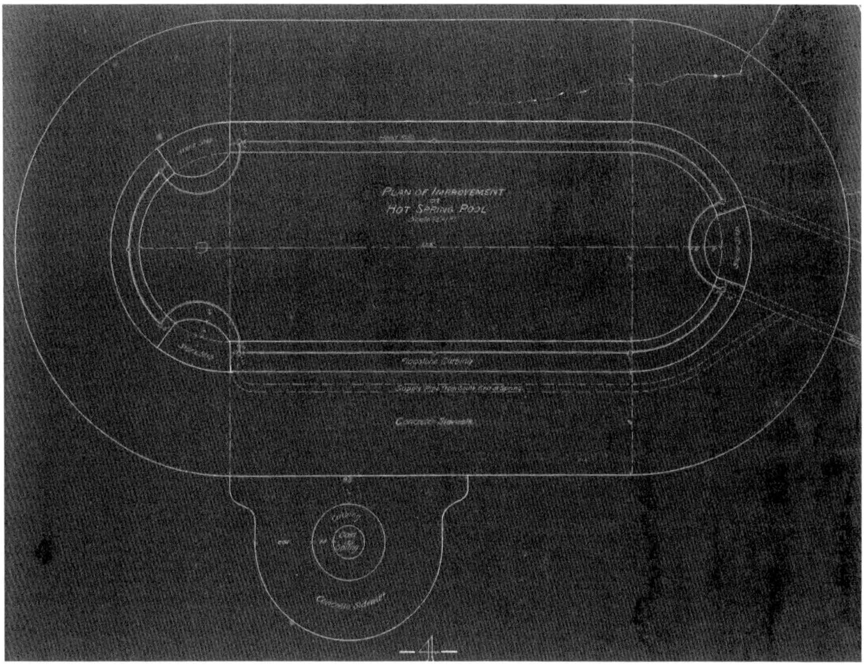

Blueprint of hot sulfur and cold spring improvement, Thomas McLaren, architect, 1902. *Courtesy of the 4UR Ranch.*

The blueprints for the Palmer-era modernization of the two springs include a larger pool for the hot springs and another immediately adjacent for the cold spring, re-walling the hot and cold springs separately.[124] There seems to be no remnant of the cold spring today, and the planned re-walling by Palmer appears not to have been implemented. Or, the actual re-walling may have encompassed both springs, such that they are now comingled.[125] Being fed by a near-surface (vadose zone) water system, it is possible that the source simply dried up, leaving the cold spring no longer discernable.

Use of the cold spring is not well-documented, and with the strong hydrogen sulfide odor, was likely difficult to drink, although often consumed. This type of water was said to have a few positive health effects. "The action of sulphuretted hydrogen [hydrogen sulfide] is said to stimulate the intestinal glands—especially the liver, augmenting secretion, and general debility."[126]

WAGON WHEEL GAP HOT SODA SPRING

This spring is classified as "Alkaline-muriated," with the most prominent ingredients being sodium bicarbonate and sodium chloride. Usually, these types of springs also have dissolved carbonic acid in them, although there were no analyses conducted for that common gas. The waters have been described as "pure, bright, sparkling and pleasant to the taste; yet the extreme alkalinity naturally prevents its use as a continual beverage. Residents have learned to sip it like coffee or hot punch. They allege it to be very pleasant, but the taste must evidently be acquired."[127]

Originally, there was a bathing house for each of the two large springs.[128] All of the springs were owned by the Henson group, but the property was split when purchased by two different entities: the Hot Sulfur Spring on the west side of Goose Creek was owned by the Palmer group and included a bathhouse and large hotel, while the Hot Soda Spring on the east side of Goose Creek, with its bathing house, was owned by McClelland and partners.[129] For a short time, Hot Soda Spring also had a small hotel associated with it. After Palmer acquired the McClelland property in 1906, the bathing house and facilities received some extensive upgrades in 1907,[130] and it is obvious that both the Hot Sulfur and Hot Soda Springs have identical walling from the Palmer era. After closure of the mill and mine on the east side of Goose Creek in 1950, owner Arthur Sharp tore down any remaining structures near the Hot Soda Spring and installed a modern steel and enamel bathtub for his ailing wife's personal use, away from the tourists in the main bathhouse. The pool discharges now as it has for some time, into nearby Goose Creek; the bathhouse and hotel are gone, and the spring is not used commercially. The 1875 Wheeler report stated a temperature of 140°F with "considerable flow," but today the temperature is an almost pleasant 109°F, with a flow of ninety gallons per minute.

The Hot Soda Spring water was known for its specific effect on aggravated cases of rheumatic and skin diseases and also for diseases of the kidneys. The water has a slightly diuretic or, in large doses, laxative effect.

> *The dissolved carbonic acid renders water palatable by imparting the "sparkle" and a slightly acidulous taste; it increases the appetite; by causing eructations* [belching] *it assists in expelling any gases formed during digestion, and in overcoming flatulence; it allays nausea and thirst and is said to increase gastric secretion and intestinal peristalsis. It combines with the carbonates to form the bicarbonates and to render the urine less acid.*

> *I would warn against the rapid and excessive drinking of any carbonated waters especially in persons with cardiac and gastric weaknesses. These waters must not be drunk ad libitum, as the amount of chlorides they contain may further weaken debilitated patients. The waters of these domestic springs are used mostly for bathing purposes.*[131]

The waters of the springs at Wagon Wheel Gap retained their credibility among the afflicted. For those suffering souls who were not able to come to the springs, entrepreneurs attempted to take the springs to them. Bottling of spring waters across the country became a large industry. According to the local newspapers, bottling of the waters from the Hot Soda Spring was a successful endeavor. The water was originally bottled by John Knoedel, a German immigrant who had lived in Leadville. He then moved to Creede in 1891, where he operated a saloon.[132]

The owner of the Hot Soda Spring, J.C. McClelland, pursued the bottling of the hot soda spring water, since he had observed that so many people drank it. He teamed up with Knoedel and formed a bottling corporation in 1892.[133] Their efforts succeeded in the early part of 1894, when "Wagon Wheel Gap Mineral Water" came on the market.

> *John Knoedel, manager of the Creede bottling works, has finally succeeded in handling the water of the hot soda spring at Wagon Wheel Gap so as to put it upon the market. The water has long been known to possess the highest medicinal qualities and now that it is on the market it is certain to command a big trade. The bottling of the water promises to become a considerable enterprise and it is a matter for congratulation that Mr. Knoedel has taken hold of the business.*[134]

The bottling and sale of Wagon Wheel Gap Mineral Water was a reasonably successful endeavor; however, Knoedel was killed in a snow slide in the winter of 1899.[135] McClelland had departed Wagon Wheel Gap by this time, but the popular Hot Soda Spring water was entered into the St. Louis World's Fair in 1904, where it received a silver medal. The award from that event hangs in the powder room of the main lodge of the 4UR resort. There were a few other Colorado waters that also received silver awards: Magnetic Mineral Water from Clark and Wolff, Pueblo; Manitou Sulphur Springs, Manitou Springs Company, Manitou; Vichy, Fred Stoekder, Canon City; Yampah Water, Glenwood Springs Company; Colorado Lithia, Pueblo; and Columbia Mineral Water, Denver. No Colorado waters won

Silver award for the Hot Soda Springs Mineral Water, St. Louis World's Fair, 1904. *Courtesy of the 4UR Ranch.*

a gold award. Poland Spring mineral water from Portland, Maine, won the grand prize.[136] Poland Spring water was bottled as early as 1859 and earned fame throughout the country and the rest of the world. Bottled for over 160 years, Poland Spring water is still enjoyed today.[137]

MORE SPRINGS

Over the years, numerous articles about the Wagon Wheel Gap Hot Springs have been published. The number of springs reported varies widely. Some reports are as high as forty—which likely included several seeps and mud pits. The most reliable number of significant springs comes from a government survey by the U.S. Geologic Service (USGS), which conducted a mineral survey of the general area and did a specific visit to the hot springs in 1911.

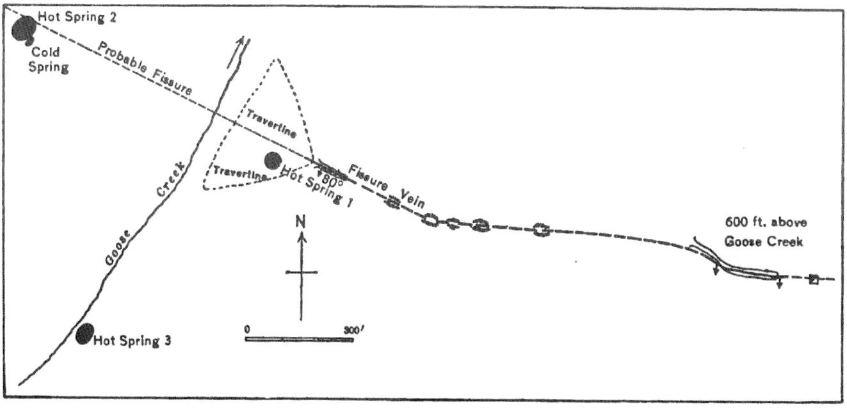

Sketch showing position of hot springs and associated mineral deposits of Wagon Wheel Gap, Colorado, 1913. Note: Spring No. 1 is the Mud Spring, No. 2 is the Hot Sulfur Spring and No. 3 is the Hot Soda Spring. *From Emmons and Larsen, "The Hot Springs and the Mineral Deposits of Wagon Wheel Gap, Colorado."*

Published in 1913, the report identified four major springs: the Hot Sulfur Spring (No. 2), the Hot Soda Spring (No. 3), the Cold Spring and another called the Mud Spring (No. 1), which was also hot.[138]

The USGS study used a different numbering system than the earlier Wheeler report, but it is interesting to note that the Mud Spring seems to have diminished to such an extent today that it is no longer obvious. The Mud Spring was referred to in a newspaper article from the *Creede Candle* on May 20, 1892: "the improved one [Hot Sulfur], the hot soda, and the mud spring,"

The USGS report includes analytical work done in 1904 and lists the temperature of the Mud Spring at 135°F. The assumption stated by the USGS report is that since "they are the only hot springs known in the area; it is reasonable to assume that they have a common origin."[139]

Yet another government study was conducted in 1976, by the Colorado Geological Survey. The mission of this effort was to collect hydrogeological data of thermal springs and wells in Colorado and assess their geothermal value.[140] A wide variety of analytes were tested for and physical measurements made on the two springs that were in evidence at that time. The data reported in the 1976 study are very similar to those from the 1904 study, although a significantly greater number of analytes were tested; therefore, not all results can be compared. Quarterly testing was performed, and minimal variation occurred throughout the year. The average annual temperatures for both springs dropped about fifteen degrees each from the earliest data from 1874, again minimal variation during the year.[141]

The activity and temperature of the springs has calmed and cooled down in the past two hundred years of available data. An observation in 1822 of geyser-like activity in the main spring, "a Spert of Watter Rose up some distance above the leavel of the Watter in the Pon and Was about the Size of a flour Barrel," was not observed in 1874.[142] The total number of hot springs today has been reduced to the two existing springs, with a drop in temperature of the Hot Sulfur from 150°F in 1874 to 138°F in 2017; and the Hot Soda Spring from 140°F in 1874 to 109°F in 2017.

The San Juan Mountains contain roughly sixty-two hot springs scattered around the region.[143] The springs located on the 4UR appear to be the only hot springs left within Mineral County, which at one point was most likely rampant with geothermal activity. As hot water travels through the fractures to the surface, it deposits minerals that eventually clog the pathways up and reduce the permeability through which the water can reach the surface. Also, consistent with the quiescent tectonic activity in the area, the cooling magma chamber responsible for heating the water may not be doing so as effectively anymore. The temperature of these springs changes with variable geothermal gradients occurring below Earth's surface. Just as the convection of heat moves liquid-like wax through a lava lamp—bubbling blobs of the material around the container—the mantle swirls and cycles hot magma around, which causes a variation in surface temperatures and warping.[144]

NOT ALL WHO CAME WERE CURED

As the Liberty Hot Springs attracted the ill and infirm, it was obvious that some would expire at the springs or on their way to or from there. Locals were buried in the nearby Creede Cemetery, and others were shipped back to their place of origin for interment. There is no record of any cemetery on the current property, although there are two known graves of young children who expired while passing through the area. Three-year-old Myra B. Ward, who apparently died while traveling with her family on the way from Leadville to Silverton in 1880,[145] is interred on the hillside north of what was the Wagon Wheel Gap stage station, with a small headstone commemorating her short life. Beside her stone is another with the name

Ruth B., Jan. 14, 1902–Feb. 1902. Young children who died while traveling were often buried en route.

> *Col. James Archer, of Denver, suddenly died very suddenly at Wagon Wheel Gap last Saturday morning. He had been suffering with rheumatism, which attacked the heart, causing almost instant death. Mr. Archer was a long-time resident of Denver, and established the Gas and Water Works, and was President of both companies at the time of his death.*[146]

> *At Del Norte on Thursday, 9th, occurred the death of R.W. Robinson, a man who was well known and highly esteemed in this city. He was formerly a large dealer in limestone here, being extensively interested in the quarrying business a few miles up the river. He was on the way to Wagon Wheel Gap for the benefit of his health, being subject to hemorrhages, but had to stop at Del Norte on account of an attack of congestion, and there he died.*[147]

> *Clayton Wetherill, well and popularly known to the citizens of Mineral county passed to the Great Beyond Thursday morning, Oct. 20, at the Hot Springs Hotel, at Wagon Wheel Gap, where he had recently been taken with a hope that the mineral water would prove beneficial. Heart trouble was the cause of his death. A minister from the valley will conduct the funeral obsequies and the interment will be at the Creede cemetery.*[148]

Few people today "take the waters" to cure paralysis, ease gout or rheumatism, soothe an ulcer or treat ailments of the liver or the heart. Bathing for medicinal purposes went out with horse-drawn carriages, a quaint but outmoded practice of people less sophisticated. Was medicinal bathing an effective technology bypassed by subsequent developments, like antibiotics, or was it was a form of quackery that resulted in mass delusion? Were all the doctors who presided at mineral springs taking advantage of the sick people who flocked there? Were all the people who swore by their bathing regimens simply deceived? Or was the proverbial baby tossed out with the bath water when balneotherapy, as it is called, was finally discarded by the modern medical profession?[149] Or, maybe, Ponce de Leon just didn't travel far enough west?

> *The* Denver News *has discovered one Ephriam Warner, is said to be 152 years old, residing at Wagon Wheel Gap. Mr. Warner is a trapper; smokes, chews tobacco and drinks whiskey.*[150]

5

FISH

Five weeks ago when I left New York I did not expect to be able to say that I have waded and soaked in the finest trout stream in America [at Wagon Wheel Gap], *and gained, in fact, my first real experience in catching the speckled beauties.... Two of my friends have caught here since the season commenced, nearly two thousand pounds of trout, all with the most ridiculously small fly hooks and fine tackle—in short, they are first-class amateurs.*

—*"Trouting in Colorado,"* Forest and Stream, *reprinted in the* Colorado Daily Chieftain, *September 7, 1875*

There is a dichotomy in the history of fishing at the 4UR. Abundant native fish and unparalleled fishing experiences for any level of expertise led to overfishing, which eventually diminished the experience. For many years, local landowners, area residents and Colorado State Game and Fish successfully struggled to restore the quality of fishing. Today, the 4UR is widely known as Colorado's premier fly-fishing ranch.[151] This is thanks in no small part to the visionary implementation of catch-and-release restrictions in 4UR streams by owner Pete Leavell in 1988. The 4UR fish logo was created to recognize the ranch's world-class fly-fishing.

Historically, fishing in the streams near the hot springs was for subsistence by Native Americans, miners and explorers. Later occupation by American settlers resulted in more people using fish as a cheap protein source, not to mention the thrill of catching as many as one wanted.

> *What fishing! One, unless they saw for themselves, would scarcely believe that trout could be so numerous. In about a half day's fishing we captured no less that one hundred and eighty-seven fish, ranging in size from a half to two and a half pounds. During our absence we caught about five hundred pounds, which* [my companion] *providently salted and packed in barrels for winter use.*[152]

THE START OF AREA FISHERIES

For many years, no control over the numbers of fish caught or kept initiated a slow decline in the total number and quality of fish. In most cases, the fish were utilized for food and eaten fresh or preserved for later consumption. The *Colorado Daily Chieftain*, July 11, 1890, relates, "The family of T.R. Zeiger don't patronize the beef butchers anymore. They are dining on trout which Mr. Zeiger is sending in large numbers from Wagon Wheel Gap." Another technique for disposing of excess fish was "gifting" them to friends and associates.

Although most sport fishermen were responsible, there were unethical fishermen who caught copious amounts of fish, by nefarious means, to sell to people living in small towns in the San Luis Valley and the booming mining town of nearby Creede. The practical reality is that fish do not keep well, and many ended up going to waste. The most heinous culprits dynamited the river, collected what fish they wanted and left others as waste.

> *A well-known sportsman who returned yesterday from a fishing trip along the Rio Grande river reports the most open destruction of trout with dynamite in the Rio Grande, the Conejos and their tributaries in spite of the state game laws which, it would seem are very weakly enforced. As an example of the state of affairs this gentleman says that D. McClelland of Wagon Wheel Gap found three men thus unlawfully killing fish in Goose Creek with giant powder. McClelland reported the case to the authorities who told him that he must have three witnesses to the offense and that if proceedings were commenced and failed to result in a conviction, he—McClelland—would have to pay all the costs. These statements very naturally put a quietus on the proceeding and the miscreants went unpunished. The Chieftain's informant says that in every pool in these streams he could have gathered up a basketful of trout that had been thus ruthlessly slaughtered. As further*

> *evidence of the bold violation of the game laws he says that trout are openly sold in Jimtown* [Creede] *at fifteen cents per pound. The lawlessness in this way is so flagrant and extensive that unless something is done the game fish of the state will in a very few years be completely exterminated.*[153]

Preliminary steps were taken to provide some control. In 1903, Colorado State Game and Fish outlawed non-licensed hunters and fisheries. In 1904, the State of Colorado funded private commercial fisheries to produce eyed eggs, raise fry for sale and produce dressed fish for commercial markets. Shortly, there were thirty-nine licensed commercial fisheries, and the Upper Rio Grande became one of the major commercial dressed fish and fish egg producing areas of Colorado.[154]

In the early 1900s, Upper Rio Grande fisheries produced more than sixty tons of dressed fish per year. That period saw a large influx of immigrants, with none of the commercial feedlots and farms for production of meat to feed the growing population. The establishment of commercial fisheries was a quick and (relatively) easy way to meet the demand.[155]

Fisheries were not new to the area. As early as 1866, Gordon Land established commercial fisheries in Conejos County. He served as Colorado fish commissioner in 1889. On the Pine River, outside Durango, the Patrick brothers established native rainbow trout hatcheries in 1885. In 1888, the Durango Rod and Gun Club seined (netted) Colorado River cutthroat trout and packed them on horses and mules to Emerald Lake on the Pine River. By 1895, W.T. Kirkpatrick hatcheries in Durango provided cutthroat trout for stocking public waters throughout Colorado. Economic stability in the country created a need for both recreational and production fishing.[156]

Commercial fishery development on the Upper Rio Grande was started by Charlie Mason, who was married to Anna Wetherill. Charlie worked alongside the five Wetherill brothers exploring ruins in the desert of the American Southwest, but Charlie was looking for other work. The Patrick brothers on the Pine River were part-time colleagues in archaeological explorations. They told Charlie wondrous tales of the business of raising fish. As Charlie thought about a new occupation, Anna's uncle Justus Tompkins, who had been with the Hayden Survey, said he knew the perfect place for a fishery on the Upper Rio Grande. In 1896, Charlie Mason homesteaded and purchased land on South Clear Creek, where he and his brother-in-law Clayton Wetherill built dams for the fishery. Charlie Mason obtained the first patented homestead claim for the sole purpose of raising trout for market and obtained the first license in the State of Colorado for raising trout for commercial sale.[157]

The introduction of nonnative species, particularly brook trout, had a major effect on fish in the Upper Rio Grande, including the 4UR. Local species were slow to grow, while other varieties grew more rapidly, thus increasing yield. Because of his relationship with the Patrick brothers on the Pine River, Charlie rode to Emerald Lake and packed cutthroat trout over Weminuche Pass to stock his new fishery. The cutthroats did not like the shallow lakes and relatively slow-moving water and did not thrive. In 1901, Charlie imported 100,000 eastern brook trout eggs from Plymouth, Massachusetts, and they flourished. The fish did so well that the next year he imported 200,000 eggs, and his hatchery became the source of brook trout in the Upper Rio Grande. Brook trout are not truly a trout, they are a char. However, Webster defines trout as "any of various salmonid food and game fishes of the genera *Oncorhynchus, Salmo,* and *Salvelinus*, having a streamlined, speckled body and usually inhabiting freshwater streams or lakes. These genera also include the salmons and the chars."[158]

During the summer of 1890, the D&RG Railroad, wishing to lay more track, contracted with timbermen to cut and deliver 100,000 crossties to Del Norte. The one hundred men and twenty teams started work in January just above Wagon Wheel Gap and by July had the order filled. Now to get the ties from Wagon Wheel Gap to the train at Del Norte. The timbermen, being from places where logs were commonly floated down rivers, confidently dumped the ties into the Rio Grande, expecting them to float serenely down to South Fork, where they would be hauled out and taken by train to Del Norte.[159] The mighty Rio Grande had something else in mind. The swift current jammed the ties into the rocks and forest detritus along the banks, where they became firmly stuck.

It took several weeks of painstakingly unjamming each tie, hauling them out of the river and loading them onto mule or horse-drawn wagons to complete the trip. The profit envisioned from the sale of the ties was severely eroded by the cost of recovering the ties and hauling them to Del Norte. Floating ties down the Rio Grande was a practice never repeated.

As General Palmer was renovating and upgrading the hot springs into an upscale resort, he recognized the need for management of the fishing experience of his guests. Since he owned all the land adjacent to Goose Creek, he made the creek a fish preserve for his guests' exclusive use, as it is today. As early as 1903, he started ordering fish and fry, both native and nonnative species, from hatcheries in Lake City and Denver, and from Hosselkus & Mason to release into Goose Creek and the Rio Grande. Fish size nomenclature, which does vary, is defined below. The growth rate of fish depends on the temperature of the water and available food.

- alevin: first hatched with a large yolk sac still attached, which they use as a food source.
- fry: at two to three weeks, the alevin absorb the yolk sac and begin to feed; one-half-to-one-inch length.
- fingerling: several weeks, about two to five inches.
- juvenile: several months up to a year, resemble an adult but not yet old enough to spawn.
- adult: fish that are mature enough to spawn, typically live for seven years.[160]

When first laid and fertilized, the eggs are called "green" and are incredibly fragile, tolerating very little disturbance. As they develop, after a short period of time, the "eye" of the fish can be seen in the egg—hence the name "eyed" egg. At this stage, the outer covering of the egg becomes resilient and tough, making it relatively easy to move these eggs as long as they are kept chilled.[161]

There were no fish in most high mountain lakes in the San Juans. As interest in recreational fishing grew, Charlie Mason and Clayton Wetherill saw an opportunity for stocking fish in these lakes and packed brookies to the remote mountain lakes and streams, including the Roaring Fork, above what became Humphreys Lake. Brook trout were hardy, grew fast, were not aggressive and provided a good source of dressed fish as well as sport. They were raised exclusively in hatcheries and were planted in many of the area's lakes and streams. Brook trout flourished and are now found in virtually every stream and lake throughout the Upper Rio Grande.[162]

In 1906, Palmer decided to build his own hatchery to allow him to stock the nearby section of the Rio Grande and Goose Creek and to be able to sell eggs and fry. A lake was needed for the fry to develop in, as well as a hatchery building. Eyed eggs could be cheaply purchased from local hatcheries. Otto Crain, a hatchery expert, was hired to manage the Hot Springs hatchery. Crain had been employed by the United States Fish Hatchery Department and was lured by the challenge of developing the Palmer hatchery.[163]

A small lake was built on the south end of the resort, along with the hatchery building, which was later converted to the ranch foreman's residence and is still used today. The hatchery was successful, and later that summer, there

Clayton Wetherill's son Carroll Wetherill (dark jacket) packing brook fry in transport cans on horses to take to remote mountain lakes and streams, assisted by Jake Mallott, circa 1947. *From the collection of the Wetherill family.*

was a coordinated effort of several private hatcheries in the area, including Palmer's, to release more than seven million fry into public waters.[164] The Hot Springs hatchery work continued for several years, hatching fry from eyed brook trout eggs and also taking native fry up to at least fingerling size in the lake before releasing.

Other people and organizations were also making efforts to maintain the fish population in the Rio Grande. The Denver and Rio Grande Railroad company contracted with Bert Hosselkus, Lost Lakes Fish Hatchery Company, to donate 100,000 fingerling rainbow trout to the Rio Grande River Fishermen's Association, to aid that body in its work of stocking the Rio Grande and its tributaries.[165] A year later, Judge Beaman from Denver, Colorado, also contracted with Hosselkus for 50,000 rainbow trout fingerlings to be planted in the Rio Grande.[166]

With the discovery of fluorspar and the intense mining operations creating conflict with the hotel operations, the death of General Palmer in 1909, World War I from 1914 to 1918, the departure of Mr. Bergey as manager of the Hot Springs resort in 1913 and the flu epidemic of 1918, the maintenance of fish was not a priority. Restocking Goose Creek was haphazard between 1912 and 1918.

In 1918, the American Fluorspar Corporation bought the hotel property, which reduced the conflicts between the two operations, and the board of directors brought Ellwood Bergey back as manager of the resort. Plans at that time were to refurbish the hotel and get it back on track. One of Bergey's first efforts was a much-needed restocking of Goose Creek. He purchased 1.5 million rainbow and native trout fry from Bert Hosselkus's Lost Lakes Hatchery.[167] As Bert Hosselkus was now one of the owners of the Hot Springs Hotel and Goose Creek, it is likely he worked with Bergey to keep the waters stocked over the next few years from the Lost Lakes Hatchery.

When the resort was sold to Bergey in 1924, he continued restocking fish from local hatcheries, as did later owners. Sometime during the ensuing years, probably related to economics, the purchase of several hundred thousand fry, of which few survived, was changed to several thousand catchable fish (nine to eleven inches), of which most survived. Deliveries would occur several times during the prime fishing months of the summer, primarily from fisheries in the San Luis Valley. "In the late 1960s, we took a load [about one thousand] of catchable fish up every other week, and split it between the 4UR [Goose Creek] and the La Garita [Bellows Creek] when the Phipps family owned both places."[168]

THE BEGINNING OF FISH MANAGEMENT

Wagon Wheel Gap continued to attract fishermen from across the country, and thanks to the efforts of many, the fishing remained extraordinary. However, fish harvesting was not managed, and excessive numbers of fish were caught, eaten or taken back to Texas and elsewhere. The general public was struggling with the idea that fish and game were limited. Game management was a new concept. State agencies were being established and charged with developing regulations for control of hunting and fishing. Anglers previously free to do what they pleased suddenly had to have licenses, and bag limits were strictly enforced. These new regulations were necessary to ensure a future for fishing. In 1917, the State of Colorado issued its first regulations in a brief pamphlet that read:

> *Trout and grayling, none less than seven inches; in running streams May 25 to October 31; in lakes over 7,500 feet altitude June 15 to October 31.*

> *Fifteen pounds in any one calendar day, twenty pounds in possession at any one time.*
> *No person shall engage in fishing for any fish without first having procured a fishing license.*[169]

About one hundred years later, an excerpt from the forty-five-page document of the 2019 State of Colorado fishing regulations states:

> *Daily Bag limit for any trout (except Kokanee): 4 fish in the aggregate: 8 fish in the aggregate in possession.*
> *Exception for Brook Trout, additional daily bag and possession limit: 10 fish, 8 inches or less in length.*
> *People 16 and older are required to buy and carry with them a fishing license to fish or take fish, amphibians and crustaceans, except as prohibited.*
> *Those under 16 can take a full bag and possession limit without a license.*
> *Colorado residents on active duty with U.S. armed forces out of state can fish free without a license while here on temporary leave, maximum of 30 days a year.*[170]

Hundreds of thousands, even millions, of fry and fish being released to the waters around Wagon Wheel Gap have been discussed. Were there truly that many fish taken, thus needing to be replaced? Of course not. The estimate for the survival of fry released in natural waters was estimated to be around 10 percent, that for the fingerlings much higher.[171] Basically, the larger the fish, the better chance of survival. The trauma of the rushing stream water on those tiny bodies, being prime munchies for larger fish and the shock from temperature changes all contributed to the high mortality rate of fry. As part of his mission to reestablish the local fish population, Colonel Humphreys, long before he built his private ranch, was a strong supporter of the effort to restore Wagon Wheel Gap area fishing. One proven way was the development of stream-side ponds along major rivers, which would allow the fry to grow to a larger size before being released into the waterway, minimizing the loss. In 1919, his first donation was for $250,000 (about $3.6 million in 2020 dollars) to the Colorado Game and Fish Department for this purpose.[172]

A couple of years later, the colonel received recognition for his contributions to the fish of Colorado. Through the Izaak Walton League, a major campaign was initiated to restock 500,000 five-inch trout in lakes and streams throughout the state. The colonel donated $350,000 for the construction of nursery ponds near Wagon Wheel Gap.[173]

The nursery ponds were a wonderful solution to young fish survival, but they had to be fed. Freshwater shrimp were a great food source and, once established, required no external oversight, as they multiplied into the millions. More ponds and more shrimp meant more fish to aid in the recovery of the fish population in streams and lakes.[174]

The subject of fish and game management was a national issue. On January 14, 1922, fifty-four visionary sportsmen met in Chicago to discuss a common concern: the deteriorating conditions of America's top fishing streams. Uncontrolled industrial discharges, raw sewage and soil erosion threatened to destroy many of the nation's most productive waterways. At the same time, the country's forests, wetlands and wilderness areas were quickly disappearing as the country's population expanded into the western states.[175]

The sportsmen formed an organization to combat water pollution named after Izaak Walton, a seventeenth-century English conservationist who wrote the literary classic *The Compleat Angler*.[176] Initially formed as a "federation of angling clubs," the Izaak Walton League of America soon broadened its goals in defense of outdoor America. Today, the Izaak Walton League's more than 43,000 members and 240 local chapters continue to build on the accomplishments of those who preceded them as defenders of the nation's soil, air, woods, waters and wildlife and make up one of the oldest conservation organizations in the United States. The most famous role of the Izaak Walton League in the early days was conservation and protection of fish, and membership was composed mainly of dedicated anglers. Referring to someone as a "Walton" meant they were avid fishermen.[177]

The colonel was committed to the principles of the league and was active in the Colorado chapter, of which he became president. Limiting the number of fish harvested, protecting habitat and assisting fish stocking were among the concepts he put in place on his own property. He was a leader who wanted fishing to be as grand as it had ever been.[178] In an interview in the *Rocky Mountain News*, August 3, 1922, Humphreys stated:

> *I will stock only cutthroat trout—no brook. I shall raise enough to stock Goose Creek and the Rio Grande. I will put in a million fry at once, and am planting fresh-water shrimp, on which they thrive near Del Norte, in the lakes to feed the young trout. This shrimp multiplies, they say, and fish love it. I will have my own hatchery; it is built and ready. My nursery lake will be the next step, then the two big lakes, Hay Press and Humphreys, where millions of trout will live; thousands are sure to go over the spillways into*

> *Goose Creek and the Rio Grande, which is right for I want to see the trout streams of Colorado again in the glory they had before they were fished out. I intend to help.*

Charles Gates Dawes was an American banker, general, diplomat and Republican politician who was the thirtieth vice president of the United States, from 1925 to 1929. For his work on the Dawes Plan for World War I reparations, he was a corecipient of the Nobel Peace Prize in 1925.[179] Vice President Dawes, his wife and their two children were at Wagon Wheel Gap as guests of Colonel A.E. Humphreys in July 1925. The vice president's focus was fishing for mountain trout in the nearby lakes and streams. On the day of his arrival, despite a heavy rain, he came in with an even dozen rainbow and native trout—the record catch of the day. The next day, he was out to beat the first day's record and to outdo other members of the party but, after landing five, hooked his finger and had to drive several miles into Creede to have the hook taken out by a doctor. The operation did not deter him, however, for he was out casting again in the afternoon.[180]

In July 1926, Colorado celebrated its fiftieth anniversary of statehood. The organizers of the celebratory event invited the vice president to speak at the semicentennial celebration in Denver. Arriving for the opening festivities on a Sunday, he departed at seven o'clock in the morning the next day with Colonel Humphreys, bound for the Humphreys Ranch at Wagon Wheel Gap. The vice president spent ten days trout fishing, enjoying the mountains and taking a break from his duties.[181]

In August 1926, Vice President Dawes was back at Wagon Wheel Gap. This trip seemed to have a competitive edge. The "fish score" on Monday night stood: Vice President Dawes, 209 caught, 86 saved; Williams, 202 caught, 77 saved; Roberts, 199 caught, 7 saved; Bartley, 151 caught, 51 saved; Mrs. Dawes, 38 caught, 14 saved: Dana Dawes, 32 caught, 12 saved; Virginia Dawes, 31 caught, 14 saved. With his toll of fish thus far, Dawes felt that he had completed what he termed the "most difficult" lap of his yearly fishing excursion—that of catching enough trout to ship to John T. McCutcheon, author and cartoonist, of Chicago. Before leaving for the West, the vice president tentatively agreed to ice and ship large numbers of trout, caught by himself, to his friends, including McCutcheon.[182]

Harvesting fish was halted altogether in 1989, when a catch-and-release program was implemented by the current owners, Pete and Lindsey Leavell. In a statement to their guests: "Under this program, we suggest that all fish caught on Goose Creek and the Rio Grande be released and returned to the

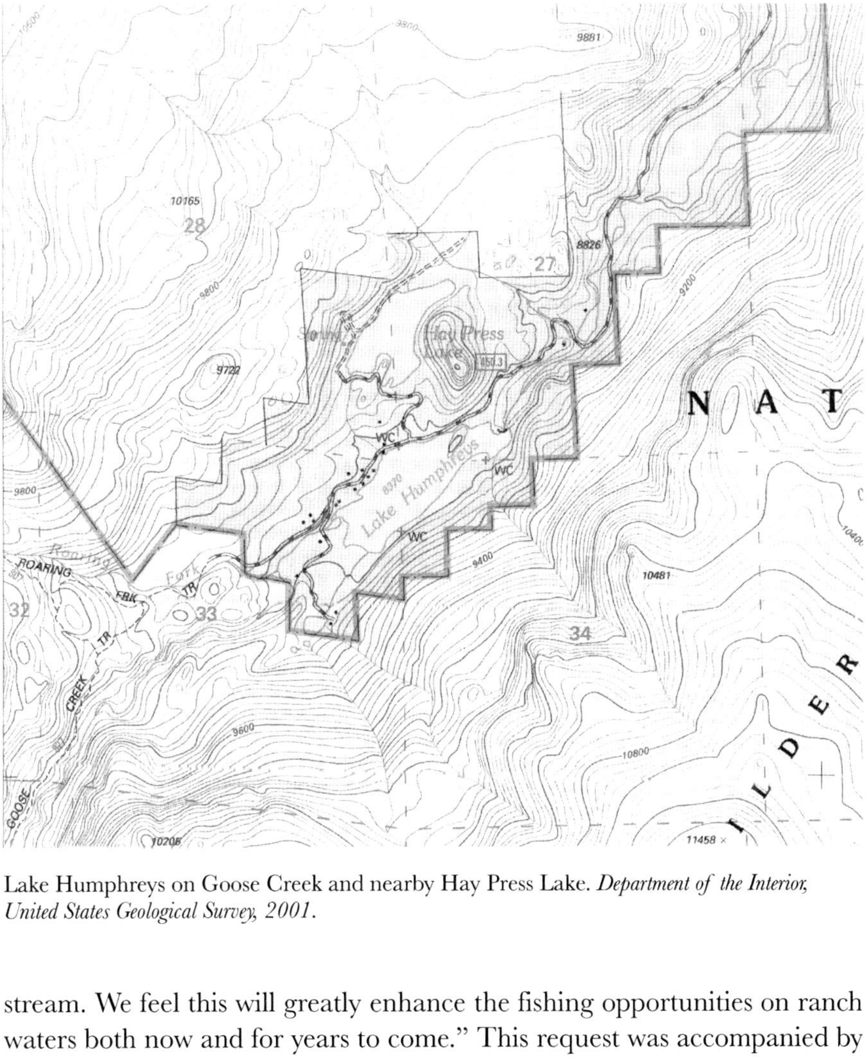

Lake Humphreys on Goose Creek and nearby Hay Press Lake. *Department of the Interior, United States Geological Survey, 2001.*

stream. We feel this will greatly enhance the fishing opportunities on ranch waters both now and for years to come." This request was accompanied by the following rules:

1. De-barb hooks before fishing.
2. If you have been fishing anywhere other than Creede within the last five months, we need to inspect your waders for the New Zealand Mud Snail.
3. Fly-Fishing Only—All fishing on the ranch is limited to fly-fishing only. This means the use of an artificial fly on a fly line on a fly reel on a fly rod. Spin fishing for kids is allowed at Walton Pond only. [Fish caught here may be kept].

4. Colorado State License—A valid Colorado fishing license is required at all times. Licenses may be purchased at the ranch office and must be carried while fishing.
5. Returning Fish to the Stream—When practicing catch and release, fish should be returned to the stream carefully. Please handle fish as little as possible—try to shake the fly loose. If you have to handle the fish, wet hands before touching the fish. Fish should be handled gently but firmly, should be kept in the water as much as possible, while handling and removing the hook, and returned to the water in an upright position. Hold the fish upright until it recovers and is able to swim away under its own power.
6. Fly Fishing Guide—A fishing guide can be provided for group or individual instruction of basic fly-fishing techniques. The office will make arrangements. Please let us know your needs one day in advance.
7. Please Keep All Gates Closed.[183]

As one drives into the 4UR after crossing the Rio Grande, there is a large pond on the east side of the road, along Goose Creek. This was initially called the Wagon Wheel Gap Trout Lake, built in 1906 by General Palmer. During construction of the improved road from the Gap up to the springs, there was a swampy place where the route had to make a curve, and it seemed a fine place to put in a fishing lake. It was renamed Leavell Lake by Charles Leavell after he purchased the 4UR in 1972. It was renamed Walton Pond by Pete Leavell in 1988, in honor of the 4UR managers during the 1970s and '80s, Katus and Joe Walton. The six-acre lake/pond was stocked over the years with different types of fish, but it is currently stocked solely with rainbow trout, and unlike other 4UR waters, the harvesting of fish is allowed from this pond.

Through the efforts of many people and organizations, including the current owners of the 4UR, the fishing along Goose Creek is world-renowned and available only to guests of the 4UR. Historically, untold numbers of fish were taken from Goose Creek, but today only catch-and-release fly-fishing is allowed in 4UR waters. Even at the weekly fish fry for the ranch guests, commercial fish are procured—neither the guests nor owners eat the denizens of the 4UR waters.

As a result of the Leavells' careful conservation of the fish on the 4UR property, restocking Goose Creek is performed once or twice a season. The determination to restock depends on two factors: the total population of

Walton Pond in the Goose Creek Valley, looking south. *Photo by Scott Hizny, 2018.*

fish—if too many have migrated out into the Rio Grande—or if they are under undue stress from fishermen. In an effort to popularize catch-and-release fishing, the Leavells instituted the Goose Creek Marathon. This popular event requires the fisherperson to catch and release a fish from each of fifteen fishing stations along Goose Creek, a distance of six miles, on foot. Recognition for completing this strenuous task is that one's name is permanently etched on a plaque that hangs in the main lodge. While many have tried, few have accomplished this feat. The earliest date on the plaque is July 1984, marking the achievement of a longtime guest from Dallas, David H. Lott, five hours and forty-five minutes. As of this writing, thirty-eight anglers have successfully completed the marathon, the longest time being ten hours and twenty-eight minutes and the shortest one hour and thirty-three minutes.

For those who eat fish, but don't like to fish:

> *Folks who want fish for food rather than fishing for sport got just what the doctor ordered near Wagon Wheel Gap on the Rio Grande recently when lightning killed an estimated five thousand trout, many of them three- and four-pounders, which were rendered easily available. But can you imagine the grouch who crabbed because the lightning didn't also cook the fish?*[184]

Goose Creek Marathon plaque that hangs in the main lodge, 2019. *Courtesy of the 4UR Ranch.*

And finally, something every fisherman even today can relate to—foot dressings:

> *I took with me from New York a pair of Frank Goode's oil-tanned moccasins, gaiter-make, with soles and heels, and had hobnails put in them for mountain travel. I never became footsore or weary…though wading for several hours of two days in the waters and on the rocky bottom of the golden Rio Grande they preserved their softness and pliability. Alas, they are departed into the hands of greedy miners, who allowed me only the choice as to whom I should bequeath them on my departure.*[185]

6

WAGON WHEEL GAP STAGE STOP AND POST OFFICE

Wagon Wheel Gap was, and is, a supply town. It was an important stage stop, and later a railroad station.

—*Perry Eberhardt,* Guide to the Colorado Ghost Towns and Mining Camps

As the stage clattered to a stop at Wagon Wheel Gap, visitors were welcomed to the hostelry there. Accommodations, food and lodging were provided for the through-traveler and for those whose destination was the fishing at Wagon Wheel Gap. The hot springs were about a mile up Goose Creek, and there were other accommodations there. Most of the time the two locations were owned and managed by separate entities, but not always, leading to confusion about which place one was referring to. The two locations were referred to as "the Gap" and "the Springs" to differentiate between them. The focus of this chapter is the Gap, which includes the Wagon Wheel Gap stage stop hotel and the Wagon Wheel Gap post office, which was housed in the stage stop for the early part of its life before moving to the train depot and later to the Springs. (It eventually closed.) In an effort to provide a cogent narrative, the hotel at the Gap is covered in this chapter, while the hotels associated with the Springs are covered in the "Early Days," "Palmer" and other chapters.

Romantic visions of gently swaying stagecoaches pulled by galloping horses along the rough roads of the Rocky Mountains were another thing altogether. Aside from the rather remote danger of bandits robbing a stage, the very real threat was the serious, sometimes fatal accidents that occurred along the treacherous "roads" of the early mining days.

> *As the stage approached the swing station, the horses going at a rattling pace, one of the lead team stumbled in a deep rut, caused by recent rains, and fell. The driver, in an attempt to hold him up with a taut line, failed to see another rut on the other side of the road, and the fore wheel ran into it, lurched the coach and threw the driver off of his seat and onto the ground. The spirited horses, feeling the slack in the lines, supposed the driver was "sending them in," and took off at a frightful pace. The driver bravely held onto the lines for some time, being dragged along beside the wagon, but eventually had to let go. The coach had 14 passengers, some seeing what was happening, leapt from the coach, sustaining a few broken bones and many bruises. The remaining passengers continued the wild ride until the horses raced into the stable yard, banged the coach off of one of the gate posts, finally coming to a stop.*[186]

WAGON WHEEL GAP STAGE STOP

About 120 acres on the north side of the Rio Grande at the mouth of Goose Creek was homesteaded in the early 1870s by William J. Hare. The homestead patent was granted on May 10, 1881.[187] Hare constructed a rough log house, corrals, pens and barns for livestock. With the opening of the San Juans for mining, Hare decided to try his luck on the other side of the mountains. Hare left for the mining opportunities in the Lake City area and sold his land and buildings to Alonzo Hubbard. Hare spent the rest of his life in Lake City and died there in 1906.[188] The first operators of the Wagon Wheel Gap stage stop took advantage of the existing facilities there and simply converted them for their use, with rooms added on as needed.

Elizabeth and John Murphy, her second husband, started their lodging career at Wagon Wheel Gap during the spring and summer of 1875, operating the Wagon Wheel Gap stage stop and hotel to support both miners heading to the San Juans and tourists visiting Wagon Wheel Gap. John Murphy went to Silverton in the late summer of 1875; Mrs. Murphy continued to run the hotel until Mr. Murphy reported that life in Silverton

Wagon Wheel Gap stage hotel looking west toward the Gap, circa 1877—no railroad yet. *Denver Public Library, Western History Collection, C-140.*

was better than life in Wagon Wheel Gap. Mrs. Murphy and her adult son, Lafayette "Lafe" Henry, joined him in the fall.[189]

> *John Murphy and William Lafayette Henry are proprietors of the* [stage] *station at Wagon Wheel Gap, who keep a stock of cigars, liquor, etc., and dish up good grub. They are accommodating gentlemen, and do, as they deserve, a lucrative business.*[190]

The stage stop was operated during the winter of 1875–76 by Alonzo Hubbard. The flow of traffic increased dramatically along the route. In 1876, Charles D. Peck and George M. Chilcott—two prominent citizens of Pueblo—purchased the property and established their hotel operation there. Although Peck was able to purchase already constructed buildings, he wasted no time in putting additions and upgrades in place.

> *We are informed that a billiard hall will soon be opened at Charlie Peck's hotel at Wagon Wheel Gap, under the superintendence of Bob Leonard.*[191]

The silver rush to the San Juans continued, and the stage stop proved profitable. Until early 1877, there had been no survey of the Gap and its environs, so there was no way for settlers to officially claim their property.[192] After the survey, there was a flurry of paperwork documenting previous property transfers. Alonzo Hubbard processed his paperwork for purchase of the property from Hare on March 20, 1877, and the next day, March 21, 1877, filed paperwork for the sale to Peck and Chilcott. Since the 120 acres was part of a homestead claim that was eventually patented, and each person could hold only one homestead claim, Hubbard sold an adjoining 20 acres to the wives, Sidney D. Peck and Jennie Chilcott, on March 21, 1877.[193]

One of the challenges at Wagon Wheel Gap were bridges across the Rio Grande. Not engineered to last like those of today, early bridges were ephemeral, maybe lasting a season or two, subject to washing away by spring floods. However, a bridge was necessary during most of the year, when the water level in the ford was too high for safe passage across the Rio Grande. With increased travel, a more convenient bridge was necessary near the station. The two existing bridges were down the river about a mile on the east side of Cottonwood Cove (which was not there then) and about a mile west right at the Gap, where the railroad bridge currently crosses. The new bridge was placed immediately adjacent to the stage station for the convenience of travelers to the Hot Springs.

> *Peck's picturesque log house, the best known and highest prized hostelry in all this region. Though of logs, the house is very roomy, and so neat and delightfully presided over by Mrs. Peck that her virtues as a housekeeper long since passed into proverb. Peck himself is a prince of landlords, open-hearted, jolly, and the champion fisherman of Colorado. From the house to the river is but a few steps, and from the pearly stream Peck coaxed the past season no less than 3,400 pounds of trout, serving the great wealth of speckled beauty upon the tables of his dining room. Directly in front of Peck's, and reached by the romantically surrounded bridge crossing the Rio Grande, is the Hot Springs Valley, up it a mile. The rate at Pecks, where 15 to 18 guests are accommodated, is from $2 to $3 per day, $12–$15 per week, and $60 per month, no deduction being made, as rooms are always in demand. Parties who camp in the vicinity can secure very reasonable rates for day board.*[194]

Charlie Peck did a great business at his hotel at the Gap. An endless stream of freight wagons passed every day, and the number of tourists and visitors continued to increase, although getting there required taking a stage from the train in Alamosa via, "an easy and direct route, open twelve

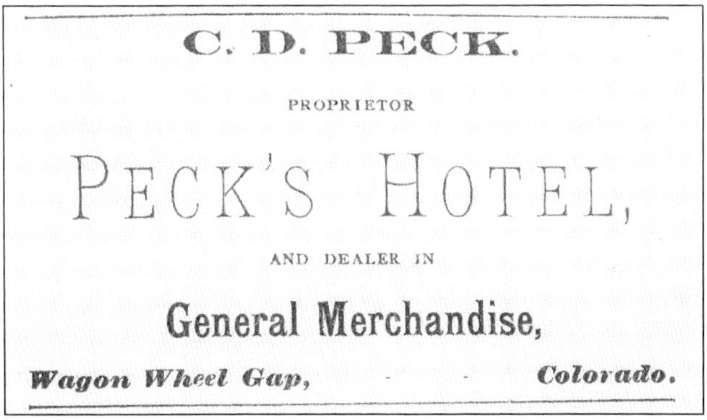

Peck's hotel advertisement, 1880. *From the 1880* Colorado Business Directory, Small Towns and Settlements, *p. 233.*

months in every year, to Del Norte, Antelope Springs, Wagon Wheel Gap, Saguache, Gunnison City, Ouray, Lake City and all other principal points in the Gunnison and San Juan counties."[195]

Sadly, Charlie's wife, Sidney, died in childbirth in August 1880.[196] Broken-hearted, and with some other bad luck, Charlie decided he could no longer run the hotel. He and his business partner, G.M. Chilcott, sold the hotel to Charles Hawkins on March 7, 1881.[197] It was purchased by Rawlinson Bevan later that spring.[198]

Sweeping changes came to the Gap with the arrival of the train there in 1883. Western Union constructed telegraph lines between Del Norte and Wagon Wheel Gap to facilitate modern communication.[199] The railroad purchased the hotel, built the depot and relocated the post office there, hiring people to act both as postmaster and train agent. Another bridge was constructed about halfway between the Gap hotel and the new depot to accommodate both groups of patrons.

In 1887, "the present terminus of the Del Norte and Wagon Wheel Gap branch of the Rio Grande R.R. is at Wagon Wheel Gap, a proper town. The place consists of a station house [depot] occupied by the railroad agent, three small houses, and a log boarding house with several additions used as a boarding house."[200] The division of work between the station agent/postmaster and the hotel manager varied, depending on the abilities of the individual, spouses or children who could share the work.

George W. Franklin and family came to Wagon Wheel Gap in 1887 to run the hotel, livery and post office. In the fall of 1889, the Franklins moved on. Although occupied by many owners, the stage hotel at Wagon Wheel Gap was long known as the "Franklin House."

When the train ceased running in the spring of 1889, all travel to the Gap and points beyond was by horse and cart or wagon. Entrepreneurs

Wagon Wheel Gap Stage stop hotel on north side of the river (*left in image*), looking east to the depot, bridge across from hotel, circa mid-1880s. *Denver Public Library, Western History Collection, WHJ-1674. Photo by William Henry Jackson.*

Railroad Depot at Wagon Wheel Gap, train, water tower and horse-drawn conveyances ready to take visitors up to the Springs, stage stop hotel was out of the picture off to the left, circa 1885. *Creede Historical Society, 427-WWG-2c1.*

The "Franklin House" stage stop hotel at Wagon Wheel Gap, managed by George Franklin family, August 1888. *Creede Historical Society, 423-WWG-1c1.*

quickly reestablished a stage line from Del Norte to Wagon Wheel Gap and other destinations farther west. The tourist trade, livery and fishing trips were major income producers at the Gap.

There was stiff competition between two livery providers that transported tourists to the Springs and to local fishing holes. The two livery businesses were a subset of the competition between the owners of the rival hot spring operations: that at the Soda Spring, including Cleghorn, and the one associated with the Hot Sulfur Spring, managed by Arthur Patten. Arthur's father, Nathaniel Patten, was managing the old stage station hotel and also operated the livery at the Gap.

The train resumed operations in 1892 to support the Creede silver boom, reducing the need for livery work, and many left the area. From 1893 to 1895, the Wagon Wheel Gap post office was closed. As a result of a lawsuit in 1892, the Pattens were not allowed to manage any property at the Springs or the Gap.[201] The Gap hotel was operated by James Murray and his mother beginning in 1893. The ubiquitous Pattens returned after clearing their legal

Wagon Wheel Gap Stage stop (*center of image*) on north side of the river, looking west to the Gap; bridge across Rio Grande near the train depot, circa 1902. *History Colorado online collection, 2000.129.237.*

Wagon Wheel Gap bridge at the depot over the Rio Grande, circa 1910. *Creede Historical Society, 433-WWG-5c1.*

troubles, took over the hotel the next year and ran it for couple of years, after which it was no longer used. The building burned down about 1909.[202]

> *Here is an old stage station, a primitive and picturesque structure of hewn logs, one-story in height, facing the south, and made cool and inviting by wide verandas extending along its entire front. Not feet away rolls the Rio Grande River, swarming with trout.*[203]

In 1902, a new road was constructed along Goose Creek from the Springs out to the depot and another bridge built as close to the train depot as was possible, no longer having any need to accommodate Gap hotel guests. The improved road and bridge were necessary to support increased traffic to the Springs brought to the place by the train.

WAGON WHEEL GAP POST OFFICE

Post offices in small settlements were essential to the pioneers. Everyone depended on newspapers and letters to keep in touch with what was going on in the world, the state and even in their neighboring communities. The post offices were usually designated rooms, or even just space, in the house of the postmaster/mistress. This was a paid position and provided supplemental income, although maybe not always worth the hassle. Being a postmistress was a respectable and common activity for the lady of the house, as she was almost always around and could interrupt her other work to serve the postal customers.

The first Wagon Wheel Gap post office was in Saguache County. Rio Grande County, which encompassed Wagon Wheel Gap, was created in 1874 by the Colorado Territorial Assembly. However, the Wagon Wheel Gap post office operated out of Saguache County until 1876, when Colorado became a state and county governments were more formalized. Thereafter, Wagon Wheel Gap post office was operated out of Rio Grande County. Mineral County was created in 1892, and the Wagon Wheel Gap post office was closed in 1893. All operations were moved to the Amethyst post office in Creede, Mineral County. This did not work well for Wagon Wheel Gap residents, so a post office was reestablished at Wagon Wheel Gap, starting in 1895 and remaining in operation until its closure. On November 30, 1954, all mail went to the

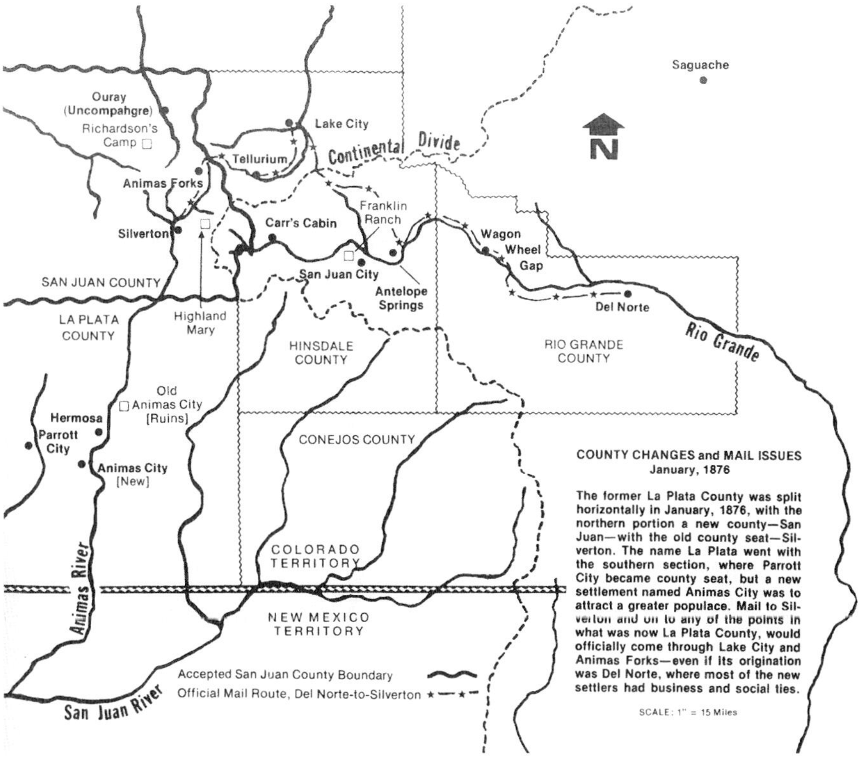

Southwestern Colorado County changes and mail issues, with road on the south side of the river, January 1876. *From* Many More Mountains, Volume 1: Silverton's Roots, *by Allen Nossaman, page 299.*

South Fork Office.[204] In June 1955, the office was reestablished as a rural station of Creede, operated only during the summer months and closed on September 30 each year. This continued for two years and ceased completely on September 30, 1957.[205]

In 1874, the mail went first to Del Norte and, from there, traveled up the river to various destinations. Mailmen were a hardy breed, using snowshoes in the winter and pack mules in the summer, followed by wagons, then trains and finally motorized vehicles.

The Wagon Wheel Gap post office was initially located in the stage station, where it remained until relocation to the train depot after that structure was completed in 1883. With the significant number of people staying at the Springs, the post office was sometimes temporarily moved up there and then back to the Gap for the winter. The last passenger train traveled to Wagon Wheel Gap in 1932, although freight still moved over the rails for several more years.[206] With the decrease in rail traffic, the post office was permanently moved near the Springs in April 1945.[207]

Just to confuse matters a bit further, the original name of the post office was Wagon Wheel Gap from 1875 until May 1893, when it was closed. It reopened in June 1895 with the name of Thornton. In 1901, the name was changed back to Wagon Wheel Gap, until it was closed in 1954. Post office name changes were made for a variety of reasons, but the location remained the same. Conversely, names were retained, but the post office was moved elsewhere. Both happened at Wagon Wheel Gap.[208]

7

EARLY DAYS AT THE HOT SPRINGS

It may be news to the new settlers to know that there are three of these hot springs at the Gap, and that by the recent corrected survey only one of them, and that the improved one, belongs to the Palmer Company. Two others, one a hot soda, and the other known as the mud spring, belong to Messrs. Cleghorn, Brastow, Ross and McClelland and are also in the forty-acre tract which contains Amethyst Hill.

—Creede Candle, *May 20, 1892*

Joel K. Mullen, Albert Mead, Henry Henson and Charles Goodwin (sometimes spelled Godwin), with money in their pockets, took up residence at Wagon Wheel Gap Hot Springs in October 1872. It was a trespass on Ute lands but nothing new for them. The proceeds from their fortuitous sale of the Ute-Ulay mine near Lake City enabled them to develop the hot springs property on the Rio Grande.[209] Around 480 acres were claimed by three of the four, Goodwin, Henson and Mead. Each received a homestead patent for 160 acres: Godwin on December 30, 1880; Henson on December 20, 1881; and Mead on March 21, 1882.[210] This property included the area along the Hot Springs (now Goose) Creek valley from its mouth to a point about a half mile above the springs.[211] There is no record of Mullen proving up on his land and obtaining a patent.[212]

The signing of the Brunot Agreement in the spring of 1874 lifted all restraint previously exercised by the entrepreneurs at the hot springs. Miners traveling to Silverton and Lake City and back were the main patrons, primarily taking mud baths in the warm, damp soil surrounding the hot springs. Demands from the traveling public were about to make significant changes to the operation. Travelers to the site in 1875 reported that improvements had been made to accommodate the bathing public, including access to a bathing house with a few rooms containing tubs, and one pool, about twelve by twenty feet. No lodging facilities were available, so people brought their camping equipment with them—standard practice for that day and time.[213]

Charles Toll, Rio Grande County attorney, visited the Wagon Wheel Gap Hot Springs and wrote a letter to his parents in Onondaga County, New York, in 1876, saying that "near one of them, quite a large bath house has been built, and around it perhaps 25 people were camped. At times there are more there, for it is a favorite stopping place for people passing in and out of the mines. The baths are very pleasant and it would be a famous place if near a more populous country."[214] Profit from the operation of the hot springs was limited, with cattle ranching and hay production being more lucrative,

Family camping in one of many tents near the hot springs with all the comforts of home, even a chair for the dog, circa 1877. Old-growth tree still standing prior to the clear-cutting of the area for lumber taken for the railroad and fluorspar mine and mill. *History Colorado online collection, 99.270.3317.*

utilizing the lush grass valleys along Goose Creek.[215] Cattle ranching on the hot springs property, which was limited or nonexistent during the Palmer and Bergey eras, was brought back in a big way during the Sharp and Phipps years until discontinued in 1988 by the Leavell family—much to the dismay of the long-time 4UR ranch manager Ed Wintz.

The *Colorado Daily Chieftain*, July 21, 1875, states: "The great necessity to make the Wagon Wheel Gap springs the most popular and delightful retreat in Colorado, is a good hotel, which the proprietor assured me would be built in another season." The stage-stop hotel a mile away at the Gap had limited availability, and there was the hassle of daily travel back and forth.

Pressure from the travelers, reflected in the press, convinced owners Goodwin, Henson and Mead to erect a first-class hotel for accommodations for tourists and invalids, a major step in attracting the wealthier tourist to the area. "The advent of a new hotel at this point, and other facilities for the comfortable accommodation of guests, must result in the making of what nature designed the springs to be, the most popular summer resort on the continent."[216] And right they were.

During 1877, the owners decided that to effectively develop the hot springs into a major resort, they needed more money and backing. Three of the original four founders—Henson, Mead and Goodwin—formed the Wagon Wheel Gap Hot Springs Company, along with three deep-pocketed gentlemen. The stated purpose of this new company was "improving and developing the land about the hot springs, and erect bathing establishments, a hotel and other buildings necessary to improve the place."[217]

WAGON WHEEL GAP HOT SPRINGS COMPANY, OCTOBER 20, 1877

That the objects for which said company is created are the improvement and development of the hot springs situated at and near what is known a Wagon Wheel Gap in Rio Grande County, State of Colorado, the construction of bathing establishments and the erection of hotels at or in the vicinity thereof, and also the construction of all other buildings, roads, bridges and other improvements which may be incidental to and necessary to accomplish the purpose of carrying on the business herein. The capital stock of said company shall be the sum of sixty thousand dollars. The Board of Directors, will consist of six persons, and shall

> *be: Charles E. Godwin, Albert Mead, Henry Henson, Adair Wilson, John L. McNeil and Hermann Schiffer. The officers of said company shall be: Charles E. Godwin, President; Adair Wilson, Secretary; and John L. McNeil, treasurer.*[218]

Charles Evelyn Godwin (Goodwin), born on February 14, 1839, in Virginia, joined the U.S. Navy in 1859 and served on the USS *John Adams* during the Civil War. He then came to Colorado, where he prospected in the San Juan Mountains and with partners discovered the famous Ute-Ulay mine near Lake City. He met and married Ann Woodruff in Del Norte in December 1877. After selling his interest in the Wagon Wheel Gap Hot Springs, he moved to Birdsnest, Virginia, where he spent the rest of his life as a farmer. Godwin died there on April 15, 1909.[219]

Albert Mead was born on January 22, 1846, in Pennsylvania. After passing through the San Juans on the prospecting trip that resulted in the location of the Ute-Ulay claims, he settled at the Springs at Wagon Wheel Gap and became one of the founders of Loma. Mead obtained a cash entry patent for 160 acres of land there on March 21, 1881. After selling his interest in the Wagon Wheel Gap Hot Springs Company, he moved elsewhere in Colorado and participated in various mining operations. He died in Rifle, Colorado, on May 22, 1914.[220]

Henry Henson was born on November 12, 1824, in Wayne County, Kentucky, and moved as a small child to Indiana. He served four years as Martin County treasurer. Henson came to Fairplay, Colorado, in the early 1860s, where he was a merchant, postmaster and school superintendent. He served as the representative from Park County to the 1864 Colorado Territorial Legislature. In 1871, he moved to Saguache, where he was a partner in a store, and it was likely there that he met Mead and Godwin. Henson Creek in Lake City is named for him. In 1876, Henson was elected to the Colorado State Senate.[221]

New partner Adair Wilson was born on November 16, 1841, in Saline County, Missouri. Son of William Adair and Mary Elizabeth (Reeves) Wilson, he was a graduate of the Masonic College, Lexington, Missouri, in 1858 and was admitted to the bar in 1860. He moved to California and on to Nevada, returning to Missouri in 1867. In 1872, he settled in Colorado. His political career included being a member and president of the Territorial Legislative Council in 1875. He also served as a Colorado state senator from 1886 to 1890 and as a Colorado Court of Appeals judge from 1897 to 1903. He died in 1912 in California.[222]

New partner John L. McNeil, born in May 1849 in Tioga, New York, pursued a career in banking. He moved to Colorado, where he was instrumental in developing several banks. John McNeil was president of the Durango Trust Company. He and his brother-in-law, A.P. Camp, were active in the banking business during Durango's early years. He established the First National Bank of Durango as a branch of Daniels, Brown & Company of Alamosa in 1881; the Glenwood National Bank in 1887; the Denver Savings Bank in 1890; and the Denver Western Bank in 1891. John died in Denver in July 1929.[223]

New partner Hermann Schiffer, an early Del Norte businessman, moved to Del Norte in 1872 and established a successful business supplying miners and travelers with clothing, dry goods, groceries and mining supplies. According to the local papers, "Schiffer & Co., are spoken of as the wealthiest and most substantial dealers in general merchandise in this part of the country. They do quite an exchange and private banking business likewise."[224] These influential and savvy men made major upgrades to the hot springs. The first was the completion of the thirty-two-by-fifty-foot two-story hotel in late 1877; it opened for business in the spring of 1878.

> *An elegant little hotel is just being finished. It is situated on a higher bench of land about a hundred yards west of the baths, and is a model of taste and good arrangement. The house contains seventeen rooms, and nearly five-thousand dollars' worth of furniture has been bought for its equipment.*[225]

Wagon Wheel Gap Hot Springs Hotel original bathhouse, cottages and outbuildings, circa 1884. *Denver Public Library, Western History Collection, C-105.*

The hotel was managed by a local woman from nearby Del Norte, Mrs. Duncan, who leased the property for ten months and is reported as "keeping a first-class house."[226] Not everyone had positive comments, though:

> *A new hotel has just been completed in the immediate vicinity of the hot spring, capable of accommodating 40–50 guests. The rate per day for transients is $2–$3 per day, by the week $12, special arrangements being made where parties remain to undergo a thorough treatment of the springs. These springs are owned by Messrs. Mead and Godwin, who do all in their power to make guests comfortable, but unfortunately for this year they have let the hotel to parties who are not calculated for this place. The house is very clean, but the table meagre, and the land-lady desires, yes insists, that her guests retire at ten o'clock (rather hard on bright moonlit nights). She objects to a noise, is also very grasping and unreasonable, taking every advantage possible.*[227]

With such negative publicity about the manager of their establishment, in the fall of 1878, the owners made a change. "The *Del Norte Prospector* understands that Ben Duval has leased the Hot Springs Hotel at Wagon Wheel Gap and will remove there with his family to take charge in a few days.[228] Duval lasted only that winter.

The owners now turned to a fellow miner they knew from Lake City who had a background in hotel management. Job C. McClelland, born in Pennsylvania on April 22, 1829, moved to Colorado in 1859.[229] He was a businessman in Del Norte. In 1878, he traveled to his home in Kansas to get married.[230] The happy couple returned to Colorado, where McClelland took a turn at mining, livery and other tourist-related efforts and was known as a jovial and competent man. McClelland took over operation of the Wagon Wheel Gap Hot Springs Hotel in 1879.

A description of the hotel in an area newspaper read as follows:

> *Kept by J. McClelland. It is a two-story frame building, containing fifteen bed-rooms, parlor, dining-room, office, etc. To the left of it the billiard hall, and almost in front of it bath houses. The springs, of which there are many, cover an area of about three hundred acres of ground. The baths are miserably fitted up, merely holes in the ground, into which one goes with the feeling that is somewhat akin to being boned. The plunge baths, however, are made more passable, the healing qualities of these waters are said to be remarkable.*[231]

The Hot Springs at Wagon Wheel Gap advertisement. *From the 1880* Colorado Business Directory, Small Towns and Settlements, *p. 233.*

In 1881, an involved, complex and confusing series of transactions began that further complicated property ownership around Wagon Wheel Gap and the Springs. Henson, Godwin and Mead sold out to "an English syndicate." The new owners were William Jackson Palmer and his wealthy Scottish friend Jas. K. Caird.[232]

There were now two major properties at the Springs: on the west side of Goose Creek, with Palmer and Caird, and on the east side sold to McClelland and his partners. For many years thereafter, there were two hot spring operations: the big hotel, cottages and bathhouse at the Hot Sulfur Spring, on the west side of Goose Creek, and the Hot Soda Spring, including the Mud Spring and Amethyst Hill, on the east side of Goose Creek. Nearby McClelland Mountain is named after Job C. McClelland.

THE RAILROAD TRAVELOGUES

The railroad was making its way west from Alamosa, and the Wagon Wheel Gap Extension was being surveyed. The Denver and Rio Grande railway reached Del Norte on July 3, 1881. The plan was to push forward from that point west to Wagon Wheel Gap.[233] The railroad actually arrived at Wagon Wheel Gap in the spring of 1883.

In an effort to increase ridership, railroads commissioned writers and arists to travel the rails and write advertising material to entice tourists. This marketing activity occurred across the country, with specific interest in the booming gold and silver mining disticts in the western United States.

Writer Joseph Gladding (J.G.) Pangborn published numerous railroad travelogues across the country. In 1878, he published *The Rocky Mountain Tourist: Arkansas Valley and San Juan Guide*, which included a brief section on Wagon Wheel Gap and the hot springs. He traveled through the area years before the rail line reached the Gap. Pangborn reports that he took the rail as far as Alamosa and from there continued to the Gap by Concord Coach.[234]

Years later, a lucrative commission from the Baltimore and Ohio Railroad for a book describing the railroad's scenic routes throughout the middle Atlantic states was offered to Thomas Moran, the painter; J.C. Pangborn, the writer; and John Karst, the wood engraver; along with a railroad representative. This group took an extended tour of the rail lines, and the product of this effort was *Picturesque B.&O.*, published in 1882.[235]

Pangborn left the group when the B.&O. project was completed in Chicago. Karst and Moran continued on to Denver, where they obtained a commission to provide illustrations for the *Colorado Tourist*, a monthly sponsored railroad publication. While there, Moran recruited his friend William Henry Jackson, who had a studio in Denver, to sketch and photograph together as they had during their years in Yellowstone. Years earlier, in 1871, Moran and Jackson were part of the first U.S. government survey of the Yellowstone region, conducted by geologist Ferdinand Vandeveer Hayden.[236] Moran's reputation was established with his painting of the Yellowstone Canyon and became so intertwined with it that he took to signing his paintings "TYM," for Thomas "Yellowstone" Moran. The nickname followed him for most of his life.[237]

The three men were joined by an "ebullient" journalist, Ernest Ingersoll, who had a commission from *Harper's Magazine* for eyewitness reports of the San Juan Mining District. Thus, the group of four headed west into the San Juan Mountains aboard a train. The commission came from both the Union Pacific and D&RG Railroads, and the area to be reviewed included Wagon Wheel Gap.[238]

Ingersoll used the information garnered from this trip for the first few chapters of *Crest of the Continent*, published in 1885.[239] He included Karst's wood block engravings from drawings by Moran. "Ingersoll contrived a readable narrative, however stuffed with guidebook chaff."[240]

Left to right: unidentified Uinta boy, Thomas Moran and William Henry Jackson, from their days with the Yellowstone Hayden Survey, circa 1871. *New-York Historical Society, Early American West Photograph Collection, PR 266, ID 88733d.*

McClelland and the Hot Soda Spring Operation at Wagon Wheel Gap

With the impending arrival of the train to Wagon Wheel Gap, the number of tourists would increase significantly, creating the need for more housing. McClelland and partners proceeded with developing the Hot Soda Spring (on the east side of Goose Creek), which had a bathing house but no hotel, into a more of a resort. Construction of that hotel was started in 1882 and completed in 1884, near the Hot Soda Spring. The new McClelland Hot Springs Hotel opened in April 1884.[241] However, heavy rain that spring closed the railroad until late July of that year, when the first train went through to Wagon Wheel Gap. Visitors were welcomed by J.C. McClelland,[242] who it appears, during 1884, was the manager for the hotels on both sides of Goose Creek. From that point on, he managed only the Hot Soda Spring Hotel on the east side of Goose Creek. McClelland purchased homesteads and expanded his holdings, including the Caldwell place, located on Caldwell Creek. He was no longer interested in managing the Palmer Hot Springs Hotel.

> *Mr. McClelland, proprietor of the hotel, and his good lady, spare no pains to make their guests comfortable. They have hotel and cottage accommodations for about sixty persons, and have had to turn off parties since the 15th day of July for want of room.*[243]

In the Wild West, property lines were approximate at best. In the early 1890s, there were efforts across Colorado to provide more accurate surveys of private land, especially in areas that were heavily claimed. Additionally, the railroads were concerned that there be accurate surveys to protect their property, and to establish "railroad sections" along their lines. Thus, government surveyors spent time in the remote areas of Colorado following the railroads and completing more accurate surveys. The updated surveys generated revised property lines, an unfortunate, but common, occurrence.

The issue came to a head at Wagon Wheel Gap in 1892, when mining claims were being placed around Amethyst Hill, as miners thought the outcropping of purple fluorspar was an extension of the amethyst (hence the name Amethyst Hill) quartz vein at Creede.[244] In the mines near Creede, amethyst quartz was the gold- and silver-bearing mineral and much sought after, but near Wagon Wheel Gap, the purple rock was fluorspar, which disappointingly did not contain precious metals. Little did they know that in a couple of decades, the fluorspar would become just as valuable.

The confusion at the Springs initiated another major survey, which proved advantageous for McClelland.

> *J.C. McClelland is very much pleased with the report of Engineer Tom Tripp who has just finished a week's work at Wagon Wheel Gap making a survey of the lines dividing the properties of Mr. McClelland and the hotel company. It has been a question for some time as to who owned the best spring at the Gap. The survey gives Mac the spring by 145 feet. He procured from the government surveyor the original field notes and set a competent engineer to work to find the true lines with the above happy result.*[245]

In 1894, as McClelland reached the respectable age of sixty-five, he decided that he had done enough in the hotel business and hired a manger to run the hotel. The hired manager apparently lasted for the 1894 season; then it was back to the McClellands to run their hotel. Over the next several years, McClelland continued to improve the property, among his mining efforts up the river.[246]

> *WAGON WHEEL GAP—One of the most delightful places in Colorado to spend a few weeks or months in the heated term is McClelland's hotel at the Wagon Wheel Gap Hot Springs. There is plenty of trout fishing and plenty of trout for everybody, and people who want bigger game can get it by going into the hills a little way in almost any direction. There is no more beautiful, magnificent or grander scenery to be found anywhere, and the table and service at the McClelland house is equal to the very best eastern hotels or summer resorts. It is really and truly a pleasure resort, fine people who are seeking a delightful, comfortable and pleasurable outing could not do better than follow the example of the 60 or 70 people who have made McClelland's Hot Springs hotel their home this season.*[247]

The 1902 season was said to be a "most profitable one" for the McClellands. At the respective ages of seventy-three and sixty-two, life was good for the couple. Unfortunately, that winter, Job's wife, Mary, fell on the stairs and lay unconscious there for over three hours. Upon regaining consciousness, there was no apparent damage, and being the tough mountain woman that she was, she soon rallied.[248] Mary's fall in the winter of 1902 was a sad prelude to other health problems that showed up the following spring. With his seriously ill wife and his own advanced age, McClelland decided to sell out his operation at Wagon Wheel Gap.

> *J.C. McClelland, who for the past years was owner and proprietor of the Wagon Wheel Gap hotel, has sold that famous hostelry and has practically severed his connections with the place he has brought up to a point which has become known and acknowledged by pleasure seekers as the leading summer mountain resort of Colorado. Mr. McClelland and wife will probably spend a few months visiting the resorts of California for the benefit of Mrs. McClelland's health, which has not been of the best lately since she suffered a stroke of paralysis several weeks ago. With the moving of Mr. McClelland from the San Luis Valley, another old resident lost. For a number of years prior to his going to the Gap he conducted the old Victoria hotel in Alamosa and so well did he cater to the public that the place became known as one of the best in the State from the standpoint of a well-supplied table. Mr. and Mrs. McClelland have many friends in Alamosa, and in fact all over the Valley, who wish them good wherever they locate.*[249]

There was really only one prospective purchaser for the McClelland property, and that was General Palmer under the Wagon Wheel Gap Hot Spring Improvement Corporation. The general authorized his attorneys to visit Wagon Wheel Gap in 1903 and develop an estimate of the value of McClelland's holdings. He was interested in purchasing all of the holdings as he expanded his resort.[250] The recorded date of sale of McClelland's holdings to the Wagon Wheel Gap Hot Spring Improvement Company was March 15, 1906.[251]

After the McClellands had been in California for several months, the *Denver Post* reported an interview with Mr. McClelland in which he stated, "I should not like to live there. Life is too monotonous and just as soon as Mrs. McClelland's health will permit, we are coming back home." [252] Mary's health did return enough that they were able to visit the following year, with the intention of moving back, "if her health could deal with the altitude."[253] Sadly, her health could not, and the couple returned to live the remainder of their lives in California. Mary died in January 1912 and Job in July 1921—at the age of ninety-two.[254]

8

THE NEIGHBORS

The land around Wagon Wheel Gap was highly prized by early settlers, with a reliable source of water and good grazing in the lush valleys. Many homesteads, official and unofficial, were established, creating a jigsaw puzzle of ownership along Goose Creek, its tributaries and the Rio Grande. Property traded hands numerous times as fortunes waxed and waned.

General Palmer purchased homesteads along Goose Creek in his quest to establish an expansive luxury resort. Most landowners sold, but a couple retained their holdings. This chapter tells the story of the neighbors of the 4UR: the Gjellum family, the Britain family and the Humphreys Ranch, and the La Garita Ranch and Cottonwood Cove on the north side of the river.

HUMPHREYS

Albert Edmund Humphreys was born in Virginia in 1860. From humble beginnings, he was a born entrepreneur. He earned the title of colonel for his service with the Governor's Guard in West Virginia. The wide-open spaces and limitless opportunities of the West called to him, and he spent the rest of his life pursuing wildly successful business endeavors, including logging, mining and petroleum exploration.[255] Much has been written about his remarkable life. Elaine Walsh stated, "When historians review the life of Colonel Albert E. Humphreys, oil dollars may dance before

A.E. Humphreys "Wildcatter Deluxe" at one of his oil fields, circa 1920. *History Colorado online collection, PH.PROP.2181.*

their eyes, for this was the source of his wealth. However, his last enterprise deserves attention, for it portrays another picture of this dynamic man who was also a dreamer."[256]

The colonel married Alice Boyd in 1887 and had two sons: Albert Junior and Ira. Both boys married and had families, providing grandchildren to be spoiled by the colonel. The one with the closest relationship to the Humphreys Ranch was Ruth Augusta Humphreys, born on November 11, 1920, oldest daughter of Albert Junior and his wife, Ruth Boettcher. The colonel had two small playhouses built for Ruth and her cousin Alice, which still exist today.[257] Ruth grew up in Denver, where she attended Kent

School. She later attended Miss Porter's School in Connecticut and Finch College in New York City.[258]

In 1943, Ruth joined the Women's Airforce Service Pilots (WASP) program and flew for two years during World War II, flying with a target behind the plane to provide shooting practice for the fighter planes. Ruth received the Congressional Gold Medal for her service during the war.[259] When World War II pilot Jimmy Doolittle visited Wagon Wheel Gap and found that Ruth had been a WASP, the two instantly bonded.[260]

Colonel Humphreys visited the Hot Springs Lodge at Wagon Wheel Gap in 1896 and enjoyed the splendid fishing. He had come to invest in the Creede mines, which he did, and coincidentally discovered the beauty and majesty of the Colorado mountains. He was hooked, so to speak, returning frequently to his favorite fishing place near Wagon Wheel Gap. As he entered his seventh decade, the colonel was a wealthy man. He returned to Colorado to invest in his dream of establishing a magnificent mountain haven for his family. He purchased the homesteads of Albert H. Pfeiffer Jr. (son of the famous frontiersman Albert Heinrich Pfeiffer Sr.), John D. Cunningham and Albert Morris Colt, creating a ranch at a fisherman's paradise on upper Goose Creek.[261]

The colonel had a soft spot when it came to fish. Humphreys had come to the region when native fish were plentiful and abundant. After years of overfishing, with minimal management of recreational fishing practices, the population had deteriorated. Humphreys took it as his personal mission to reestablish the glorious fish of Colorado.[262] His milling operation along East Willow Creek in Creede had effluent known as "slime" that was allowed to discharge into the creek. When informed that slime was harmful to the fish, the colonel instructed his managers to build a settling pond for all of the effluents from his operations—long before the Environmental Protection Agency was around. This required an additional outlay of funds, but for Humphreys, the benefit was worth it.[263]

During the next seven years, Humphreys focused on oil exploration elsewhere in the country. Upon his return, he visited the Hot Springs at Wagon Wheel Gap, did some fishing and met with his business associates in Creede. The colonel's continuing concern for fish is related in a *Creede Candle* article dated August 12, 1911: "Humphreys appeared before the association's members and advised them that slimes from the big mill would be turned into the flume [and not the creek]."

In the summer of 1919, he completed a deal with the Colorado State Game Commission to establish fish nursing ponds to allow fry to grow to a

View of the Humphreys Mill and aerial tramway power plant near Creede, Colorado, 1890–1910. *Denver Public Library, Western History Collection, X-61959.*

Colonel A.E. Humphreys, circa 1920s. *From the collection of Bill Dooley.*

larger size, allowing them a greater chance at survival when transplanted into rivers.

A few weeks later, a major incident of dynamiting fish occurred in the Rio Grande between Deep Creek and Wagon Wheel Gap, leaving hundreds of dead fish floating in the river. This was a blow to fish protector Humphreys, and he made serious commitments and provided support to catching this criminal. The community, having been sensitized to the need for protection of the local fish population—at least partially through the colonel's efforts—was outraged "and threatened that the culprit would endure some rough handling besides what the state would do to him."[264]

In August 1921, the colonel cut short his trip to Wagon Wheel Gap on account of an ulcerated tooth, which may have led to his more serious illness. The *Creede Candle*, December 31, 1921, reported:

> *Col. A.E. Humphreys, formerly of Creede, is seriously ill and his recovery is doubtful. He has amassed a large fortune in the oil fields of Texas and is now rated as the wealthiest oil magnate of the west. With death hovering near Col. Humphreys has not forgotten his fellow man and with his great wealth he wants to better the conditions of the deserving, and mankind in general. Mr. Humphreys has been a prospector, a miner, a promotor and speculator in turn, and just as he had achieved his great success in the oil fields, he was taken by illness which may prove fatal. Through all the vicissitudes of life Col. Humphreys has been a man among men and has accomplished some good in the world.*

This illness did not end his life but may have been something of a wake-up call. Shortly after this, he began in earnest to develop his summer resort, called Humphreys Camp at Wagon Wheel Gap, and to pursue his lifelong mission to help the fish in this part of Colorado. Money was no object.

The colonel had purchased several hundred acres of land to build his fish and water improvement projects. One project was a large dam on Goose Creek and a hydroelectric plant, with the resulting lake (Humphreys Lake) encompassing an area of fifty acres to be stocked with fish. The second was another lake (Hay Press Lake) constructed at a site eight hundred feet above the first, with a small existing lake with a dam twenty feet high. The expenditure for both lakes was around $100,000. All construction materials had to be hauled in by hand or by pack animals, and the concrete had to be hand-mixed on site.[265]

In the summer of 1922, Humphreys and some of his family spent much of the summer supervising and directing construction projects. The centerpiece was a large log lodge with a spacious recreation room, a sunroom, six double bedrooms and three baths. The dining room, kitchen and extensive pantries were located in a separate building. Nearby was another large building with several more bedrooms and three baths. A six-car garage, stables for horses, tennis courts, a swimming pool and boathouses created a family playground. Servants quarters were in a separate building, and a comfortable six-room modern house was provided for the year-round caretaker, who was instructed to allow others on the property to fish or use the facilities only with written permission from the Humphreys family. Neighbors and friends were always graciously approved for fishing privileges, which remains true today.[266] The colonel kept a crew of workers busy. Not until the hard winter months were the workers able to take a break.[267]

The colonel's excitement over the nearing completion of some of his construction projects led him to invite the entire area to a lavish Labor Day picnic to help him celebrate. The invitation was made in the early summer, and enthusiasm for the event was spreading. He delegated the management of details to a good friend from Denver, Dr. David Bayliss, who was spending the summer at the camp. Contracts were let for food and drink; extensive preparations were made, and anticipation around the area was high.

> *Col. Humphreys last week received a large consignment of pedigreed bull-frogs that sing bass, which he had placed in his reservoir. Just what his object is, is not stated, as to whether a musical event is to be pulled off, a French feast provided, or he is simply going to raise the frogs and save the hops.*[268]

> *Col. Humphreys has contracted with Bert Hosselkus for 3,000 pounds of trout for the fish fry on Labor Day at the Humphrey resort.*[269]

Unfortunately, the event did not happen. One report said that Dr. Bayliss was taken seriously ill toward the end of August, and along with another

Workers constructing the ninety-foot concrete Humphreys Dam on Goose Creek above the 4UR, 1923. *Creede Historical Society, 2928-HR-53.*

health issue with the colonel, no one was able to complete the preparations. Another story didn't mention any illness but said that the bridge across the Rio Grande near Wagon Wheel Gap had been condemned and would not be safe for the numbers of visitors. This second reason may be credible, as local papers reported just a couple of months after that the colonel teamed up with the folks at the fluorspar mill to build another bridge across the Rio Grande. That bridge is still in use today, although it has received remedial work several times over the years, and the current owners are evaluating options of upgrade, repair or replacement.

The building operations continued at the resort during the spring, summer and fall of 1924. During the next few years, the colonel had his family and guests at his resort as much as possible during the summers, ensuring that all of them loved and appreciated the mountains and outdoors as much as he did.

Charles G. Dawes, vice president of the United States from 1925 to 1929, was a friend of A.E. Humphreys prior to his election. Dawes was also an avid fisherman and took several trips to Wagon Wheel Gap to fish, the families becoming close. After Dawes's election in 1924, he had to suspend his fishing trips, but after a hiatus of two years, he was again able to make his trek to Wagon Wheel Gap with his family.

Tragedy struck just a few years later. After suffering from an attack of double pneumonia in Houston, Texas, the colonel returned to Denver, where he was recuperating. He planned a trip to Wagon Wheel Gap and hoped that the expedition would restore his health, as it had in previous times. However, the colonel's involvement in the Teapot Dome Scandal of 1921–23, was coming back to haunt him. The U.S. Senate was investigating oil leases, and early in 1927, the Supreme Court ruled that the leases had been corruptly obtained. Many involved in the scheme, including the colonel, would be called to account.[270] Ordered to testify before a congressional committee investigating the scandal, he committed suicide in his Denver mansion after a Sunday family dinner on May 8, 1927. Although rushed to a nearby hospital, he never regained consciousness. Newspapers reported the story with profound grief and honor to his generous philanthropic efforts.[271]

After Colonel Humphreys's death in 1927, all of his holdings went to Albert Junior and Ira. Both were experienced businessmen and had major roles in administration of the family holdings, having learned at the incomparable knee of their father. Much has been written about the successes of the two boys. The Humphreys Ranch at Wagon Wheel Gap was preserved for the private use of the family and was never a commercial enterprise—per the wishes of the colonel. Having come to the ranch as children, the two boys shared their father's love and respect for the area. After the colonel's death, the ranch was used sporadically by the family, with maintenance and oversight, but little improvement.

As the Humphreys family was not always in residence, the job of caretaker fell to a series of men, the length of service attesting to the good working conditions:

- Max Martinez, 1923–1953, thirty years
- "Bud" Martinez, 1953–1973, twenty years
- Bill Dooley, 1973–2013, forty years
- Casey Adelman, 2013 to present

Ruth and her husband, D.R.C. "Darcey" Brown, a founder and president of the Aspen Ski Corporation, would come to Humphreys at Wagon Wheel Gap for weeks at a time during the summers.[272] In 1968, Albert Junior died, and Ruth Humphreys Brown bought the lodge from her father's and uncle's estates.[273]

After years of benign neglect and lack of modernization, Ruth took up the tasks of installing a modern water system, putting in foundations and new roofs for all of the buildings, building a residence for herself and a major overhaul to the dam on Humphreys Lake.[274] The work was done with respect and consideration for the historic aspect of the buildings,

Ruth's maternal grandfather was Charles Boettcher, who between 1900 and 1905 helped organize the Great Western Sugar Company, the Ideal Cement Company, Western Packing Company, Capitol Life Insurance Company and several real estate and investment firms. He and his son, Claude, established the Boettcher Foundation in 1937, and family members, including Ruth Humphreys Brown, have continued to support its many philanthropic interests. Ruth's paternal grandfather, Colonel Humphreys, founded the Humphreys Foundation in 1922, which over the years benefited a variety of social causes. Coming from strong family traditions of philanthropy, in 1959, Ruth established the Ruth H. Brown Foundation, which has given grants to many nonprofit organizations in Colorado and across the country.[275]

Ruth Humphreys Brown died on December 30, 2010, at the age of ninety. In her memory, and in keeping with the heritage of her family, her children created a name-grant for the construction of the Ruth Humphreys Brown Theatre in Creede. This project was a double honor, as Ruth was a theater major in college but had to abandon that pursuit to maintain marital harmony. She won in the end.

Charles Leavell and partner William Farah purchased the neighboring 4UR in 1972. After a few years, Farah fell into financial difficulties and

Ruth Humphreys Brown Theatre, Creede, Colorado, 2019. *Photo by Scott Hizny.*

needed to divest himself of his interest in the 4UR. Leavell approached Ruth Brown to see if she was interested in purchasing Farah's share, which she did in 1986. The complicated co-ownership of the 4UR that started in 1872 continues to this day. The two major property owners agreed to protect access along the creek and ensure that the Humphreys property remained private and did not become landlocked.

The colonel included a small hydroelectric plant during his original construction efforts.[276] The Humphreys Ranch was powered solely by that micro-hydro project from 1924 until 1980. Due to increasing maintenance issues and increased demand, the family developed a project to install a 42-kilowatt (kW) plant. The ranch was hooked to the grid and buys back electricity needed for the ranch, although this plant can provide backup power if the grid goes down. In 2011, a third, large 310 kW system was installed, and all power is sold to the grid.[277] Today, the original power plant remains in place but has not been operated for many years.[278]

The family maintains the ranch as a personal retreat. A popular activity during the winter months is cutting ice from Humphreys Lake, a carryover from the early days, when all ranches cut their own ice to use for summer refrigeration in the icebox. Maybe even more important was the availability of ice to pack the numerous fish that were caught, not to mention for the evening cocktail hour. Cutting ice to sell to folks living in towns and to the railroad was also an essential activity. This was a great opportunity to supplement limited winter income, and many local men spent the cold winter months doing the hard work.

> *The American Fluor Spar Co., of Wagon Wheel Gap, has contracted to furnish the D&RG railway with 10,000 tons of ice. W.H. Swinehart and son, Bill, Jr. left Thursday morning to join the ice cutting crews at Wagon Wheel Gap.*[279]

BRITAIN

As early as 1883, the Henry Clay Caldwell family was coming to Wagon Wheel Gap. Caldwell was a judge of national renown, presiding over the Eighth U.S. District Court of Appeals.[280] The judge homesteaded 40 acres on the northern edge of the Springs, in a beautiful isolated canyon with a stream that was named after him. The patent was granted in October

1900, and he soon requested another homestead for an additional 120 acres (making 160 total) that was patented in December 1905.[281] The judge built a fine mountain cabin in 1899 and called it the Aloha Lodge; the family spent the next several summers there.[282] The judge stepped down from the court in 1903 and spent as much time as possible at his mountain retreat, although his retirement was remarked with regret by the highest government officials in the country, including President Theodore Roosevelt.[283]

> *In his later years he* [Caldwell] *decided to make his summer sojourns in Colorado; he selected an isolated mountain glade near Wagon Wheel Gap, which furnished a broad and beautiful open space at its foot, narrowing as it ascended into the mountains. Through it coursed a clear brook which took its rise in the mountain side. There, away up the narrowing glen, towards the source of the rivulet, in the midst of a natural park luxuriously wooded, and with the timbered mountains rising on either side and at the rear, he built a commodious summer abode, amply supplied with water piped from the brook, and in the large sitting room of which he erected a huge fireplace—such as he had seen in his father's house and warmed his youthful limbs before. To make the reminiscence more complete, he equipped this fireplace with a long iron crane like those of the olden time, provided with a hook on which constantly hung a teakettle over the fire which was never suffered to die out.*[284]

Unfortunately, two years later, for health reasons, Caldwell had to sell the lodge and return to his home in Arkansas full time, preceding his death in 1915.[285] Incorporated into the Palmer estate, the Caldwell property and lodge were utilized by General Palmer and his elite guests, especially the Humphreys family.[286]

As part of the Palmer estate, the old Caldwell property was included in the purchase by Ellwood Bergey in August 1924. The Aloha Lodge burned down in the 1930s, leaving only Caldwell's notable fireplace standing. After Bergey's death early in 1943, his wife, Gertrude, inherited the property and married Harold E. Cowieson in November 1943. The couple was not interested in running the resort, so during the winter of 1943–44 most of the property was sold to Arthur Sharp; Gertrude retained about six hundred acres on Caldwell Creek. The Cowiesons rebuilt the lodge and lived there for many years. After the death of Harold Cowieson in 1964 and the death of her son Ellwood Bergey Jr. in 1966, Gertrude found living in the remote area too isolated and sad. She sold the property to Adam "Ad" Britain in 1969.[287]

Ad and his family endeavored to spend the summer months at the ranch, and he often invited associates and friends to hunt and fish. His son, Howard Britain, recalled a summer when his dad bought a Palomino horse from ranch manager Ed Wintz on the 4UR. Ad and Howard went down to collect the horse but did not take any tack with them. Ad told Howard to ride the horse bareback over to their place on Caldwell Creek. The horse was having none of it and promptly bucked Howard off. Ed provided a lead rope for the halter, but Howard was in the dirt again. Loaning him a bridle, Ed had to watch as Howard came unseated a third time. Not to be deterred, young Howard mounted a fourth time and proceeded a ways down the road. When Ad came driving by in the pickup, it spooked the horse and caused yet another unplanned dismount. Howard led the horse home. When he arrived, he asked Ad if he wanted to work the horse, to which Ad replied, "Not just now, turn him loose in the pasture." [288]

In 1995, at the age of seventy-five, Ad passed away and the property went to his children and second wife. The family decided to sell half the ranch to provide for the second Mrs. Britain. Today, the Britain family owns 350 acres, and grandchildren are well on their way to becoming stewards of the land they love.[289]

In the early days of Wagon Wheel Gap, children were sent to Del Norte to school and later to Creede. There were few children and, therefore, no interest in or need for a school at the Gap. With the establishment of the fluorspar mine and mill in 1918, which employed many men, some with families and children, there was an urgent need for a schoolhouse for the children.

> *For the erection of school house at Wagon Wheel Gap, Colorado, frame building on concrete foundation, the building 18 x 24 feet. The same to be completed no later than the tenth of September, 1918. Plans and specifications can be seen at Wagon Wheel Gap Post Office. Bids will be opened July 15, any and all bids subject to refusal. By order of the School Board, District No. 1. E. Glendenning, Secretary.*[290]

> *The Wagon Wheel Gap school began the term this year on Wednesday, September 7,* [1921]. *Miss Harriet Youngman, a teacher from Williamsport, Pa., where she has taught for a number of years and also in the high schools and a graduate of the University of Chicago as instructor. The school term will be for nine months. The enrollment started with fifteen pupils, the second month shows an increased attendance and the prospects are favorable for the Gap to have a splendid school this winter.*[291]

> *Miss Ann Ashley, the popular school teacher at Wagon Wheel Gap has resigned owing to ill health and returned to Creede the first of the week. Miss Sara Chapman, of Monte Vista, has accepted the position as teacher at the Wagon Wheel Gap school to fill vacancy.*[292]

The little red Fremont schoolhouse started classes in the fall of 1918. Katherine Collins Rasmussen, a former student, remembers that the schoolhouse was white with green trim in 1923, although it was always referred to as the "little red schoolhouse."[293] It was officially called the Fremont school, because of the conviction of local residents that the area was named after the fourth, ill-fated Frémont expedition that lost a wagon, or wheels, at the place, which was later proved to be specious. Ellwood Bergey deeded land to the school district in 1924 along Caldwell Creek.[294] The schoolhouse continued to operate until 1948, when most of the men at the mine had been laid off and moved away, taking their families with them, and there was no longer a need for a school at the site.

Ad Britain was a sporting goods representative. He sold many forms of hunting, fishing and other related equipment. After he retired from that

Fremont School at Wagon Wheel Gap, circa 1932. Mrs. Hazel Lewis was the teacher. Written on back of photo: "Rex Deaner, Bruce Barksdale, David Blackburn, Bobby Blackburn, Hazel Lewis, Carolyn Blackburn, Edna Cassit." *Creede Historical Society, 2563-BF-8 [2563-WWG-16.].*

business, he purchased sports clothing and miscellaneous items during the winter in Texas for sales he would have during the spring and summer at the old Fremont schoolhouse. The Britain family purchased the acreage where the school sits and are working to protect and preserve the structure.[295]

Gjellum

When Thad and Lena Elliott moved to their second homestead along Goose Creek about 1907, their homestead patent being finalized in 1912, her parents and siblings remained on the homestead that is now part of Humphreys Ranch several miles away. Lena complained about being lonely and the trek up to the Pfeiffer place to visit her family being too far for easy traveling. Thad, the loving husband, helped Lena's sister Elizabeth Velette Pfeiffer, soon to be Mrs. Jess "Curny" Higgs, to homestead 160 acres across Goose Creek, her homestead patent being finalized in 1912.[296] Having her sister close to be company and to help with the children was a blessing for Lena. As years passed, the Palmer estate was expanding, and the eldest Elliott son, Lester, wanted to go to high school. Thad and the family moved from Wagon Wheel Gap to Monte Vista. They sold the property at Wagon Wheel Gap in 1912 to General Palmer, although they were able to summer their cattle and horses there, bringing them down to Monte Vista in the winter.[297] In December 1921, Thad suffered a major injury from which he never fully recovered.[298] Eldest son Lester died at the age of eighteen in 1922 of typhoid fever, and he was followed by Thad in January 1923, also of the fever.[299]

Across Goose Creek, Elizabeth married Curny Higgs shortly after she moved to her homestead. Together they lived and worked, raising one daughter. As years passed, Curny developed major medical issues, for which he was treated by Dr. Gjellem in Del Norte. The medical bills piled up, and the Higgses' financial situation was dire. Curny offered the doctor his 160-acre ranch at Wagon Wheel Gap in lieu of payment of his medical bills, with enough cash from Dr. Gjellem to enable Curny and his wife to live out the rest of their lives. Dr. Gjellum accepted the offer, and the deal was completed in August 1944.[300]

Arthur B. Gjellum was born in 1890, grew up in eastern Colorado, graduated from Denver University's medical school and interned at Mercy Hospital in Denver. He married his beloved "Billie," two years his junior, in 1917, and they moved to Del Norte, Colorado, where he set up his medical practice.[301]

Dr. Gjellem served during World War I from August 1917 until the spring of 1919, returning to Del Norte, to his wife and the first of their four children. He was a captain in the medical corps and received two citations for bravery in 1919.[302]

Dr. Gjellum had a private practice as a physician/surgeon and worked at the Del Norte Hospital. He became a fixture in the small community, and many longtime families in the area have stories to tell about the beloved Dr. Gjellem. After the end of World War II, he suffered from serious hip degeneration and was forced to retire. When the opportunity arose to purchase the ranch at Wagon Wheel Gap and enjoy time with his family and fishing, he left his practice and moved to the ranch during the summers.[303]

Following in his adored father's footsteps, the second-eldest son, James Eric, was a second lieutenant during World War II. He was colorblind, and the U.S. Army Air Corps turned down his application, so he joined the Canadian Air Force. He became an expert at night flying and was then recruited to the U.S. Army Air Corps. He was in Great Britain from April 1941 to October 1942. Out of his squadron of eighty-eight men fighting during the Blitz of London, he was one of only two survivors. Because of his unique night-flying skills, he returned to the United States to work as an instructor and test pilot for the new radar system and night flying. Tragically, he died during a test flight in 1943 as a young man of twenty-two.[304]

The doctor lived to a ripe old age of ninety-seven years, passing away in 1987; Billie died in 1950. They are buried in the Del Norte cemetery.[305] The property at Wagon Wheel Gap passed down to the surviving children and remains in the family as a mountain retreat and hunting lodge. Great-grandchildren of the doctor are growing up with the appreciation and love for the outdoor life experiences of the Colorado mountains.

COTTONWOOD COVE

Cottonwood Cove resort was started in 1945 by Nell and Bibs Wyley. Wilbur Watson Wyley, the fourth of four children, always had to wear hand-me-downs from his older brother, which were often bib overalls, earning him the nickname of Bibs. As an adult he refused to wear bib overalls, but the name stuck.[306]

Nell was raised in South Fork, graduated from high school and attended business school in Waco, Texas. She met Bibs while working in Monte Vista. They were married on November 2, 1941, about a month before the bombing of Pearl Harbor. Bibs went into the military but was missing three fingers on one hand, so he was not allowed to go overseas. Bibs served with the Military Police stationed in Denver. Nell went with him and worked for Rio Grande Motorway, but after about a year, Bibs contracted scarlet fever and was medically discharged. They returned to the San Luis Valley.[307]

Bibs lost those three fingers as a nine-year-old boy, when he was playing with blasting caps at his uncle's house in Monte Vista. Hearing the loud bang and Bibs's screams, his uncle ran to render assistance. Having been warned repeatedly not to play with blasting caps, Bibs thought he would be in trouble, ran away from his uncle and hid. He was eventually found and treated but lost three fingers. According to his son Ken, that never really slowed him down.[308]

Upon Bibs's release from the military, Bibs and Nell decided to pursue a life in the dude ranch business. Bibs recalled a beautiful picnic ground from his youth around Wagon Wheel Gap. Bibs and his brother Clinton looked at purchasing the Wagon Wheel Gap resort for sale at the time, but decided that there would not be enough work or money for two families to coexist there. The two families went their own ways. Bibs and Nell created Cottonwood Cove Resort just around a bend from the 4UR entrance on the Rio Grande.[309]

In 1945, Nell and Bibs obtained a one-hundred-year lease for the land for ninety dollars a year from the Denver and Rio Grande Railroad and started building a dude ranch. The first baby, Kay, came along shortly, so Nell and the baby lived in Monte Vista and Bibs in a tent at the site. Once his first cabin was completed, with virtually all of the work being done by Bibs, he brought his little family home. By 1946, the family opened their Cottonwood Cove resort with six cabins, the main lodge, a restaurant—and a new baby, Gea.[310]

Some of the cottonwood trees had to be cut to make room for cabins on the north side of the road. The Cove was a rustic resort, with wood stoves and no electricity or running water for a couple of years. The Rural Electric Association put in service to the Cove in 1949, and the cabins were eventually plumbed. The Wyleys had horses and took guests on pack, fishing and hunting trips.[311]

In 1948, the third and last child, Kenneth, was born. By the mid-1950s, Nell and Bibs had built fourteen cabins. The family lived at the Cove

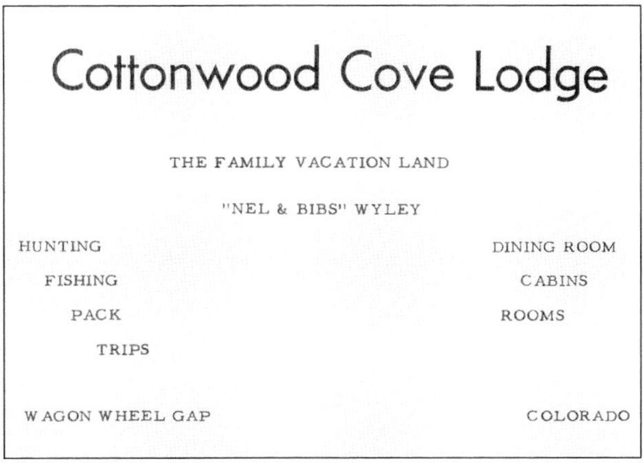

Above: Bibs and Nell Wyley in Cottonwood Cove Lodge, circa 1950. *Creede Historical Society, CHS 3418-HR-62.*

Left: Cottonwood Cove advertisement, 1959. *From* The Creede Yearbook, *1959, p.48.*

Main lodge at Cottonwood Cove, circa 1950. *Creede Historical Society, CHS 3529-CS-75.*

year-round. The summers were wildly successful, but the winters were slow. To help make ends meet, Bibs and Nell remodeled a building in Creede to be a bowling alley. The business was sold in 1967. That building is now the Kentucky Belle grocery store. Bibs served as a Mineral County commissioner for eighteen years. As years passed, the hard work at the resort took its toll on Bibs's health, and they sold their beloved Cove in 1977. At that time, the resort boasted twenty-seven cabins, a lodge with a hall, a horse stable, pastureland and eighty head of horses. The Wyleys moved to their home in Creede, where Bibs died in 1978 and Nell in 2014.[312]

La Garita Ranch (Meaning Gateway or Lookout in Spanish)

> *Ducked down below the dike of the third lake, the mustached man with a passion for trout fishing was astounded by the enormous strike on his first cast, and by the ensuing battle to land what turned out to be a 5-pound rainbow on the lead fly, and a 3-pound Brook trout on the dropper. However that happened—call it La Garita magic—he made up his mind on the spot to buy the place from the widow* [Jesse] *Thorne. The year was 1908, and the young executive from Denver with a background in steel, Lawrence C. Phipps, fell hook, line and sinker in love with the La Garita Ranch.*[313]

Across the Rio Grande to the north was another beautiful mountain valley with a crazy patchwork of parcels of land along Bellows Creek.

George W. Thorne moved to Colorado Springs as a young engineer and made his fortune in real estate development there, specializing in resort development. In 1891, when he was fifty-two years old, he married a society belle named Jesse Rowe, who was twenty-nine years old.[314]

Because of Thorne's experience and interest in developing resorts, when he discovered the beauty of the Bellows Creek area, he purchased property from various homesteaders and subsequent owners.[315] He and Jesse filed for homestead claims of their own in 1890, 1892,and 1894.[316] At the time of George's death in 1905, the Thorne estate was about 1,400 acres. The Thornes had invested considerable money in substantial improvements, creating artificial trout lakes and making the property a state-licensed park and preserve.[317]

The Thorne family, which soon included four children, lived summers at their mountain ranch, maintained their permanent residence in Colorado Springs and spent their winters in California. George contracted tuberculosis in the fall of 1904 and was confined to the Glockner sanitarium in Colorado Springs for most of the winter.[318] When spring came, he moved to Bellows Creek and enjoyed what he could of the summer there, until he died in July. Jesse, with four children from the age of thirteen down to a toddler, sold the estate to Lawrence C. Phipps and moved her children to California.[319]

The purchase is documented in the *Denver Post* on March 3, 1908. The beautiful estate is described as being contiguous to the holdings of General Palmer of the Hot Springs Hotel. Phipps was interested in making improvements to the buildings on the property and improving the game preserve. However, local critters had something to say about the nature of the game reserve:

> *The Phipps fish and game preserve, located above Wagon Wheel Gap, was visited by a bobcat several nights ago and ten pheasants of long and beautiful plumage were bagged by the bob. Lawrence Phipps has an estate of 1,400 acres on Bellows Creek and has enclosed five acres with a ten-foot wire fence in which enclosure he is raising pheasants. The preserve is in charge of S.E. Land, formerly Superintendent of the Denver Fish Hatchery. On the night of the bobcat's visit, Mr. Land was awakened by a commotion in the pheasantry and got his gun. He was there just in time to see the cat climb down the outside edge of the fencepost and disappear into the night. There will be a new fence at the Phipps pheasantry.*[320]

Lawrence C. Phipps Sr. developed the property into an exclusive hunting and fishing resort, at one time encompassing about 2,400 acres on both sides of the Rio Grande. The excellent fishing expected on the La Garita Ranch in Bellows Creek required stocking and management, accomplished with an on-site hatchery, which hatched eyed eggs and also raised fry. S.E. Land, a longtime fish culturist from the San Luis Valley, manager of state fish hatcheries and previously Colorado State Fish commissioner, was hired to manage the fishing.[321] The May 14, 1910 *Creede Candle* reported that "S.E. Land of the Phipps's Ranch on Bellows Creek has secured 145,000 rainbow trout fry which have been placed in the Phipps hatchery. They are ultimately to be deposited in Bellows Creek."

Lawrence Phipps was a U.S. senator from Colorado from 1919 until 1931.[322] His terms as senator expanded his already considerable circle of influential and powerful friends. Well-known names were often guests at the senator's La Garita hideaway, including other senators, generals, current and future presidents and other politicians.

A *Creede Candle* article, August 28, 1920, said, "Senator Phipps and party consisting of U.S. Senator Frances E. Warren, General [Black Jack] Pershing and E.W. Hart of Omaha and their wives paid Creede the honor of a short visit late Friday afternoon. The General's party is resting at the home of Senator Phipps, near Wagon Wheel Gap." Sadly, the general's wife and three young daughters died in a tragic house fire in 1915, leaving his son,

La Garita Phipps Ranch cabins, 1918. *Creede Historical Society, 3946-PC-113.*

John "Black Jack" Pershing visiting La Garita Ranch with son Warren, preparing for a pack trip with the Phipps family. Pershing is center left wearing an army hat, his son thought to be the boy on his left, circa 1925. *Creede Historical Society, 2404-P 323.*

Warren, the only survivor. General Pershing was best known as commander of the American Expeditionary Forces in Europe during World War I. The general retired from active duty in 1924 and was able to spend more time with Warren. The general died July 15, 1948.[323]

> *This will be Mr. Hoover's fourth visit to Colorado within the past year, two of them political trips and two non-political. A fishing trip in the Wagon Wheel gap country and an address before the American Metal Mining Congress comprised Mr. Hoover's two extracurricular visits.*[324]

There was a visitor of another kind at the La Garita Ranch. An oft-told Phipps family story relates a common paranormal event in the La Garita lodge, especially in rooms 1 and 2. Alice Blood, a ranch caretaker, was running from the lodge to the barn to deliver a message, when she slipped in the mud, fell and broke her neck, dying instantly on August 12, 1971. Her ghost was said to haunt the lodge; late at night, when everything was quiet, doors would open or close and odd sounds were heard. No formal investigation was ever conducted, and the lodge is no longer in existence.[325]

The Phipps family sold about 90 acres on the south side of the river, and that area was developed for home sites, now known as Wagon Wheel

Gap Estates. After Lawrence Phipps Sr. passed away in 1958, his son Allan R. Phipps took over and developed the La Garita Ranch into one of Colorado's most desirable recreational properties. The approximately 1,880-acre property included outstanding fishing on two and one-half miles of the Rio Grande, nearly three miles of Bellows Creek, four lakes, seclusion and direct access to the surrounding Rio Grande National Forest.[326] Several generations of families from throughout the country enjoyed the ranch through membership in the La Garita Club. Club buildings were classic log structures reminiscent of the dude ranches built in the early 1900s—but with modern amenities.

In 1982, the Phipps family contacted the Nature Conservancy and asked for an evaluation of their property in order to design a conservation easement. They wanted protection of the land's unique and scenic values through the easement and wished to donate that to the conservancy. The restrictive easement was completed under the direction of Allan's son Tony Phipps. The cabins can be repaired and the fishing ponds maintained, and livestock can graze the lush meadows, but none of the 1,400 acres can be subdivided for housing tracts. Allan Phipps, who had "pissed with the big dogs" for years, became emotional when reminiscing about fishing on the

View of the La Garita Ranch and La Garita Club, circa 2010. *Denver Public Library, Western History Collection, AUR-818.*

La Garita with his dad, saying that "this conservation easement was the most important deal he had ever done."[327]

After the death of Allan Phipps in 1997, the La Garita Ranch remained in the Phipps family, owned and operated by the Wagon Wheel Gap Associates partnership, consisting of Allan's children: Graham, Tony and Mindy.[328] The family sold the La Garita Ranch in 2014 after operating it for over one hundred years. The new owner has made it into a private ranch, tore down all of the old buildings and no longer accepts guests.[329]

9

THE PALMER ERA

The place in a year or two, I apprehend, will prove to be one of Colorado's most fashionable resorts.
—Colorado Daily Chieftain, *July 21, 1875*

Well, it took longer than a couple of years, lots of money and a man of vision to truly make the place into one of Colorado's most fashionable resorts. Much has been written General William Jackson Palmer's diverse projects: mining, construction and, most of all, railroads. The story of the general's involvement with the hot springs at Wagon Wheel Gap is a little-known tale. This chapter focuses on development of the hot springs at Wagon Wheel Gap into a world-class resort, including functions of a sanatorium.

As an idealistic young man, Palmer traveled to Europe, became enthralled with railroads and made the bulk of his eventual fortune in the railroad business. A brevetted general during the Civil War, he returned to his passion of railroads in 1865. At the age of thirty-four, he married Mary Lincoln Mellen, known as "Queen," thirteen years his junior, on November 8, 1870. That year, the Denver and Rio Grande Railroad was incorporated, including Palmer as one of the directors. The Palmers settled in Colorado Springs, of which the general is widely recognized as being the founder. The Palmer's first child, Elsie, was born on October 30, 1872, at the Glen Eyrie mansion.[330] Palmer had apartments in London and New York and a mansion in Mexico. When

Left: General William Jackson Palmer in his home in Glen Eyrie, circa 1880. *Denver Public Library, Western History Collection, Z-310.*

Right: Mary Lincoln Mellen "Queen" Palmer, circa 1880. *Colorado Springs Pioneers Museum, A71-223.*

possible, the family traveled with Palmer, but he was a part-time husband, often gone, and Queen was young, alone and of frail health. An excellent presentation of the life of Queen Palmer may be found in Stephen May's *A Kingdom of Their Own*.[331]

In 1880, Queen suffered a heart attack while pregnant with their second daughter, Dorothy, born at Glen Eyrie. Queen went to England for the birth of her third daughter, Marjorie. Queen often lived on the East Coast of the United States or in England, and in 1886, she and the three girls moved permanently to England, thinking the lower altitude and milder climate would be better for her. Palmer traveled to England once or twice a year to be with Queen and their daughters, although he was an absentee husband for much of their marriage. Queen died in England at age forty-four on December 27, 1894. The three girls returned to the United States to live with a father they really didn't know at Glen Eyrie in Colorado Springs, Colorado.[332]

D&RG WAGON WHEEL GAP EXTENSION

The D&RG was a land-grant railroad that received millions of acres of land from the federal government. Alternating sections of land along the rail line were sold to finance the cost of construction of the railroad. Purchasers of the land were most often immigrants from Europe, primarily Britain and Scotland, who had been enticed to move with promises of a better life and unlimited opportunities in the western United States.[333]

> *The interdependence of U.S. railroad expansion and immigration shaped the lives of thousands of migrants. Company pamphlets, posters and handbills reached across the Atlantic, and in England Sir James Caird and Richard Cobden were recruited into the advertising campaigns. It became a massive propaganda exercise, much of it exaggerated and deceptive, to generate a flow of immigrants and westward moving settlers.*[334]

The beloved Scottish jute baron Sir James Caird was generous with his money and one of Scotland's most successful entrepreneurs, noted for his interest in providing financial aid for scientific research. He was one of the sponsors of Sir Ernest Shackleton's ill-fated Antarctic expedition of 1914 to 1916. The ship's boat, the *James Caird*, was named in recognition of Caird's contribution, as was the Caird Coast of the Weddell Sea.[335]

Caird was hired by U.S. railroads as a spokesman. On his advertising campaigns across Europe, Caird made the acquaintance of Palmer, and the two men became friends. Palmer invited Caird to the United States to visit and work with him. Being of an age with each other, highly intelligent, ambitious and adventurous, the two men embarked on several investments in southern Colorado together as early as 1877.[336] Likely, Caird provided the bulk of the capital and Palmer the vision. Caird returned to Scotland around 1881, never returning to the United States, although his business relationship with Palmer lasted for many years.

The D&RG planned a route west from Pueblo over La Veta Pass, through the San Luis Valley and possibly points beyond.[337] Planning ahead, surveying and obtaining permits required traveling along the proposed route and meant that the general and Caird saw first-hand the different enterprises being developed in the San Juan Mountains. On their way through Wagon Wheel Gap, they visited the hot springs with the thought of developing the area sometime in the future, with the hot springs available for use as a sanitarium. Palmer and Caird started quietly buying up property in the area as early as 1881, with the purchase of eighty-two acres from Abraham R. Bevan, including the hot springs property.[338] It was during that summer that the D&RG reached the nearby town of Del Norte, about thirty miles east of the Gap.

Over the next couple of years, a significant effort was made by the D&RG, under Palmer's direction, to complete the tracks from Del Norte to South Fork in 1882 and on to the Gap in 1883. This was a boon to business at the hot springs, making the trip from points to the east much easier and faster. Palmer and Caird purchased the 480-acre Wagon Wheel Gap Hot Springs Company from its President Abraham Bevan early in 1883.[339]

> *The Denver and Rio Grande Railway is now completed to Wagon Wheel Gap, and trains are running regularly. The completion of the road to the Gap opens to the public what is sure to become the most popular watering place in the West. It possesses both a hot and cold mineral spring; is situated upon the Rio Grande River, a historic stream surrounded by magnificent scenery; is a paradise for the hunter and fisher, and is unexcelled as a health resort. Wagon Wheel Gap has a bright future before it, and the opening of the railroad is an event worthy of note in its history.*[340]

ABSENTEE LANDLORDS

For its early life, the hot springs operation was managed by J.C. McClelland, who had managed the Hot Springs Hotel since its earliest days for Henson and partners. With the change in ownership, McClelland took out a three-year lease for management of the hotel and springs in the spring of 1881.[341] As McClelland obtained his own property, with projects and establishments to tend to, he left the Palmer hotel for others to manage starting the summer of 1885.

> *To rent or lease for a term of years Wagon Wheel Gap Hot Springs hotel. This hotel is situated on the Rio Grande River at Wagon Wheel Gap, one mile from the Denver and Rio Grande Railroad and is famous for its curative waters and spring. It is also surrounded by one of the best cattle ranges in Southern Colorado. Thirty-two large bedrooms and good kitchens and offices and bath houses, bedsides family accommodation.*

> *Extra excursion trains run constantly to this point through the summer. Rent moderate and immediate possession. Apply to A.R. Bevan, Del Norte, Colorado.*[342]

This advertisement attracted the attention of Nathaniel K. Patten, his wife and adult son, Arthur, from Creede. Arthur had been postmaster at the Gap in 1883. The family relocated to manage the hotel in the spring of 1885, starting a long tenure of the Pattens in the Wagon Wheel Gap area. Mrs. Patten was acknowledged in the local paper for hosting an event at the hotel to honor the burial of former President Grant at his death in August 1885.[343]

> *A number of vehicles were in waiting at "the Gap" to convey the party to the Hot Springs hotel, a mile west of "the Gap" at the springs. An excellent supper was ready, to which all hands did ample justice, after the appetizing ride of the afternoon over plowed fields and irrigating ditches. The hotel is kept in excellent shape by Patten & Son. Mr. Arthur Patten, the son, is clerk and spares no pains to make the guests feel at home. Mrs. Patten presides in the kitchen, and sees that everything runs ship shape.*[344]

Business at the hot springs was booming, and there was demand for more housing. Discussion took place, and proposals were made for extensive improvements at Wagon Wheel Gap, including an artificial lake and a big hotel.[345]

Palmer and Caird didn't take an active role in the management of the hotel and springs, the Wagon Wheel Gap Hot Springs Company being primarily an acquisition company. The facilities that had been in place since the 1870s were getting long in the tooth and sorely in need of upgrades. Clamor continued for improvements to be made at the Springs, and in the late fall of 1889, a new company was formed to make improvements to the resort. Incorporation papers were filed early in the following year. At the same time, the railroad decided to cancel trains from Del Norte, starting in the 1889 season.

WAGON WHEEL GAP IMPROVEMENT COMPANY, FEBRUARY 1, 1889

The Wagon Wheel Gap Improvement Company was formed to:

- Acquire, lease and purchase lands and real estate
- Build and maintain irrigation ditches
- Construct and maintain roads, reservoirs, water courses
- Acquire, hold and develop mineral resources
- Produce ore and other mineral substances and to prepare the same for market.

The board of directors were William A. Bell, Thomas J. Fisher and John E. Lundstrom. All were Colorado Springs residents and longtime friends and business associates of General Palmer.[346] Palmer and Caird were the largest stockholders. The shell company allowed them to get out of some of their other relationships and start to consolidate everything under the umbrella of a corporation, in the trusted hands of William Bell.

Dr. William A. Bell, an English gentleman of wealth and enterprise, was a natural associate of Palmer.[347] Although Palmer has more name recognition, Dr. William A. Bell is recognized as one of the founders of the D&RG and one of the pioneer developers of Colorado Springs and other areas of southwestern Colorado.[348]

Palmer and Bell started the *Colorado Springs Gazette* together and sold it in 1877.[349] For many years, Bell was vice president of the D&RG under Palmer, often acting in his stead when he was unavailable.[350] Palmer and Bell were active in philanthropic efforts, donating 1,500 acres of land to Colorado College for a School of Forestry, including buildings and water. The two men engaged the services of Gifford Pinchot, first head of the U.S. Forest Service, to aid in staffing the department.[351]

Thomas J. Fisher, a younger man, was manager of many Palmer interests, later a co-investor on several other projects and a lifetime associate of the general.[352]

As the years progressed, General William Jackson Palmer and James K. Caird purchased property around the Gap, especially near the hot springs, in the name of the Wagon Wheel Gap Improvement Company. They owned the hotel, the main spring and bathhouse and several cottages.

> *Colorado Springs capitalists have within the past six weeks quietly taken up all the vacant land in and about Wagon Wheel Gap, and it is said by those secret to their scheme is to establish there one of the finest summer resorts in the southwest.*[353]

In May 1891, the partnership of Palmer and Caird sold their holdings in the Wagon Wheel Gap Improvement Company for $50,000. Local newspapers reported,

> *This is grand news for the people of this section, because it is supposed that the transfer will do away with the tie-up that has existed on the property in question for many years. The change doubtless means improvement of the Gap property and in any event is favorable to the country as compared with the ownership of Palmer and Caird. The change in ownership of the Gap property the* PROSPECTOR *considers greatly to the advantage of this entire section.*[354]

This exchange of monies allowed Caird to dissolve the partnership with Palmer and recover his investment at the Gap. Likewise, it allowed Palmer to gain control as the single largest investor in the Wagon Wheel Gap Improvement Company, managed by his friends Bell and Fisher.

> *The transfer of the property of Palmer and Caird at Wagon Wheel Gap to the Wagon Wheel Gap Improvement company has been made and the deed recorded in Rio Grande county. The sale includes about 900 acres of land and the entire hotel and hot springs property. It is not known yet whether this transfer means that the D. A R.G.* [D&RG] *will be induced to run summer trains to that paradise of fishermen.*[355]

The lack of a train running to the Gap from 1889 to 1892 did not seem to deter any of the usual influx of summer tourists, as evidenced by numerous articles that told of many traveling to Wagon Wheel Gap for extended periods of time during the summer months.

> *Mr. and Mrs. Mealey and Mr. and Mrs. Ed Smith will start in wagons tomorrow for Wagon Wheel Gap. They expect to remain there till September and propose to have a good time.*[356]

> *W.F. Boob returned from Wagon Wheel Gap yesterday. He reports that the camber of camps at the Gap is greater than it has been for some time, and that everyone who is there is having a splendid time.*[357]

The train tracks between Del Norte and Wagon Wheel Gap received some attention during 1891 in anticipation of reopening them to support the Creede mining boom.[358] It was not until 1892 that the Creede boom made extending the line from Wagon Wheel Gap to Creede financially feasible There were some railroad politics involved. From the *Colorado Daily Chieftain* of July 24, 1891, we learn that "commencing today the D. & R.G. will hereafter run trains to Wagon Wheel Gap on Monday, Wednesday and Friday of each week."

In the spring of 1892, there was trouble about who was the manager of the hotel at Wagon Wheel Gap. The owners decided to give the lease to M.M. Cope. The Pattens claimed they had a valid lease, which sent the case to court. From the time of the contested lease in May 1892, the Judge in Del Norte "quashed the summons" in June, which allowed Cope to manage the hotel during the summer of 1892, opening in early June and

THE WAGON WHEEL GAP

HOT SPRINGS HOTEL

—IS OPEN FOR THE SEASON OF 1894—

SPLENDID TROUT FISHING:
A DELIGHTFUL BATHING RESORT.

SPECIAL ATTENTION TO INVALIDS.

ANALYSIS OF WATER:

Upon analysis, the water of the main spring is found to contain the following constituents to the gallon: Carbonate of lime, 18.08; carbonate of magnesia, 1.98; sulphate of soda, 6.13; chloride of sodium, 6.84; silica, 0.63; organic matter (hydro sul.), 7.00. Total solids, 41.65. Hydro sulphate gas, 7 grains in 19.2 cubic inches. Temperature, 148° Fahrenheit.

JOHN ZANG, LESSEE.

Zang's Wagon Wheel Gap Hot Springs Hotel advertisement, 1894. *From the* Creede Candle, *June 29, 1894.*

closing in September.[359] In the summer of 1892, Nathaniel Patten resigned as postmaster at the Gap, and the family moved to Creede.

Mr. Cope lasted only the season of 1892. An ebullient German immigrant, John Zang, owner of Zang's Hotel (now the Creede Hotel) in Creede, was offered the opportunity to run the Hot Springs Hotel in 1893. With Mrs. Zang readily able to manage their Creede Hotel, John, with his Teutonic enthusiasm for work, eagerly took over the Hot Springs Hotel in 1893, attracting a pilgrimage of guests from Creede.[360] The next year, John Zang was back at the Hot Springs Hotel with a formal opening on June 8, 1894.[361]

The *Creede Candle*, the major source of information about Wagon Wheel Gap, was not in operation from late 1894 until the spring of 1904. Short notes in other area papers relate simple statements, such as "The hot springs at Wagon Wheel Gap are being put in order for the use of bathers and tourists."[362] Likely not much was going on at the Springs during many of those years, as General Palmer was consumed with recovering from the death of his wife in 1894 and caring for his three girls.[363]

MODERNIZATION OF THE WAGON WHEEL GAP HOT SPRINGS

As early as 1898, there were reports of a planned grand resort being proposed at Wagon Wheel Gap.[364] In 1901, Palmer retired from the D&RG and turned his attention to his family and local enterprises. Realizing a clear profit of $6 million from the sale of his share of the D&RG, he gave a substantial amount of money to former employees, charities and universities.[365] In 1902, he sold his interest in a Mexican railroad for a couple of million and started serious investments into Wagon Wheel Gap resort.[366] Colorado Springs architect Thomas MacLaren, who was designing upgrades to the general's Glen Eyrie property in Colorado Springs, was hired to do the design for the improvements proposed at Wagon Wheel Gap.[367] The projects to be implemented in phases over a several-year period included construction of a new bathhouse, a large barn, a water system, a sewer system and remodeling the hotel, as well as painting and numerous needed repairs and upgrades. The general purchased more homesteads in the area to increase the size of his planned resort.[368]

Thomas MacLaren, born on February 19, 1863, in Scotland, received advanced degrees in architecture. His older brother James died of

Thomas J. MacLaren, architect, circa 1911. *Pikes Peak Library District, 263 11475.*

tuberculosis, and Thomas developed symptoms of the disease as well. A dry climate was advised, so Thomas moved to Colorado, first to Denver, then to Colorado Springs. MacLaren is highly regarded as the designer of landmark churches, libraries, schools and homes—many of which have been listed in the National Register of Historic Places.[369] Becoming acquainted with Palmer, and interested in sanitariums because of his own illness, MacLaren interpreted Palmer's grand vision into reality.

In the summer of 1902, the first of the major renovations was completed.[370] With money no object in getting the work done in time for the summer season, "R.J. Verner, of Colorado Springs, has the contract for the work of making improvements at the Hot Springs Hotel, Wagon Wheel Gap, and is putting on all the mechanics he can get."[371]

The bathhouse was a classic wonder in the Spanish Mission style.

> *The bath-house, one of the most carefully and best-appointed bathing establishments in the United States, was erected in 1902. Of liberal dimensions, it possesses the unique feature of having both ladies' and gentlemen's inside hot-water swimming pools. Adjoining each pool are commodious resting rooms provided with rockers and willow couches. Encircling the dressing rooms are enclosed individual dressing compartments. To meet special requirements* [for the invalids] *the bath-house is provided with bedrooms having private bath tubs attached.*[372]

> *Next year, no doubt, will see a crush at the Gap owing to the splendid improvements made by the owner of the property, General Palmer. Over $100,000 has been spent and more will be expended along the same line next year. Old patrons of this famous resort would not know the place now.*[373]

A.E. Gates, a Creede resident since 1892, wrote in a letter,

> *The Hot Springs Hotel was a favorite for families; often on a Sunday after church, we drove down for Sunday dinner and a swim in the pool. The*

> *plunges were in the same building but in separate rooms. One for men, one for women. We rented bathing suits from the management. The suits* [for women] *consisted of bloomers, a full skirt, long sleeves and long black stockings. No wonder none of us ever learned to swim.*[374]

The manager of the Wagon Wheel Gap hotel in 1902 and 1903 was Jacques Bussert.[375] He had been the steward at the Antlers' Hotel in Colorado Springs, and Palmer knew him.[376] Bussert departed after the 1903 season to be the proprietor of the National Hotel in Cripple Creek the following year.[377]

The improvements to be completed over the winter of 1903 for the 1904 season were estimated to cost around $50,000. They included a flood-control ditch to divert waters from above the resort to the Rio Grande River, fencing, new lawns and installing a complete electric light system. Palmer made Goose Creek a fish preserve for the private use of his guests, a policy that lasts to this day.[378]

In 1904, a landmark year, Ellwood Bergey was first hired as the manager of the Hot Springs Hotel, leading to an association that would span almost forty years. He worked as manager of the hotel for the Palmer estate until 1913, then for other owners, and eventually purchased the property, as related in chapter 11.

Endless problems with the bridge over the Rio Grande continued to plague the resort. Many years, in the spring, the bridge needed to be repaired or replaced.[379] At that time, there was no dam on the Rio Grande—there would not be until 1912—to control flooding that occurred every spring during runoff. Not only was there an issue with the water rising, but the bridges were encased in ice from the winter as well. Spring floods came pushing water and other ice, straining the abutments of the bridge. In the early spring of 1905, Palmer (or his representative) went to the Mineral County Commissioners and said, "I will rebuild the bridge and portion of road as necessary, but then it will be mine and closed to any other traffic." The potential for mines was already on the horizon, and the county commissioners decided that they would spend the money for the bridge and keep the bridge and road open to the public.[380] The bridge was completed the next year and said to be "one of the best in the county."[381] However, Mother Nature was not to be denied, and the bridge had to be replaced yet again in 1909.[382]

Notice
Private Property
The owners assume no
liability to the public and
reserve the right to close
the bridge at any time.
Do not ride or drive over
this bridge faster than
a walk, or drive droves of
cattle or horses over it, or
drag logs across it.[383]

With the bridge taken care of for the time being, Palmer continued to implement his plan of phased improvements. During the winter of 1905 and spring of 1906, the road from the Wagon Wheel Gap station to the resort was constructed. The boulevard was twenty-five feet wide, built on an even grade, with drainage as necessary, about a mile long, with a solid base suitable for year-round travel and the convenience of tourists. No longer a rough two-track trail, this road was the "finest mountain road in the state," at a cost of $12,000. This effort included installation of a telephone line into the resort.[384]

In the spring of 1906, major construction costing $75,000 and employing over one hundred men was rushed as much as possible to accommodate the 1906 tourist season starting in June. These projects had been on hold until Palmer was able to purchase more of the homesteads and ranches along Goose Creek that were in the way of drives, boulevards and fishing:

- fish hatchery and nursery pond, and a road extended to the south toward Humphreys Ranch,
- fish lake at the swampy area at the bend of the road (now called Walton Pond), and
- modern livery barn stocked with fine driving and riding horses and carriages.[385]

The significant improvements to the resort were recognized by many, especially in comparison to the original facilities provided in the 1870s.

> *That the improvements at Wagon Wheel Gap are well worth seeing and could the original locators, Squire Henson, Charley Peck and others, who*

View of the Hot Springs Hotel with cottages and the hotel with porch and verandas. Wooden walkways connect the buildings, circa 1910. *Denver Public Library, Western History Collection, CHS.X5212.*

> *have passed over the great divide, they who put up the rude log cabin bath-house and welcomed the old San Juan pioneers for their annual baths, could they but return they would gaze in astonishment at what General Palmer and his wealth has done, but it is questionable whether the old timers would enjoy the present luxurious accommodations with as great relish as they did the whole-souled generosity, accompanying the flap-jacks, sowbelly* [bacon] *and poor whiskey dealt out by the pioneers of pioneers.*[386]

> *The cottage feature predominates, so that about one-third of the guests are accommodated in the main building and the remainder in the cottages, which are connected with the hotel by substantial walks with rustic railings. They are models of neatness and convenience, affording a privacy not usually found in a hotel.*[387]

THE BEGINNING OF THE END

A consummate equestrian from his years in the Civil War, General Palmer became personally involved in the acquisition of the fine riding horses for his new livery barn. A carload of riding horses was shipped from Colorado Springs to Durango. From there, he and some friends rode overland from Durango to Wagon Wheel Gap. The trip took about two weeks in late August 1906.[388] Surely the best of times to be in the Colorado high country.

Palmer spent several weeks at Wagon Wheel Gap, but he returned to Glen Eyrie to celebrate his seventy-first birthday on September 18, 1906. An unconscionable accident happened to the general on October 27, 1906—just weeks after his cross-county ride from Durango to Wagon Wheel Gap. Riding with his daughters and friends at Glen Eyrie, not on his usual horse, he was thrown as the unfamiliar mount shied. Landing on his head, he broke two vertebrae in his back and, for a time, was near death. Physicians were summoned from Denver to complement his own in Colorado Springs.[389]

Across the state, newspapers carried headlines of General Palmer's near-fatal injury. Almost daily updates were provided, and his condition slowly improved, although he was mostly paralyzed for some time. He conducted business at his home and eventually purchased an automobile for travel, which he had previously despised and had banned from all of his properties.[390]

Meanwhile, work at Wagon Wheel Gap continued. Upgrades and improvements to beautify the place were rushed feverishly for the opening of the hotel in June 1907. One interesting upgrade was the installment of "box hair" mattresses in all the rooms. Horsehair mattresses are luxury items, obtained today from $20,000 up to $150,000. Horsehair is critical. The tail hair is braided by hand, then unwound, to give it more bounce. Every single curled strand functions like a tiny spring, providing support and pliability. Because each horsehair strand is also a hollow tube (unlike human hair), the material acts as a miniature airway to wick moisture away so there's no sweat buildup.[391] The high-end mattresses were necessary because of the constantly growing class of wealthy families who liked to have the comforts of home.[392]

Back at Glen Eyrie, the eldest Palmer daughter, Elsie, was married on the evening of January 20, 1908, to Leopold Hamilton Myers, of Cambridge, England, a business associate of the general for several years. Reverend A.N. Taft, rector of Saint Stephen's Church, performed the ceremony, and the bride was given away by her father. After the ceremony, Mr. and Mrs. Myers left for New York, thence to Italy, and settled in England.[393]

Almost a year and a half after his accident, the general succumbed. He had been ailing for several weeks, so his passing was not unexpected.[394] Elsie had recently had her first child and was notified to return with all haste, which she did, bringing her ten-week-old baby. The general had requested that she come and had hoped to name the baby. Elsie and baby made it to Glen Eyrie before her father expired on March 13, 1909, at the age of seventy-three.[395]

William J. Palmer as an older man, circa 1906. *History Colorado online collection, PH.PROP.4933.*

The general's funeral was a major production, as he was beloved by the people of Colorado Springs, known throughout the state and parts of the entire country. Reverend Taft performed the funeral. The pallbearers were men of long-standing acquaintance with the general: Colonel D. C. Dodge of Denver; Leopold Hamilton Myers, the general's son-in-law; Major Henry McAllister; Dr. W. A. Bell; Thomas J. Fisher; F.C. Thornton; F. Greene; Dr. W.F. Slocum; W.L. Sclater, brother-in-law of General Palmer; E.C. Van Deist; and W.W. Postlethwaite.[396]

Although Palmer and Bell had many successful businesses together and were lifelong friends, after both men were gone, their children instigated lawsuits between the two families. A dream for litigation attorneys, this case took over twelve years for a final ruling.[397]

Renewing and Extending the Corporate Life of the Wagon Wheel Gap Improvement Company, February 11, 1909

The Last Will and Testament of William J. Palmer released his holdings in the Wagon Wheel Gap Improvement Company to his three daughters and son-in-law, Leopold Hamilton Myers.[398] They maintained the Wagon Wheel Gap Improvement Company and renewed the 1899 incorporation, which had a life of twenty years. The children and in-law were intent on holding on to the resort, and the Palmer family remained the largest stockholder.[399]

Ellwood Bergey continued to manage the hotel and hot springs operation. In 1910, he informed the local paper that the Wagon Wheel Gap Improvement Company had started building three cottages of six rooms each. Estimated cost for each cottage was $6,000 or more.

> *These new buildings, as well as the rest of the buildings will be fitted with new plumbing fixtures, including porcelain baths and sinks with hot and cold-water faucets, and the latest modern toilet. The fresh water comes from a reservoir built along Pierce Creek* [still used today]. *It is said that an electric plant will soon be installed by the Improvement Company for the benefit of the hotel and adjoining cottages and other buildings. When this is done, this already famous resort, known now all over the world for its scenic beauties and the high qualities of its fishing grounds, will not lack one modern feature that is now deemed essential to the comfort of mankind.*[400]

A telegraph line was put into the Gap as early as 1893, years before telephone lines were available all over the country, especially in a backwater like Wagon Wheel Gap. A single party line was available for several years, but it was next to impossible to call with so many people vying for time on the line. In July 1910, the Colorado Telephone Company's workmen started stringing new wires from Creede to the Hot Springs Hotel at Wagon Wheel Gap, which would provide a single party line, a significant improvement for patrons of the resort.[401]

There were more complications at the resort. Mineral discoveries and claims across Goose Creek led to problems. The primary issue was the common road used by both hotel guests and mining wagons to get over the Rio Grande at the depot. Ellwood Bergy, who had investments and interest in promoting the mine, was at odds with the Palmer heirs. He stayed through the 1912 season, but anticipating some involvement with the mine, tendered his resignation to the Palmer heirs in January 1913.[402]

The Palmer estate contracted with a previous manager, Jacques Bussert, to manage the hotel in 1913, 1914 and 1915. Bussert was an experienced hotel man and had been at the Hot Springs Hotel in 1902–3—prior to Bergey's arrival.[403]

> *Hot Springs Hotel, Wagon Wheel Gap will be open for the season Sunday, June 7th* [1914]. *The management solicits the patronage of Walsenburg citizens. Week end rates. Rates, $13.00 per day and up. Also, one large furnished room for light housekeeping $15.00 per mo.*

One 5 room cottage furnished for light housekeeping, $15 per month. J. BUSSERT, Manager.[404]

World War I started in Europe in July 1914, and although the United States did not declare war on Germany until April 1917, the effects of the war were felt long before that. Bussert maintained,

No more will the American millionaires fill up the resorts of Europe. Many of these resort towns are now over-run with soldiers. The palatial spring houses have been destroyed along with the cathedrals and other public buildings. Millions had been expended by most of the European governments to provide comforts and luxuries for the health seekers of the world who came to take the waters. Since the war the American health resorts will now come into their own.[405]

In the late summer of 1915, Jacques Bussert got himself into trouble regarding nonresident fishing licenses. Bussert was charged with falsifying the residence of two young fisherman, stating that they were from Colorado, when they were really from Kansas City. Bussert was fined thirty-five dollars. Special Game Warden O'Rear reported "that if he had been one month earlier, he would have had most of the tourists at Wagon Wheel Gap under arrest, as they had no fishing license at all."[406]

The conflict with the mining operation across Goose Creek, complicated by Bussert's fishing license scandal, left the door open for another manager. The next manager took out an owner-financed mortgage with the Wagon Wheel Gap Improvement Company to purchase the hot springs operation. A.H. Jordan took possession in the spring of 1916 and operated the resort for two years.[407]

The First World War, from 1914 to 1918, the Spanish flu pandemic of 1918 and operation of the adjacent fluorspar mine affected the resort to the point that Jordan was not able to make a go of it, despite glowing reports in local newspapers. The resort was a local attraction but did not bring in enough wealthy patrons from across the country to sustain profitable operations. With the focus on winning the war, the mine was in full operation, and the endless conflicts between the mine people and the resort people were coming to a head. Jordan defaulted on his loan, and the Palmer estate, under the Wagon Wheel Gap Improvement Company, sold the property, ending the thirty-eight-year Palmer association with the place.

10

THE FLUORSPAR MINE AND MILL

The Fluorspar mining proposition at Wagon Wheel Gap is assuming very extensive proportions. It is owned and operated by S.B. Collins and B.C. Hosselkus, principally. We are told that they shipped approximately 400 tons to the C.F. & I. during April, the lowest car of which was 84 per cent pure and ranging from that to 92 per cent. As long as steel mills run there will be a market for fluorspar on a profitable basis. This venture is practically new, about five months old and promises to be numbered among the big propositions of Creede camp. They are now employing about ten men. Their mines are about one mile from the Wagon Wheel Gap depot, where their product is loaded with teams.

—Creede Candle, *July 5, 1913*

This chapter discusses the impact of the operation of the fluorspar mine and mill from 1913 to 1950. The effect on the resort was significant in the early years of the mine's operation. The mine was a couple hundred yards directly to the east from the resort across Goose Creek. Proximity and competing priorities made for ongoing confrontations between the two operations. The biggest issue was the single road, over a mile long, that ran between the mill and the railroad depot at the Gap. Heavily laden wagons carrying ore rumbled down the road, and equally heavily laden wagons trundled back up the road carrying coal to fire the boilers. Patrons of the resort in small hacks had to dodge the heavier wagons or be stuck in the dust behind them.

Mill and mine openings of C.F.&I. Company fluorspar mine looking east from opposite side of Goose Creek Valley, Wagon Wheel Gap, Colorado. Hot Springs resort in foreground. 1926. *Department of the Interior, United States Geological Survey Denver Library Photographic Collection, bef01325. Photo by Ernest Francis Burchard.*

Looking east to operating fluorspar mill from the resort, black coal smoke and billowing steam. Bridge across Goose Creek in foreground, circa 1920. *Courtesy of the 4UR Ranch.*

There also was the noise of rock crushers in the mill, smoke from burning large amounts of coal and negative interactions between patrons of the resort looking for peace, solitude and relaxation and the rough-and-tumble miners. The mine/mill and the resort were geographically separated by Goose Creek: the Hot Sulfur Spring and resort on the west side and the mine operations and Hot Soda Spring on the east side. Resort patrons were no longer able to use Hot Soda Spring.

FLUORSPAR

Before World War I, the rattling of sabers across the ocean spurred a demand for more steel, and the making of quality steel demanded fluorspar, which is calcium fluoride. U.S. Geological Survey geologist Ernest F. Burchard wrote, "Fluorspar is one of the nonmetallic minerals of moderate intrinsic value the demand for which, has increased greatly since the beginning of the European war, on account of its usefulness in the metallurgic, ceramic, and chemical industries, especially in the manufacture of open-hearth steel, enameled ware, and hydrofluoric acid."[408] He stated that the concentration of calcium fluoride in the ore from the Wagon Wheel Gap mine was one of the highest among mines around the country—therefore, quite valuable. The railroad from the Gap to the open-hearth steel mills in Pueblo made it even more attractive for the western production of steel.

Steel making is significantly enhanced by the addition of fluorspar as a flux, something added that chemically allows the metal mixture to flow, or melt, more easily. Iron ore and coke (carbon) are heated to create a liquid mass, and impurities from the ore must be removed from the mix to form pure steel. The stony waste matter separated from metals during the smelting or refining of ore is called slag. The addition of calcium fluoride changes the chemical nature of the slag, allowing it to absorb more impurities, resulting in a purer steel.[409]

In 1911, Shrive B. Collins, then Mineral County surveyor and a deputy U.S. mineral surveyor, recognized the lovely purple quartz rock as fluorite. With his degree in mine engineering, Shrive knew that fluorite was an important material in the making of steel. With trouble coming in Europe, Russian fluorspar would no longer be available, and an American source would be required. For several years, disappointed miners prospecting around Amethyst Hill found fluorite, which looks a lot like amethyst but

Shrive Collins at Wagon Wheel Gap, circa 1915. *Creede Historical Society, 3372-LF-38c1.*

fails to contain silver and gold. (The real amethyst found in the mines around Creede does.)[410]

It took the knowledge, energy and conviction of Shrive Collins to make the mine and mill a reality. Teaming up with his fishery business partner, Bert Hosselkus, the Colorado Fluorspar Mining Company was incorporated on September 12, 1912.[411] They approached the Wagon Wheel Gap Improvement Company and secured a ten-year lease of land and water from Palmer's heirs. By 1913, development had progressed to the extent that five thousand tons of fluorite had been shipped to the steel mills in Pueblo. During 1914, the mine was idle, but it reopened in 1915 and was worked intermittently until its closure in 1950.[412]

WORKING TOGETHER

On September 1, 1916, the Colorado Fluorspar Company was officially defunct and inoperative, replaced by the American Fluorspar Mining, Leasing and Transportation Company, which was incorporated to operate the mine and mill with an expanded scope.[413] In addition to Shrive and Bert, two other Creede men, Wallace Leary and Win LeZotte, were added to the list of owners.[414] Recognizing the need to develop alternate access to the railroad station, the company put in place a plan to construct a surface tram track on the east side of Goose Creek from the mill to the rail siding. The track would cross the Rio Grande at the old wagon bridge on the east side of the Goose Creek delta, downstream from where Cottonwood Cove is now.[415] The old bridge soon proved unreliable, and another one constructed in 1921 served for the remainder of the project.[416]

The conflicts between the mine/mill and resort became untenable. The resort and mine folks decided that the best solution was for the mining company to purchase the resort, which it did in the spring of 1918.

> *Buys Hot Springs Hotel. This week a business deal was transacted whereby the American Fluor Spar Mining company became the owners of the Hot Springs Hotel at Wagon Wheel Gap. The transaction included the buildings and the entire amount of land. The new owners will not attempt to run the hotel. The purchase was made in the interest of their mine. The American Fluor Spar Mining company has experienced much difficulty at the hands of the hotel people regarding the wagon road as well as other matters. By the purchase of the property all difficulties will be ended. The hotel buildings and part of the land will be for sale.*[417]

As the need for fluorspar waxed and waned, 1920 was a boom year, and the mine was hiring as many men as it could find. In order to supplement housing, the resort was closed to the public and used to house the miners. "The body of General Palmer would turn over in his grave if it could see miners inhabiting the fashionable Hot Springs Hotel at Wagon Wheel Gap. The proprietors of the place have found that there is more profit in mining the rich deposits of fluorspar than there is caring for the tourists."[418]

> *We are informed that the Fluorspar mine at Wagon Wheel Gap, has near 80 men now on the payroll.*[419]

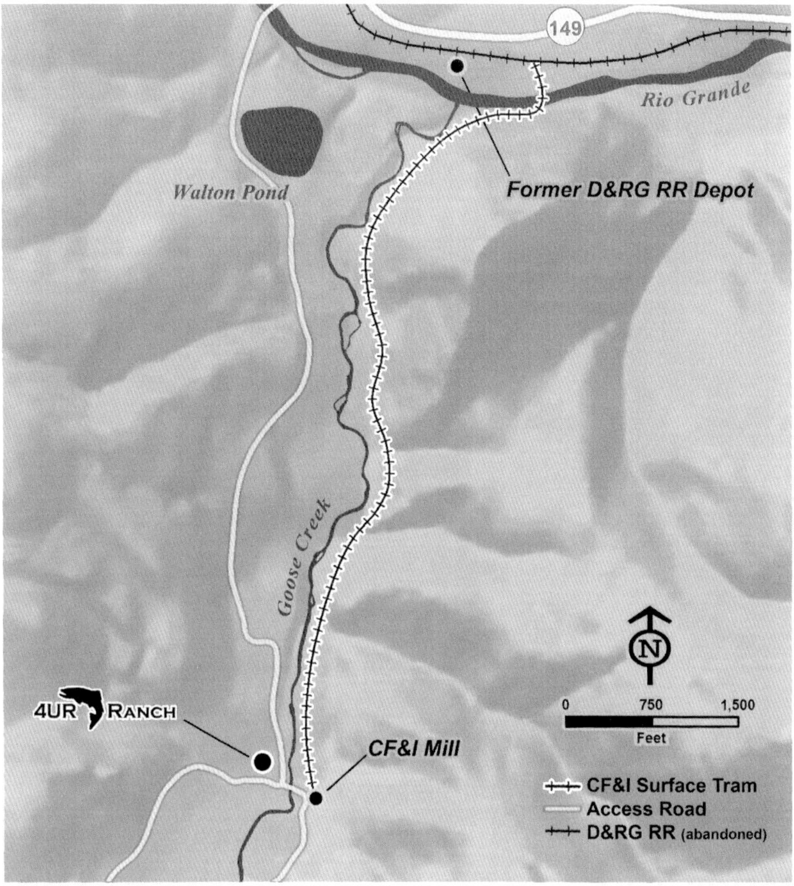

Surface tram along east side of Goose Creek from mill out to railroad. Note re-routed Goose Creek near the mill. *Cartography by John Evaskovich, from Copeland and Vendl, "The Wagon Wheel Gap Fluorspar Mine."*

Early in the spring of 1921, mining activities were to be suspended about the middle of May and not resumed until the end of the hotel season. Bergey was to open the hotel to tourists that summer. However, in May it was determined that the mine would continue operations during the summer, so for a second year the hotel was closed to tourists, which made an impact on the businesses of the area that depended on visitors.[420]

> *At present we are badly in need of a good hotel, capable of caring for one hundred guests. It does not necessarily mean that this hotel should be in the town of Creede, but one on the Rio Grande river, the greatest trout fishing*

> *stream in all the wonderful west, is a necessity right now. During the past season* [1920]*, when the Hot Springs Hotel at Wagon Wheel Gap was closed, the visitor was up against it for accommodations unless he carried an outdoor outfit.*[421]

As employment at the mine and mill fluctuated wildly, people turned to an unexpected activity: raising lettuce. With a short growing season and nighttime frosts occurring frequently at 8,400 feet in elevation, the area was not known for agriculture. However, lettuce is a cool-season crop and could withstand some cold weather. There were two drivers for this activity: blight in some of Colorado's iceberg lettuce crop and the lucrative market for head lettuce.[422] Since the Wagon Wheel Gap region was essentially virgin, as far as raising crops, there was no chance of blight, and area ranchers/farmers decided to give the expected profitable crop a try. This was not an isolated effort at Wagon Wheel Gap but attempted in other high-altitude parts of the state, especially in mining camps that were idle.[423]

Work was implemented to dig irrigation ditches to bring in water for the lettuce, and men took crash courses in lettuce farming. In the fall of 1921, lettuce was shipped out in carloads, making Wagon Wheel Gap a hub of activity. Plans were made to build a major lettuce handling station at the Gap, since lettuce had to be shipped in ice or in refrigerated rail cars. From ten acres of lettuce planted at the Gap, five carloads were shipped out that summer.[424]

Creede Candle, October 16, 1920.

The lettuce business continued through 1922 and 1923 but petered out as growers struggled with vagaries of high-altitude weather, including nighttime summer freezes. It was easier to produce a reliable crop in other parts of Colorado. Although Shrive Collins had signed up to plant 150 acres of lettuce on the mine/mill property in 1922, that July, the American Fluorspar Company resumed regular work and had enough contracts to ensure steady, but limited, production for the remainder of the year. A few workmen were hired, and operations were restarted.[425] Across Goose Creek, Ellwood Bergey was able to open Wagon Wheel Gap Hot Springs resort to tourists during the summer months, while he retired to Colorado Springs for the winters.[426]

In 1924, with ongoing limited production, major changes occurred at Wagon Wheel Gap. The American Fluorspar Company was sold to the Colorado Fuel and Iron (CF&I) Company. The sale of about 200 acres of mining lands and the mill were part of the $240,000 deal for one of the largest U.S. fluorspar deposits.[427] Ellwood Bergey was able to purchase the hotel and environs and 3,800 acres of land for about $60,000.[428] Something about being in the right place at the right time.

THE COLORADO FUEL AND IRON (CF&I) COMPANY

The Colorado Coal and Iron Company (CC&I) was formed in 1880 when three Denver and Rio Grande subsidiaries controlled by General William Jackson Palmer merged. These were the Colorado Coal and Steel Works Company, the Central Colorado Improvement Company and the Southern Colorado Coal and Town Company.[429] The company's holdings included thousands of acres of iron ore lands and even more coal bearing lands in southern Colorado. Palmer decided to construct the steel production mills not in Colorado Springs but farther south in Pueblo, closer to coal supplies. Railroads needed steel rails, and Palmer was in the railroad business.[430]

The CC&I's purpose was primarily to manufacture rails for the railway. In 1890, as most of his rail lines were in place, Palmer relinquished his position. The new president merged the CC&I with Rockefeller's Colorado Fuel Company, creating the well-known CF&I Company.[431]

The fluorspar mill operated at a low capacity from 1924 through 1931 but was inactive in 1932 and 1933, the depths of the Depression years.[432] The separation of the mining operations on the east side of Goose Creek, with

East side of Goose Creek, workers walking to their residences from the C.F.&I. Company mill at Wagon Wheel Gap Hot Springs, circa 1926. *Department of the Interior, United States Geological Survey Denver Library Photographic Collection, bef01321. Photo by Ernest Francis Burchard.*

From the Wilson Tunnel level, looking west at the resort, circa 1926. Note the tram towers, used to haul ore down to the mill. *Department of the Interior, United States Geological Survey Denver Library Photographic Collection, bef01318. Photo by Ernest Francis Burchard.*

the resort on the west side, seemed to work well—especially since the Goose Creek surface tram was used to haul fluorspar and coal and there were no longer road conflicts.

In the early days, ramshackle housing was provided for itinerant miners in the form of tents and hovels along both sides of Goose Creek. In 1927, a major flood on Goose Creek took out most of the shantytown.

With the approach of World War II, the demand for U.S.-produced steel increased, and in 1934, Wagon Wheel Gap fluorspar operations cranked up to meet the demand for the coming war effort.[433]

As the mine and mill became more productive, resulting in a significant influx of year-round workers, better housing was established for the workers on the west bank of Goose Creek. Some single-family dwellings small enough to move on the railroad were moved to the Wagon Wheel Gap site from the Orient iron mine at the northern end of the San Luis Valley, both mines being owned by the CF&I and under the same superintendent. In 1932, the Orient mine closed, and the superintendent moved full-time to Wagon Wheel Gap.[434]

Another shutdown attributed to the Depression occurred from October 1937 through April 1939. After that, the mine and mill operated for several years until its final shutdown.[435] The mine and mill operated just across Goose Creek from the guest ranch, but guests essentially had no interaction

Goose Creek flood of 1927, taking out most miners' shacks and tents. Looking west, roof of bathhouse just visible, resort properties were minimally impacted. *Creede Historical Society, 2575-BF-19.*

Housing for C.F.& I. miners east of the resort, but west of Goose Creek, view looking southeast, circa 1935. *Creede Historical Society, 851-FF-1.*

with those activities. Despite their proximity, the mine and resort seemed two separate worlds.[436] The summer of 1950, after processing 118,023 tons of fluorspar concentrate, the mine and mill were closed and everything put in cold-standby.[437] This meant that all machines were shut down and left in place in case the country needed to start processing fluorspar in the future.[438] The equipment in the mill remains today as it was then. After the closure of the mine and mill, and with significant renovation and demolition, the resort made use of the miners' housing for its employees, which continues to this day, known as Ranch Staff Row.

The mine was never reopened, and the CF&I management decided to divest themselves of the property. In 1982, the CF&I sold the surface rights of the six patented mining claims to Charles Leavell but retained the mineral rights.[439] The mineral rights were purchased by the Leavell family in 1996.[440]

Since the closure of the mine and mill in 1950, little was done to stabilize and protect the mine workings. Longtime ranch guest Mary Mortimer Chapman recalled that the young children of resort guests, a group of about six ranging from six to fourteen years of age—being left to their own devices—would wander over and explore the mine entrances and tunnels. She remembered being amazed that one of the tunnels had icicles in it, even during the warm summer months.[441] These unauthorized explorations occurred during the 1950s, shortly after the mine had ceased operations, but were presumably curtailed as the mine workings began to deteriorate. The accessible underground workings at the mine site were evaluated in the early 1990s and found to be "in an active state of collapse and extremely dangerous."[442] Therefore, the Leavells, as owners of the mine property, made plans to close the mine portals for safety and insurance reasons.

In 1992, Bob Kirkham, a reclamation specialist and geologist with the Inactive Mine Program of the Colorado Mined Land Reclamation Division (now the Division of Reclamation, Mining and Safety) examined the mine for hazardous openings and environmental problems. Several hazardous mine openings were documented. However, likely due to the water agitation process with no chemicals used, no significant environmental problems were noted.

Nine hazardous openings were safeguarded later that summer and fall at the Wagon Wheel Gap Fluorspar Mine. The closure work included backfilling two adits (a horizontal passage leading into a mine for the purposes of access or drainage) and one shaft; installation of a corrugated steel pipe with a galvanized steel bat gate at an adit to allow bats continued access into and out of the underground mine workings; and construction of nearly six thousand linear feet of barbed wire fence to limit access into open stopes, collapsed stope complexes and an open cut.[443]

Recently, the roof of the adit collapsed behind the corrugated steel pipe with bat gate, and human entry into the adit was again possible. The Leavells had the steel pipe and gate removed, then backfilled the adit.[444]

THE MINE AND MILL

In 2018, the owners of the Wagon Wheel Gap fluorspar mine and mill, Pete and Lindsey Leavell, consistent with their vision of historic preservation, initiated work to develop a nomination for listing the fluorspar mill in the National Register of Historic Places. The nomination was approved in April 2019. Specific details of the mine and mill's history, construction and operation are found in that document and several others and will be summarized here.

The high-grade fluorspar ore, at least 96 percent fluorite, was sorted off and shipped to East St. Louis, Illinois, for manufacture of hydrofluoric acid.[445] The less-pure fluorspar ore was taken from the various mine levels along the ore tram system to the mill, where the processes of reduction and separation were started. The ore was collected in a large holding bin near the portal of the tunnel. The ore was "trammed" from this bin on the aerial tramway about 1,500 feet down the hill to the mill. The ore would be dumped at the top level of the mill into a Grizzly with 2-inch openings, which allowed the fines to pass directly and the boulders to be sledged through to start the milling process. Mules pulled the ore carts back up to the various mine levels.[446]

The walls of the vein were weak and irregular and the ore friable, resulting in large amounts of timber needing to be used to make operations safe. The cost of timbering was high and remained so for the duration of the operation of the mine. Spruce was plentiful locally, and a sawmill was established near the mill building that provided lumber for

Looking east from the resort, tailings piles and tram towers visible, circa 2012. *Photo by Robert Berquist.*

the mine. The aerial tram to the upper level was used solely for moving timber up to the mine, not for bringing ore out.[447]

The mill separated the fluorspar from waste rock, a process involving crushing, separation and re-crushing. The finely crushed material was introduced into an agitated water cell to separate the final product by specific gravity. The mill used mechanical power from the steam engines, water and compressed air. No chemicals were used in the separation process, and the mill waste was dumped nearby. No environmental contamination resulted from the activity.[448]

The processed concentrate, considered metallurgical grade, was sold to the CF&I mills as flux for their open-hearth steel furnaces at Pueblo.[449] The concentrate was collected in bins and loaded into surface transport through chutes constructed to allow filling without direct handling—in other words, no shoveling. The concentrates from the mill were loaded into steel tram cars that could hold about 1,500 pounds each. A short train of about twelve ore cars was pulled down to the railroad along the tram track by mules, where the ore was unloaded onto standard-gauge railroad cars. The returning cars were loaded with coal from the CF&I mines or other supplies to be brought up to the mill.[450]

Unique to this mill, the use of steam was continued until the mill stopped operations, even though other mills had converted to electricity. The steam boilers burned coal to heat the water to generate steam for the operation of the mill. Since the mine did not work 24/7, the two boilers had to be started every day the mill worked to provide steam for the operations. This was an essential and somewhat difficult job, entrusted to reliable workers, and took about an hour to get up and running.[451] The two large Hendrie and Bolthoff 115-horsepower boilers were fed coal by shovel, and water was pumped up from nearby Goose Creek, which had been rerouted to the east to bring the water closer to the mill. A complicated method was utilized to pre-heat and pre-pressurize incoming water prior to introduction to the boilers.[452]

The primary mill engine was the Murray-Corliss steam engine, manufactured by the Murray Iron Works in Burlington, Iowa. The engine had a bore of fourteen inches, a stroke of thirty-six inches and an eight-foot diameter flywheel that used a one-and-a-quarter-inch hemp rope to deliver power through a series of bull-wheels and pulleys. The engine is truly one of the great treasures of the mill.[453]

The other main mill engine was manufactured by the Skinner Engine Company in Erie, Pennsylvania. This is a complicated mechansim that

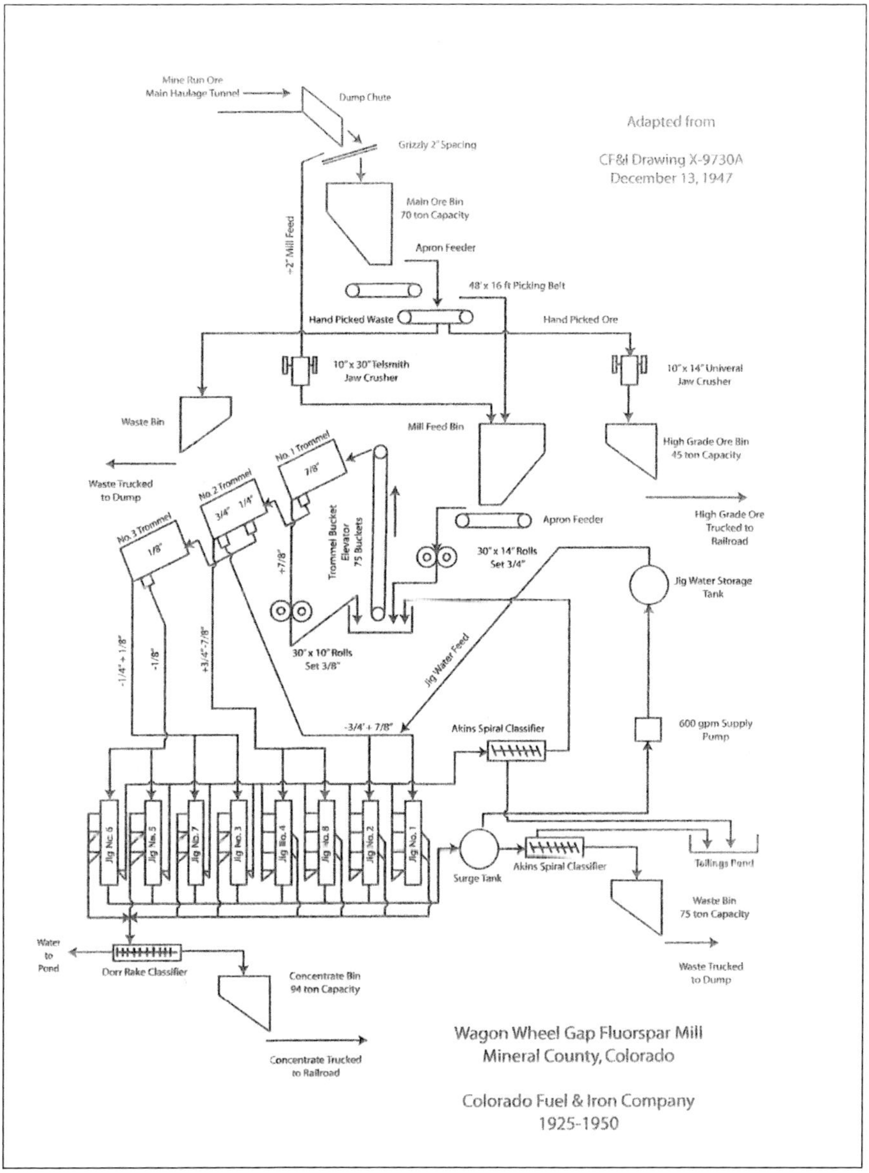

C.F.&I. fluorspar mill diagram. *From Copeland and Vendl, "The Wagon Wheel Gap Fluorspar Mine."*

Mule-drawn tram cars taking processed ore from the mill out to the Wagon Wheel Gap tipple over the bridge across the Rio Grande, circa 1930. *From the collection of Kenneth Wyley.*

HISTORY Colorado

This is to certify that the

Wagon Wheel Gap Fluorspar Mine and Mill

has been listed in the

National Register of Historic Places

by the

United States Department of the Interior

on

April 22, 2019

Holly K. Norton, Ph.D.
Deputy State Historic Preservation Officer

Certificate of listing of the Wagon Wheel Gap Fluorspar Mine and Mill on the National Register of Historic Places, 2019. *Courtesy of the 4UR Ranch.*

includes a dual-fly wheel and an auto-lubricating system. This engine is also a treasure of the mill.[454]

The mill was constructed "hell built for stout" to withstand the incredible pounding and vibration that resulted from mill operations. Timbers were made from old-growth trees harvested locally and red cedar imported from the Northwest,[455] but the ravages of time have affected the exterior of the building. Heavy winter snows have damaged the roof, and although temporary remedial measures have been taken by the owners, there has been partial roof collapse. The arduous task of stabilizing the mill is now in process.

11

OWNERS

Bergey, Sharp and Phipps

It seems almost incredible that during this [twentieth] *century and the previous one, a single disease, tuberculosis, was responsible for the deaths of approximately a thousand million human beings. There can be little doubt that the discovery of the cure for tuberculosis changed human history.*

—*Ryan, Frank, MD,* The Forgotten Plague: How the Battle Against Tuberculosis Was Won—And Lost

For many years, hot mineral springs, found all over the world, were the hoped-for cure for bacterial infections, primarily tuberculosis. Although they had some palliative effect, there was truly no cure for bacterial infections until the understanding of the disease process and creation of effective diagnosis and treatments. Robert Koch (1843–1910) is recognized as isolating the *Mycobacterium tuberculosis* in 1882, more commonly known today as *Tuberculosis bacilli* (TB). It wasn't until years later that the medical community embraced the concept of bacteria. In 1895, William Roentgen (1845–1923) discovered X-rays, and with that came the ability to detect lung diseases, including the deadly TB. Although the medical world understood the how and the why, it could not yet cure the deadly infections caused by the bacteria.[456]

Significant research efforts were made by pharmaceutical companies to discover or synthesize antibiotics to treat the infections caused by an assortment of identified bacteria. Slavarsan for syphilis was discovered in 1905, Prontosil (precursor of sulfa drugs) and penicillin in the late 1920s.

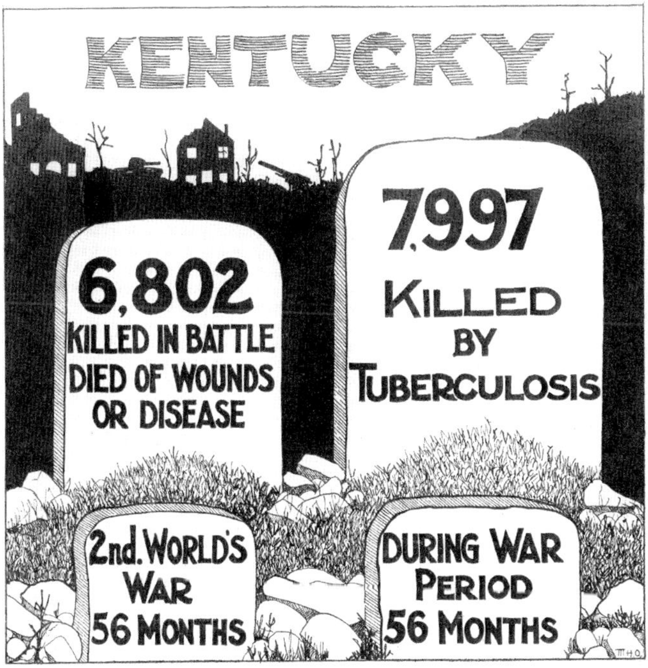

The War against Tuberculosis is not over.

TB in Kentucky is still more deadly than War.
TB took 1195 more Kentucky lives than
World War II in the same period of time.

Early TB can be cured. The X ray finds it early.

Enlist now in the war against TB

Have your chest X-rayed.

KENTUCKY TUBERCULOSIS ASSOCIATION
620 SOUTH THIRD STREET, LOUISVILLE

Kentucky Tuberculosis Association Ad, circa 1945. *Used with permission of the American Lung Association.* Early Research and Treatment of Tuberculosis in the 19th Century, *courtesy of the Claude Moore Health Sciences Library, Historical Collections, at the University of Virginia.*

But it was streptomycin in 1944 that was found to be the truly effective antimicrobial agent against tuberculosis.[457]

Mortality rates from TB had been steadily declining in Western countries as the disease was better understood and precautions were taken to limit the spread of the bacterial infection—isolation in sanitariums, for example. Now armed with an effective drug, an aggressive TB control program was implemented in Europe and the United States. In the 1940s, the rates of TB infections and deaths plummeted.[458] In recent years, the rate of infections has stabilized, and in 2014, around one thousand cases of TB were diagnosed in the United States, which has the lowest rate of TB in the world. The disease is not conquered, as the persistent bacteria still exists, but it can be cured if treated early.[459] Hot springs used as sanitariums saw a sharp decline in use as the rate of TB infections and deaths went down. Some resorts became defunct, but others found ways to develop other attractions to draw a different clientele. As a professional hotel man, Ellwood Bergey was employed as manager of the Broadmoor Hotel in Colorado Springs, which opened in the summer of 1915. Tragedy struck that same summer with the death of his wife, Jennie Hamilton, with whom he had one daughter, Beulah.[460]

Bergey spent one year at the Broadmoor, and the summer of 1916, he was reported to be in Antelope Park (near Creede) with his daughter, Beulah, spending the summer there. The following year, they were again at Wagon Wheel Gap.[461]

After the sale of the holdings of the Wagon Wheel Gap Improvement Company to the American Fluorspar Company, the inexorable Ellwood Bergey was soon back on the scene at the Wagon Wheel Gap Hot Springs Hotel. A *Pueblo Chieftain* article dated May 3, 1918, announced,

> *Ellwood Bergey of Colorado Springs was unanimously elected manager of the Hot Springs Hotel at Wagon Wheel Gap. Mr. Bergey announces that extensive improvements on the property are being planned and will be completed this spring. The famous hot boiling springs will be enclosed in a new concrete ellipse and the waters piped direct to the swimming pools and baths by underground conduit. All the rooms in the main hotel will be refinished and redecorated. Goose Creek will be stocked with 1.5 million rainbow and native mountain trout from the Lost Lakes Hatchery.*

Fortunately, the fishing at the Wagon Wheel Gap Hot Springs was still a draw, and Ellwood Bergey knew how to maintain a good finny population in

Goose Creek. Other outdoor activities including hunting, hiking and pack trips became the fare of the day—when guests were not fishing. Having made an incredible purchase of 3,800 acres of prime pastureland and forest along Goose Creek, as well as all of the buildings associated with the hot springs, Ellwood Bergey was in good shape. With prior experience as the hotel manager from 1904 until 1913 for Palmer, and then from 1918 until 1924 as manager of the resort for the American Fluorspar Company, Bergey had intimate knowledge of every inch of the place.

Bergey worked to return the Wagon Wheel Gap Hot Springs Resort to its former glory. Under his management, Wagon Wheel Gap Hot Springs was reported to be "rapidly regaining its old-time popularity. Its most numerous patrons are the people of the San Luis Valley who know about it."[462]

A major change made to the resort was the removal of the elevated walkways, which were replaced with wide, graveled paths with good bases. Women no longer had long flowing dresses that had to be kept out of the mud and grime, necessitating the elevated walkways. Bergey wanted guests to be well provided for and to enjoy their stay but also wanted some accountability on their part, leading to his published house rules, primarily focused on fishing, which was an essential part of the resort.

NOTICE

1. The hotel is not liable for the loss of money or other valuables unless deposited with the management for safe keeping.
2. Guests wishing to have washing done will please apply at the office.
3. Fishermen are asked not to leave their rods, creels or boots on the hotel or cottage verandas.
4. Guests desiring any extra service performed by help will please make such arrangements at the office.
5. There is no charge for lunches consisting of sandwiches, fruit, etc.
6. Lunches for picnic parties are charged extra.
7. Meals served in rooms 50 cents.
8. Meals served in the dining room outside posted hours will be charged extra.
9. Minimum rate without private bath $6.00 per day each for two in room. With private bath, minimum rate $8.00 per day each for two in room.

Fishing Regulations

1. Nine-inch limit. Keep only trout measuring 9 inches and over.
2. Use a basket creel. Pack trout in willows, not grass.
3. Clean all trout soon after being caught. They are not good when carried about all day uncleaned.
4. Local mountain trout are among the world's most delicate and healthful food when promptly cleaned and properly cooked.
5. Guests are asked not to give away or ship trout taken from Goose Creek.
6. Bait and spinner fishing are not permitted in Goose Creek.
7. Guests stopping at the hotel for a single day are not accorded the fishing privileges.
8. You must have a license before being allowed to fish. Resident license $2.00. Non-resident license $3.00.

Meal Hours
Breakfast 7:00–8:30
Luncheon 12:00–1:00
Dinner 6:00–7:15

The hotel cannot maintain service in the dining room unless guests observe the above hours.

When the fluorspar mill next door was operating regularly and miners and their families took up local residence, the wives of the miners were available to do much of the work at the resort: laundry, cleaning and some cooking, although Bergey was a food aficionado and hired professional cooks. The availability of employees associated with the mine and mill allowed the resort to function with fewer full-time employees and enabled the miners' families to be better off. Bergey was insistent that the place be spit-spot and the food top-notch.[463]

In the early spring of 1919, fifty-one-year-old Bergey married Gertrude "Trudi" Smith, a young woman of nineteen years, at the Broadmoor in Colorado Springs.[464] While Bergey and wife Trudi were managing the resort, their only son, Ellwood Jr., known as Bill, attended grades nine through twelve at New Mexico Military Institute in Roswell, New Mexico. In a letter dated April 15, 1935, Bergey wrote some long-distance parenting advice to fourteen-year-old Bill, encouraging him to

Wagon Wheel Gap Hot Springs resort, bathhouse on left, hotel and cottages, circa 1920s. *Creede Historical Society, 727-BPR-43.*

lighten up: "You go around with a much too sober look, which to others likely appears too severe, and I want to suggest that you start in with a more pleasant look, a smile when you meet and speak to people, and a little word of wit and an occasional 'wise-crack'—all of which you can do very well when you wish. Be careful about early to bed and rising at the proper time in the morning. This means much to you in the way of feeling fit."[465]

For many years, Bergey maintained the old hotel in order to accommodate the greatest number of guests, as many were still coming for health issues. He could accommodate up to one hundred people in his rooms, several of them single rooms, and his prices were reasonable at six dollars and up.[466]

As Bergey reached the venerable age of seventy, with some attendant health problems, he had enough of operating the large resort and dealing with all of its unending maintenance issues. He decided to start the process of selling the property. In a letter to his son, Bill, in the spring of 1938, Bergey laments that "about the only word I use around the place is Fix," and mentions that the sale of the place "remains uncertain."[467]

To promote the sale, Bergey developed a sales brochure listing all of the features and their respective value. He was selling this as an investment property, and many area businesses looked at it, but it was not sold prior to his death. Bergey was seriously ill for several months and died of a heart attack in June 1943 in Colorado Springs, where he is buried.[468] He left his much younger wife, Gertrude, with the resort, which she sold to Arthur G. and Geneva Sharp in November 1944. Gertrude kept about six hundred acres on Caldwell Creek, which became the Britain inholding of the 4UR, as discussed in chapter 8, "Neighbors."[469]

CHIEF FEATURES WITH ITEMIZED VALUATION

3,500 acres range and timberland	35,000
500 acres hay and meadow land	20,000
Reservoir, water and plumbing system	40,000
Main building	15,000
Bath house	35,000
No. 1 Cottage	5,000
No. 2 Cottage	2,500
No. 3 Cottage	3,500
No. 4 Cottage	4,000
No. 5 Cottage	12,000
Casino	2,000
Stable	3,500
Aloha Lodge (Caldwell Creek)	5,000
Trout Hatchery, with nursery lake	1,500
Miscellaneous buildings	5,000
Hotel furnishings	10,000
Canyon driveway and bridges (up to Humphreys Ranch)	10,000
Six-acre lake, with Trout (Walton) Pond	5,000
General improvements	6,000
Hot Mineral Springs	50,000
Total	**$270,000**

THE SHARP YEARS: 1945–1959

> *A relative newcomer to the dude ranch business is Arthur G. Sharp,* [Class of] *'28, who taught English at Colorado College before World War II. After release from the Red Cross in 1945, he bought Wagon Wheel Ranch, 8500 feet up in the Colorado Rockies and restored the ranch to accommodate some 40 guests happy to pay $95 a week for superb trout fishing, riding and bathing in hot mineral springs. He also maintains a fine herd on his 3,000 acres.*[470]

Arthur Gideon Sharp was born on September 18, 1905, to Arthur (Senior) and Louie Sharp. Arthur Sr. was a self-made man and president of the Exchange National Bank in Colorado Springs. He was an acquaintance of General Palmer, and that is likely how the connection to the Wagon Wheel Gap Hot Springs was made. Arthur Jr. married Geneva McElwain in 1932. He was an English professor at the Colorado College, where he also served on the board of trustees from 1955 to 1959. Arthur Sr. died in 1936, leaving everything to his son. The Sharps purchased the Wagon Wheel Gap ranch in 1943. There was one daughter, named Louie after her grandmother, and a son, who died as a young child.[471]

Arthur adored life on his Wagon Wheel Ranch at Wagon Wheel Gap. After about fourteen years, Geneva started having serious health problems, and getting out of the high altitude was a priority. They sold the ranch and moved to a lower altitude in 1959. She died two years later, at the age of fifty-six. Selling the ranch broke Arthur's heart. Years later, his granddaughter asked him to take her to the ranch she had heard so much about. When they got to the gate, he said he could not go in—it was too sad.[472]

During the later Bergey years, little major maintenance had been performed at the resort. Arthur Sharp came in and made some sweeping changes. He erected corrals near the barn and built the cattle shipping facility across the Rio Grande on the north side by the highway. The bridge over the Rio Grande, then as now, was not able to handle the weight of a cattle truck. Tom Wartman hauled his cattle from Monte Vista to those holding pens and drove them up to his Forest Service summer grazing south of the Wagon Wheel Ranch. Today, ranchers who graze on nearby Forest Service leases still use the roadside facilities for loading and unloading cattle.[473]

Near the cattle shipping facility, Wagon Wheel Ranch, Ed Wintz (*left*), Rod Wintz (*center*) and Louie Sharp (*right*), circa 1955. *Courtesy of Kate Myers, granddaughter of Arthur Sharp.*

Another major project was demolition of the old hotel and construction of a new lodge. The old hotel, originally built in 1878 and remodeled significantly by Palmer in 1903, was torn down in 1948 and replaced with the current lodge. No longer used for housing guests, it became the main ranch house and dining room. This reduced the number of guest accommodations at the Wagon Wheel Ranch from one hundred guests during the Bergey years to twenty rooms. Guests now stayed only in the cottages, as they do today. The separate dwelling units, in which guests are housed in small groups, was a holdover from the sanatorium days. The cottages were referred to as the low cabin, the gate cabin and the high cabin.[474] Cottage names were later changed. The cost went up to fifteen dollars, then to seventeen in 1959.[475]

The old Palmer bathhouse was still in operation for the guests, although not in the style of previous years. Not all of the baths and pools were working. There were ongoing battles between the generations about the temperature of the water, which was controlled by the addition of cold water. A cold spring with a metal lid was used for chilling canned or bottled beverages.[476]

Inside of new main lodge built by Sharp, circa 1948. *Courtesy of Kate Myers, granddaughter of Arthur Sharp.*

Guests would come to stay a week, a month, or even the entire summer. Some brought their own furniture, making the place just like home. The reduced number of guests enjoyed a weekly communal fish fry and evenings of camaraderie with plays, skits and music provided by themselves.[477] Arthur was a great storyteller and entertained the guests, especially the children, in the evenings after supper at the Palmer house, providing enduring memories for guests. During this time, Geneva and her staff could clean the lodge and get ready for the next morning.[478] Guests reported that this created a family feel that was rarely duplicated elsewhere—it continues to this day.[479]

Some years, the Sharps lived at the ranch year-round, dealing with the cold and snowy Colorado winters. Other years, they moved back to Colorado Springs. They lived in a cottage next to the lodge, and the ranch foreman lived in the old Palmer hatchery, which had been converted into living quarters.

Arthur was an avid and accomplished fly-fisherman. He and Geneva developed the numbering system for the fishing stops along Goose Creek that is still used. Fishing was popular, even with the State of Colorado–

Arthur Sharp with his catch, circa late 1950s. *Courtesy of Kate Myers, granddaughter of Arthur Sharp.*

imposed limits on the number of fish caught. Many people did catch and keep them up to the limit. Once a guest hoarded dressed fish in his bathtub to take home, using the plentiful ice provided every evening on the porches of the cottages for cocktails. One of the maids spotted the fish and informed Arthur, who promptly threw the guest off the property and asked him never to return.[480]

Guests who did not want to spend all of their time fishing were taken on pack trips into the mountains by ranch wranglers. When she was old enough, daughter Louie Sharp took many tourists out on day rides in the surrounding mountains. Known as Lou, she was a tomboy and as tough as the cowboys.[481]

After a few years of rebuilding the tourist operation, Arthur Sharp got into cattle ranching, starting small and building up a good herd. Arthur developed and registered the 4UR brand in 1945.[482] The Wagon Wheel Ranch raised Herefords and would de-horn, brand and castrate bull calves in the spring. Wintered at the ranch, man and beast were glad to see the

Pack trip leaving from the old hotel, circa mid-1940s. Wrangler Ed Wintz leading pack-string of unidentified tourists. *Left to right*: Louie, Geneva and Arthur Sharp on the porch. *Courtesy of the 4UR Ranch.*

From left to right: Arthur Sharp, fellow cattle rancher Tom Wartman and Wagon Wheel Ranch foreman Harry McClure, circa 1950. *Courtesy of Kate Myers, granddaughter of Arthur Sharp.*

spring thaw. The Princeton-educated English professor loved chasing cattle branded with his own 4UR and the whole Wild West experience. His ranch foreman from 1945 to 1952 was Harry McClure. Ed Wintz, who had been a ranch wrangler for several years, took over in the spring of 1953. Wintz worked as 4UR ranch foreman for forty years under three different owners, retiring in 1993.[483]

Arthur loathed to leave his ranch, relishing the strenuous but rewarding work—something his Princeton friends just couldn't understand.

> *Arthur Sharp of Wagon Wheel Ranch, Wagon Wheel Gap, Colorado, writes that the reunion "comes at a bad time for a dude rancher." That may be, but Arthur, plan to come to the 1953 round-up anyhow.*[484]

Arthur also was an artist and spent warm summer days on a hillside above the ranch painting, an activity he did not continue after he left the ranch. A beautiful landscape scene painted by Arthur Sharp hangs in the 4UR lodge today. Arthur Sharp lost his Geneva in 1961, did not remarry and departed this earth in 1987, never having returned to his beloved Wagon Wheel Ranch after he left in 1959.

ALLAN R. PHIPPS: 1959–1972

When his neighbor and good friend Arthur Sharp announced he had to sell his Wagon Wheel Ranch to move his ailing wife off the mountain, Allan Phipps, one of the owners of the La Garita Ranch, purchased it on November 10, 1959. The Phipps family now owned the La Garita Ranch on the north side of the Rio Grande and the Wagon Wheel Ranch on the south.[485]

For over a century, the Phipps family made significant contributions to the state of Colorado. In 1901, Lawrence Cowle Phipps Sr., a self-made multimillionaire in his mid-thirties, moved from Pennsylvania to Colorado, divorcing his second wife. Phipps wanted to live and raise his children in Denver. He did not want to make more money but was determined to invest what he had "in health and happiness." Phipps Sr. later became a beloved U.S. senator from Colorado from 1919 to 1931.[486]

The third Mrs. Phipps, the former Margaret Rogers, married Lawrence in Denver in 1911. She was an accomplished musician, and her love of

A view of the La Garita mountains, the Palisades and Shirley's barn, which Charles Leavell built for his wife, Shirley, taken June 2018. *Photo by Scott Hizny.*

Ranger, the horse, crosses Goose Creek, late October 2018. *Photo by Scott Hizny.*

Hot sulfur spring and the historic Palmer bathhouse, no longer in use, 2019. *Photo by Robert Seago.*

Little Medicine, the modern 4UR hot springs indoor/outdoor pool facility, at dusk, circa 2012. *Photo by Emily Minton Redfield.*

The Hot Soda Spring, with private bathtub for the less intrepid from the 1930s, no longer used, taken 2019. *Photo by Scott Hizny.*

The Hot Sulfur Spring and aspens looking south, fall 2018. *Photo by Scott Hizny.*

The historic Commodore cabin on the 4UR, circa 2012. *Photo by Emily Minton Redfield.*

The Holy Moses, a historic cabin on the 4UR. *Courtesy of the 4UR Ranch.*

Image 9: Purple fluorite (CaF2) with white rhomboid barite (BaSO4) from Wagon Wheel Gap mining district, Colorado. Specimen housed in the Adams State University Geology Museum, 2019. *Photo by Ashley Bosa.*

Volcanic dacite columnar jointing, known locally as the Palisades. *Courtesy of the 4UR Ranch.*

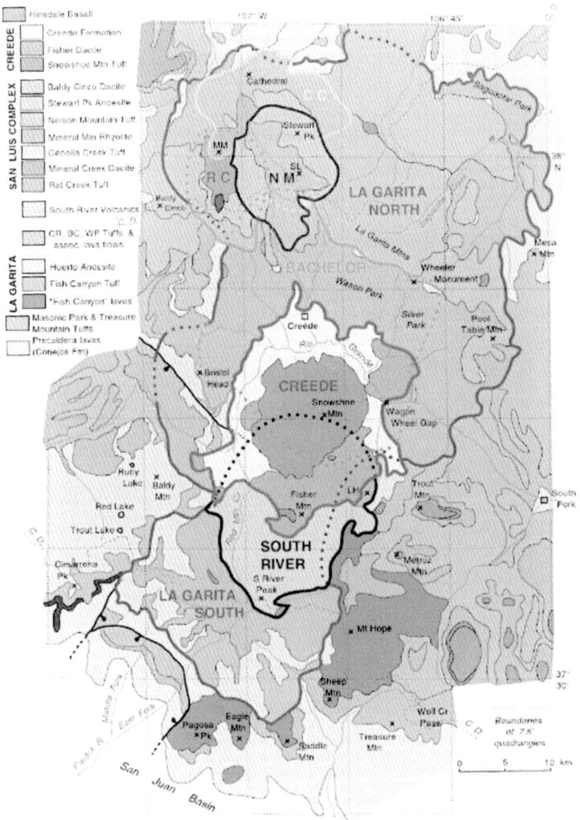

Left: Figure 2: Geologic map showing the remnants of the Creede and La Garita Calderas. *Modified from Larsen and Lipman, "Exploring the Ancient Volcanic and Lacustrine Environments of the Oligocene Creede Caldera and Environs, San Juan Mountains."*

Below: Image 2: A brecciated fault (outlined) is noticeable within the Wagon Wheel Gap geology. Notice the different rock textures on either side of the fault. *Modified photo by Scott Hizny, 2019.*

Image 3: Schlieren (vertical lines), a type of plastic deformation rock texture, 2019. *Photo by Scott Hizny.*

Image 7: Layered ash-tuff, greenish hues likely a result of the hydrothermal activity related to mineral depositions, and deuteric alteration, 2019. *Photo by Scott Hizny.*

CF&I Fluorspar mill at the 4UR, early morning fog, 2017. *Photo by Scott Hizny.*

Boilers from Hendrie and Bolthoff, Denver, Colorado, and auxiliary equipment, circa 2012. *Photo by Robert Berquist.*

Flywheel of the Murray and Corliss steam engine, with hemp rope, circa 2011. *Photo by Robert Berquist.*

Skinner engine with centrifugal governor and belt powering overhead line shafts, circa 2011. *Photo by Robert Berquist.*

Fremont schoolhouse, Wagon Wheel Gap, circa 2018. *Denver Public Library, Western History Collection, AUR-812.*

Young child's grave marker on hillside above Wagon Wheel Gap stage stop, 2019. *Photo by Scott Hizny.*

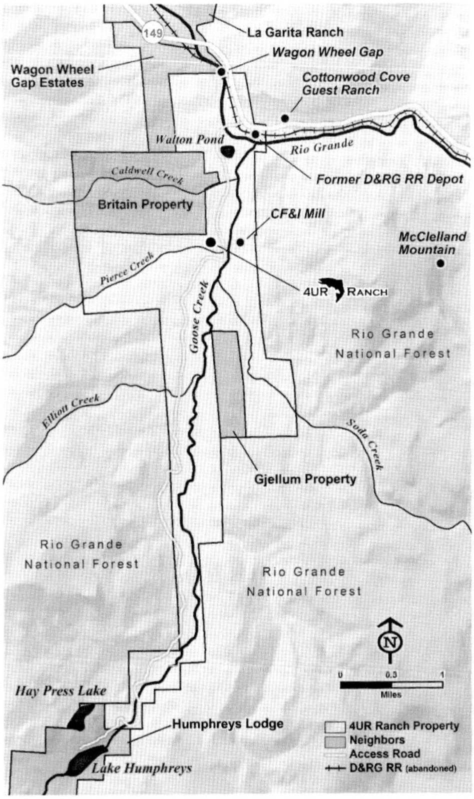

Left: Properties neighboring the 4UR. *Cartography by John Evaskovich, 2019.*

Below: A group of "Doolittle Raiders" fishing at Humphreys Lake, circa 1982. Left to right: William Marsh "Bill" Bower pilot of plane no. 12 of 16 in the "Doolittle" raid over Tokyo; Robert "Bobby" Hite, copilot of plane no. 16; Richard A. Knobloch, copilot of plane no. 13; General James Harold "Jimmy" Doolittle, pilot of plane no. 1; and Richard E. "Dick" Cole, copilot of plane no. 1, last survivor of the mission, who passed away on April 9, 2019, at the age of 103. *Photo by Keith Rodgers, courtesy of Art Jones.*

Painting of Wagon Wheel Ranch by the owner at the time, Arthur Sharp, circa 1950, presently hanging in the lodge of the 4UR. *From the collection of the Leavell family.*

The anonymous painting of the Wagon Wheel Gap from the 1880s, which led to the writing of this book. *Photo by Scott Hizny, 2018.*

Remains of Elliott homestead cabin, circa 2018. *Photo by Jen Judge, courtesy of the 4UR Ranch.*

Cloud lying low in the Elliott Creek draw on the west side of the Goose Creek valley, September 2018. *Photo by Scott Hizny.*

Fishing on Goose Creek, circa 2018. *Photo by Jen Judge, courtesy of the 4UR Ranch.*

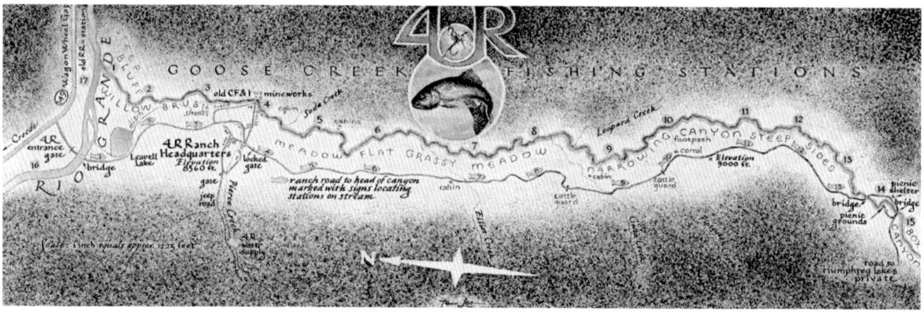

Tom Lea painting of the fishing stations along Goose Creek at 4UR Ranch. *From the collection of the Leavell family.*

Left to right: Lindsey Leavell, Pete Leavell and Mary Lee Leavell Pinkerton, July 2010. *From the collection of the Leavell family.*

Leavell family photo taken in 2007 at the 4UR on the occasion of Shirley's ninetieth birthday, her last visit there. *Back row, from left to right*: Charles S. "Pete" Leavell, Lindsey Leavell, Jenny Leavell, Shirley Leavell, Matthew Winston, Brian Leavell, Mary Lee Pinkerton, Jay Smith and Shelly Winston; *front row, from left to right*: Fred Winston, John Terrell Winston, Walker Smith and Audrey Smith. *From the collection of the Leavell family.*

Sunset in the Wagon Wheel Gap, a view of Ute Peak, November 2018. *Photo by Scott Hizny.*

Early morning fog fills the Wagon Wheel Gap and sits over the Rio Grande, 2017. *Photo by Scott Hizny.*

music and the arts was a focal point for her cultural and philanthropic activities. She played a major part in the founding of the Denver Symphony Orchestra and was active with the University of Denver, the Central City Opera House Association, the Denver Museum of Natural History and the St. John's Cathedral choir.[487]

Lawrence had a son and daughter from his first marriage, two girls from his second and two boys with Margaret. The last two brothers, of very different temperaments, were born in Denver—Allan on October 3, 1912, and Gerald on March 4, 1915.[488] Being sons of a U.S. senator, the brothers grew up in Washington, D.C., spending summers and holidays at the La Garita Ranch.[489]

Allan, a straight-A student, attended Oxford University in England as a Rhodes Scholar and earned a law degree from University of Denver Law School in 1937. Gerald studied English at Williams College in Massachusetts and was quoted as saying he settled for "gentleman's grades." Allan practiced law for the Denver Tramway Company, and Gerald worked for the Denver & Rio Grande Western Railway.[490]

They loved Denver, and Gerald often joked it would take an act of Congress to get them to leave. He was right. When Congress declared war on Japan, both joined the U.S. Navy. Allan served as a lieutenant commander in the South Pacific. Gerald served in an official position in Washington, D.C. After the war, they returned to Colorado, Allan to practice law, and Gerald to start his own construction business.[491]

Allan guided development of the Winter Park ski area, where a run is named for him. He served the University of Denver for forty-five years as a trustee and donor. Allan received the university's prestigious Evans Award in 1980 for his civic contributions, which included heading the Presbyterian/St. Luke's Medical Center board of managers and being active in the Denver Symphony Society and the Colorado chapter of the American Red Cross. "Allan saw himself as being part of a prominent family with a huge responsibility to the community," son Graham Phipps said. "This was a duty."[492]

Most longtime Coloradoans will remember that the Phipps brothers saved the Broncos. Allan and Gerald bought the struggling Denver Broncos professional football franchise in 1961 to keep it from being moved to Atlanta, then built the club into a Super Bowl contender in 1978. Gerald Phipps is the only non-player among twenty-three Broncos enshrined in the Ring of Fame at Broncos stadium at Mile High. The brothers sold the team to Edgar Kaiser in 1981.[493] Gerald died in August 1993.[494]

Allan married his first wife, Doreen, in 1934, and they had two boys and a girl: Graham in 1936, Anthony "Tony" in 1943 and Mindy in 1946.[495] Allan and Doreen divorced in 1953.[496] Allan married Clara Van Schaack in 1955,[497] and they were together until his death at the age of eighty-four in 1997.[498]

Allan's sense of responsibility to the community was evident with his willingness to help Arthur Sharp by purchasing the Wagon Wheel Ranch. Allan and Clara Phipps were the owners and hosts of the 4UR for the next thirteen years. They continued to run Hereford cattle from the Sharp herd, and Ed Wintz was retained as ranch foreman.

The use of the name *Wagon Wheel Ranch* became problematic because Gertrude Bergey Cowieson used that name for her property on Caldwell Creek. To avoid neighborly entanglements, the Phipps place was called the 4UR, after the brand. The 4UR Ranch at Wagon Wheel Gap became and remains the registered name of the property.

In 1963, on its three thousand acres, the 4UR could accommodate about forty guests in three large cottages, each within one hundred yards of the main ranch lodge at a cost of twenty dollars per day. Most rooms had twin beds, and all beds had inner-spring mattresses (not horsehair). Excellent fishing was maintained in Goose Creek, with generous stocking of "fighting trout." Only fly-fishing was allowed in both the private section of the Rio Grande (since they owned both sides for some distance) and Goose Creek. The hatchery lake was kept stocked for novice fishermen. Horseback riding and pack trips were available for an extra cost. The Palmer bathhouse was used for hot mineral baths, and a new outdoor swimming pool was built and heated with "fresh, filtered" water to 76°F. Instructions were given for guests to fly to Denver or Pueblo and rent a car from there.[499] One could fly into Alamosa, but there was neither surface transportation nor rental car availability from there.

Being the well-heeled son of the nationally prominent Phipps family, Allan's ownership of the 4UR attracted well-known names. Graham Phipps tells of the year he and his wife were assistant managers at the 4UR and Walt Disney and his wife came to stay a few days. Walt was interested in finding a location for *Little Britches* and wanted to see if the 4UR would be appropriate. (It was filmed in Jackson Hole.) Walt, a taciturn man not given to socializing with other guests, did not enjoy the 4UR tourist passion for fishing. Known for his love of animals, Walt spent his time in the corrals with the horses and cattle and with ranch foreman Ed Wintz, with whom he developed a friendship.[500]

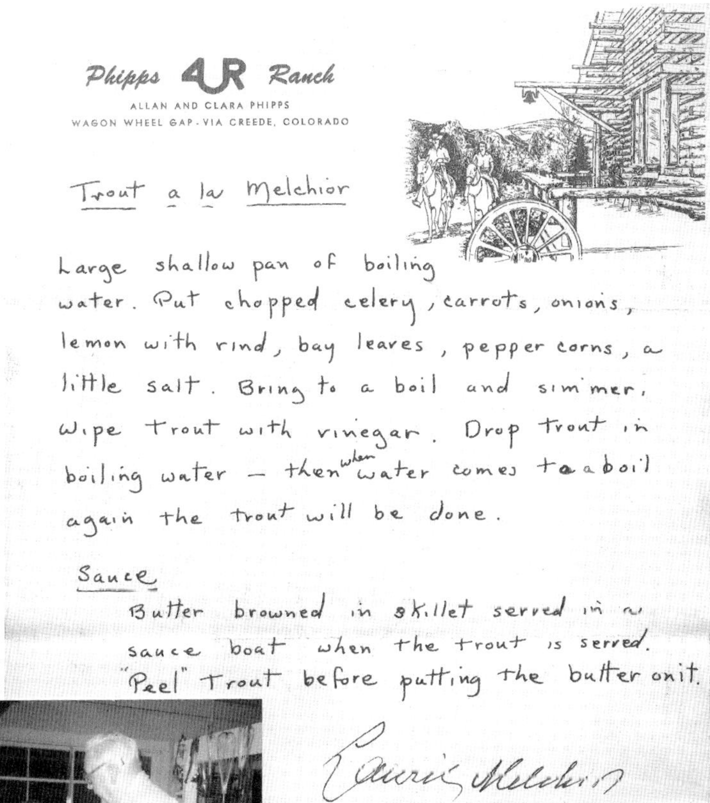

Phipps 4UR Ranch
ALLAN AND CLARA PHIPPS
WAGON WHEEL GAP - VIA CREEDE, COLORADO

Trout a la Melchior

Large shallow pan of boiling water. Put chopped celery, carrots, onions, lemon with rind, bay leaves, pepper corns, a little salt. Bring to a boil and simmer. Wipe trout with vinegar. Drop trout in boiling water – then when water comes to a boil again the trout will be done.

Sauce

Butter browned in skillet served in a sauce boat when the trout is served. "Peel" trout before putting the butter on it.

Lauritz Melchior

Toni Davlin Shaw, hostess of the 4UR, with Melchior, listening to his fish recipe and discussing the appropriate wine to go with it, circa 1970. *Courtesy of the 4UR Ranch.*

Lauritz Melchior, a Danish-American opera singer, was considered the preeminent Wagnerian tenor for three decades in the mid-1900s and has become the quintessence of his voice type. Late in his career, Melchior appeared in movie musicals and on radio and television.[501] He loved to fish and visited the 4UR periodically.

Allan Phipps, in Creede, circa 1960s. *Creede Historical Society, 5703-P-659.*

Toni and Chuck Davlin worked as managers for the La Garita and the 4UR for many years during the Phipps ownership of the 4UR. Son Doug Davlin remembers helping his parents, and during the summers of his high school years, he was in charge of mowing the lawns and keeping fireplaces stocked with firewood—both seemingly endless tasks.[502]

In the summer of 1972, Allan, then sixty years old, decided to sell the 4UR. Allan was quoted as saying, "It's not an easy thing to run a ranch, you know. My wife and I will want to do a little traveling, and we will be able to do that now. My wife and I have spent years building up the clientele, and now we want to take it easy a little bit."[503] The 4UR was sold to Charles Leavell and William F. Farah on December 15, 1972.

12

LOST LAKES

The Lost Lakes are two small bodies of water occupying rock basins of a high bench at the north side of the Rio Grande canyon three miles west of the center of the San Cristobal quadrangle. The bench surrounding the lakes is occupied by many rock hills and ridges, the smooth surface of which displays the effect of ice, which during the Wisconsin stage moved across this upland. The lakes are well stocked with trout and are a favorite spot of fishermen from Creede the San Luis Valley. On the densely timbered slope surrounding the Lakes there is much wild game so that the spot is ideal for fisherman or hunter.

—*Wallace W. Atwood and Kirtley F. Mather,* Physiography and Quaternary Geology of the San Juan Mountains, Colorado

The two-lake complex of Lost Lakes is not contiguous with the 4UR and is about a two-hour drive from the main ranch, mostly on dreadful roads. So why is it in this book? An interesting family story reflects the snap decision-making ability of the highly successful Charles Leavell. About the time that Charles Leavell purchased the 4UR, he went on a fishing trip to Lost Lakes, which is in a breathtaking location, with a local realtor who had facilitated the 4UR sale. Shrive Collins's descendants were anxious to sell the Lost Lakes property, and the realtor knew Leavell had the wherewithal to purchase it. While they were fishing in a boat on the lower (larger) lake, a plane/helicopter flew over. The realtor remarked, "Oh, that is such and such, who is looking at buying these lakes." The competitive Charles Leavell,

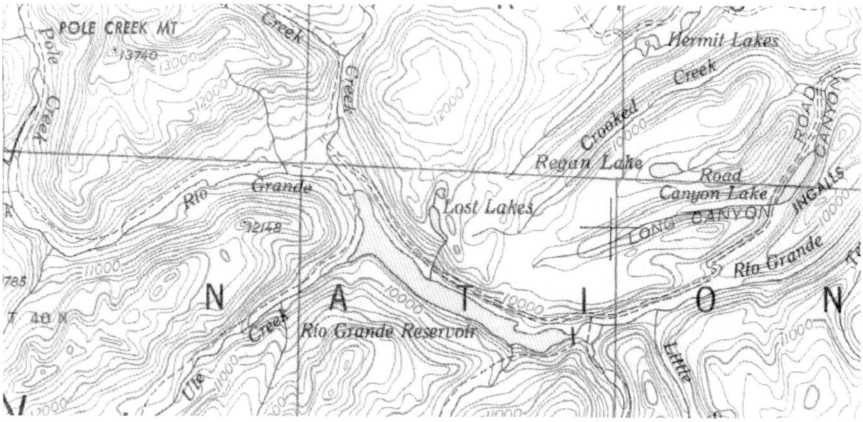

Location of the two Lost Lakes near the Rio Grande Reservoir. *Department of the Interior, United States Geological Survey.*

never a man to be beaten in any enterprise, said "I'll take it." The two men hurried back to shore and into Creede to finalize the deal. The overhead plane/helicopter was purely serendipitous.

The Lost Lakes property was purchased by Charles Leavell and his partner William Farah in August 1973. Some years later, Farah ran into financial difficulties and sold his share of Lost Lakes to Leavell. From 1973 to the present day, Lost Lakes has remained in the Leavell family.

The development of Lost Lakes involved another highly successful entrepreneur, Bert C. Hosselkus Sr., who established one of the most successful commercial fishery businesses in southwestern Colorado. While the stage was still running from Del Norte to Silverton in the 1880s, Bert was a driver and saw many places along the route that he believed would be good locations for fisheries. One such location was near Stage Station Flat, on the top of Finger Mesa. His good friend and eventual longtime business associate Shrive B. Collins built dams on several small lakes in the area, including the Lost Lakes, to store water. He then sold the water to San Luis Valley farmers for irrigation.[504]

Shrive had moved to Del Norte, Colorado, with his family and was a graduate of Del Norte High School in 1897. Growing up with the nearby Creede mining boom in the 1890s, Shrive was fascinated with geology and mining. He was not interested in simply being a hard-rock miner, so he pursued a degree in mining engineering.[505] He received a degree as an engineer of mines (EM) from the Colorado School of Mines in 1901.[506] His first job was to survey the Continental Divide from Durango to Lake City.

From above Lost Lakes, view of the Rio Grande Pyramid (*far right peak*), circa 1930. *Creede Historical Society, 3660-WF-18.*

This allowed him to see much of the San Juan country, leading to his ability to identify the potential of numerous small lakes for storage of irrigation water. Shrive met and married Hallie Chapman from Creede. Her father, Lewis J. "Lute" Chapman, did the bulk of the construction work on the small lake dams, including Lost Lakes.[507]

Hosselkus received a homestead patent for 160 acres that encompassed both of the Lost Lakes on June 30, 1909.[508] Homestead patents were typically worked for five years to "prove up" before the patent was granted. Hosselkus was reported to be residing at Lost Lakes as early as July 1900.[509] A small homestead cabin was built on the lower lake to support the fishery operations, but it is now in ruins. Bert worked with other fishery men to get started. Nearby neighbor and expert fishery man Charlie Mason had developed his Hermit Lakes fishery into a successful resort for fishermen who came to Creede on the train. Bert thought that would be a good use of his beautiful Lost Lakes, but the remoteness and inaccessibility proved too much for a successful resort, and Bert continued to look for other business opportunities during the winter months in nearby Salida, Colorado, where he purchased an interest in the Saddle Rock restaurant.[510]

In 1904, Hosselkus teamed up with Charlie Mason and silent partner Shrive Collins to create a new hatchery along the Rio Grande just east

From left to right: A. J. Major, owner of the store they are standing in front of; Bert Hosselkus and his daughter, Millie; and an unidentified man, circa 1920. *Creede Historical Society, 5697-P-653.*

of Creede that was called the Lost Lakes Hatchery. This led to some confusion over the years between the lakes themselves and the business operation. However, it was an extremely successful business and allowed Bert to become one of the major fishery men of southwestern Colorado. Every year, millions of eyed eggs and fry were delivered locally and around the world.[511]

Bert used Lost Lakes as a private hatchery and did not allow fishing of any kind. With no native species, all fish in the Lost Lakes were planted. Bert made Lost Lakes into a cutthroat trout fishery, from which he sold eggs and fry. He was careful not to introduce other species of fish as he did on many of his other lakes.[512] A series of caretakers of the Lost Lakes stocked the lakes with rainbow, native and brook trout.

Lost Lake no. 1, with homestead cabin, circa 1930. *Creede Historical Society, 3667-WF-25.*

Remains of Lost Lakes homestead cabin. *Photo by Scott Hizny, 2018.*

Hosselkus leased many of Shrive Collins's small lakes for his fish culture business, and he and Collins became partners in the fishery business, either owning or leasing lakes in which to raise fish, including Lost Lakes, Reagan Lake, Santa Maria and the Road Canyon Reservoirs along Crooked Creek. The upper lake at Road Canyon was used only for water storage and was not stocked with fish. The lower lake, made deeper and larger by raising the height of the dam, had many different species of fish in it over the years. Hosselkus experimented unsuccessfully with Kamloops and steelhead salmon. German tench flourished, which allowed him to ship about two tons of dressed fish every two weeks during the summer months.[513]

Partners for many years, Shrive Collins and Bert Hosselkus got caught up in the mining fever associated with the fluorite deposits found near Wagon Wheel Gap. Shrive, being a mining engineer, identified the fluorspar vein in 1911 and convinced Bert that the fluorspar mine was a good investment. The two began another chapter in their long business association in 1913 with the formation of the Colorado (later, American) Fluorspar Mining Company.[514]

As the major shareholders in the American Fluorspar Mining Company, Collins and Hosselkus obtained the mining rights and land for the fluorspar mine. They shortly purchased the hot springs resort as part of a package deal in 1918.[515] As the mine came into full operation and profits were flowing, Hosselkus found that his heart was with the fishery business, so he and Collins decided to amicably "split the sheets" and went their separate ways in 1922, although they remained friends for the rest of their lives. As part of this deal, Shrive Collins gave up his interest in the Lost Lakes Fish Hatchery, which was transferred to Hosselkus; the Road Canyon Reservoir and Regan Lake also went to Hosselkus, but Lost Lakes went to Shrive Collins.[516]

Two years later, Collins sold out his interest in the fluorspar mine to the Colorado Fuel and Iron Corporation and the hotel property to Ellwood Bergey.[517] Hosselkus did continue his Lost Lakes Hatchery and fishery business, involving his large family, which eventually took it over upon Bert's death in 1943. The complex of various lakes and leases were eventually dissolved. The Road Canyon Reservoirs and Regan Lake were sold to the State of Colorado in 1956.[518]

After a short stint in World War I, having been wounded and gassed, Ted Walker, returned to his hometown of Creede, married and took over as caretaker at the Rio Grande Reservoir. He also leased nearby Lost Lakes. The two conditions of his lease were to take fisherman there and keep the lakes stocked. After Ted Walker, Howard Kennell—a local fishery man, who grew up in the Creede area—took rainbows and native cutthroats out of Lost Lakes from 1929 to 1934. Wallace Wright and Billy Wills had the lease for Lost Lakes for a few years afterward.[519]

Carroll Wetherill took over the lease after World War II and ran it for many years, until it was sold in 1973.[520] True to the start of his life above a fish hatchery, Carroll Wetherill spent his life as a mountain man, guide and fish culturist. Purchasing Lost Trail Station in 1936, he developed a small fish hatchery on the ranch, collecting cutthroat eggs from nearby Lost Lakes. Grandson Bill tells stories of going with his grandfather Carroll to collect eggs in the early spring, when the cutthroat spawn. In the high-altitude lakes, spring is slow in coming, so there was still snow and ice over the lake. Grandpa Carroll would stand in the freezing water catching fish with his bare hands and stripping the eggs into a large washtub, once in a while grabbing a male and squirting in some semen to fertilize the eggs. Bill would soon be frozen and go stand by the fire, but Grandpa Carroll seemed to be oblivious to the cold and worked with ice frozen on his arms.[521] Shrive's daughter Katherine remembered taking pack trips to their property at Lost Lakes as a family. She recalled always wanting to have Carroll Wetherill go with them, because "he always knew where the fish were hiding and everyone was able to catch fish."[522]

Modern cabin at Lost Lakes. *Photo by Scott Hizny, 2018.*

Shrive died in 1954, leaving Lost Lakes to his two daughters. They formed the S.B. Collins Ranches Inc. and continued to employ Carroll Wetherill as caretaker for the operation of Lost Lakes. In 1973, after losing one of their longtime caretakers at the ranch in Del Norte, they sold Lost Lakes and the ranch at Del Norte. Charles Leavell purchased Lost Lakes, and once again, both the Wagon Wheel Gap Hot Springs and Lost Lakes were under one owner.[523]

Leavell had a new cabin built there shortly after purchasing the lakes. Ranch foreman Ed Wintz had the cabin constructed at the 4UR, disassembled it and hauled it up to Lost Lakes, where it was reassembled. This took about five round trips in a ranch truck.

For some years, Leavell hired a full-time caretaker during the summer months, but he discontinued the practice in 1988. The duties of the caretaker were as follows:

Keep poachers out
Pick up all litter on property, and along the road going in and out.
Keep cabin neat and clean. Have food in cabinets neatly arranged. Keep container tops and table clear and clean.
Air out sleeping bags occasionally.
Have a large supply of wood and kindling cut always.
Keep area around cabin raked clean.
Be willing to work on any project necessary in the way of improvements on the property.
Keep boats and accessories in good repair and clean.
See that fishermen are aware of the rules. They are not allowed to keep Native trout. Make sure all fishermen sign register book.
Fishermen may use lures if they cut two of the three hooks off.
Call in by two-way radio every morning at 7:15 a.m.
Cook for overnight guests. Row the boat for them if they desire. Make their stay enjoyable.

On May 8, 1987, the outlet conduit (pipe) downstream of the head-gate on the lower Lost Lake was compromised. A break in the pipe released a large amount of water that cut a deep gully in the outflow stream channel from the lake and took out a portion of the Rio Grande Reservoir Road. The U.S. Forest Service quickly repaired the impassable road and replaced five culverts.[524]

The flood event triggered several actions. First was repair of the broken pipe at the lower Lost Lake dam to prevent further erosion. Charles Leavell had actions in place for those relatively simple repairs, but the state engineer decided that the dam was "washed out" or at least damaged to the extent that it was no longer reliable and that a new dam would have to be engineered for reconstruction.[525] As a result, Leavell was to foot the bill for a major renovation of the dam and surrounding area.[526] The dam was successfully repaired and approved by the state engineer in October 1987.[527]

It turned out that the Lost Lakes dam was actually on Forest Service land, necessitating a special use permit for Leavell personnel to work on the dam. More accurate land surveys in the 1970s resulted in changing many Forest Service inholding and private property boundaries, usually to the detriment of the landholder. The redrawn lines in recent years gave the public access to both lakes, and the entire outlet/dam system was on public land.[528]

Having the dam on Forest Service property was a potential obligation to the government. Maintenance, repairs and unavailability of liability insurance were all issues that motivated both Charles and the local Forest Service office to initiate a land exchange. The original 1909 Hosselkus homestead of 157 acres would be augmented by 146 acres of additional land, including the dam system and both of the lake boundaries, bringing the total up to 302 acres. This was finalized on December 2, 1987.[529] All problems associated with the dam and lakes were now solely Charles Leavell's responsibility.

Another issue then arose. The flood from Lost Lakes made the San Luis Valley Irrigation District (SLVID) and the state water engineer staff fully aware of the potential source of water stored in Lost Lakes. All information had been and was in the public domain, but not in the public consciousness. With Colorado's incredibly complicated, closely controlled water rights, the microscopic investigation began. The priority rights of the Rio Grande Reservoir and Lost Lakes, water storage amounts and beneficial use issues were carefully reviewed. In the fall of 1990, the position of the SLVID and state water engineer was that Lost Lakes water rights were junior in priority to those of the Rio Grande Reservoir, such that they could administer a call for water in Lost Lakes as necessary to fulfill downstream user water demands.[530]

Losing the Lost Lakes water would decimate the fishing and recreation at the lakes. Therefore, Charles sued the SLVID for a more equitable solution to the Lost Lakes water situation. The case was made that the SLVID had abandoned its priority rights over the past many years when it did not make any calls on the water. The case was resolved favorably to Leavell, with the final decree issued on February 28, 1992. The Rio Grande Reservoir still has the senior priority right, but a complicated system was put in place to calculate how much water could be stored and how much released, based on a rolling ten-year average, with some exceptions, resulting in most of the water remaining in Lost Lakes.[531]

Lost Lakes remains a private fishing spot, open only to the guests or approved visitors of the 4UR. The Leavell family retains ownership of Lost Lakes and takes responsibility for management and stocking fish. All rainbow and cutthroat fish must be released, but brook trout may be kept, and it is encouraged that fishermen do so.

13

LEAVELL FAMILY

Charles Leavell was in construction, and his company had major projects all over the world. He was chairman of the board of Leavell Development Co., a wholly owned subsidiary of Rio Grande Industries. Leavell Development was formed to acquire and operate the business and properties of Leavell Enterprises, Inc., Frizzell Co., and Texas Homes, Inc., all of which were acquired in transactions in May 1970. Fellow Texan and friend William Farah, the slacks magnate, teamed up to purchase the 4UR in 1972.

—Rocky Mountain News, *September 9, 1972.*

CHARLES AND SHIRLEY LEAVELL

Charles Holland Leavell was born on February 26, 1911, in El Paso, Texas, to Charles Holland Leavell Sr., a real estate broker, and Mabel Walton, a piano teacher. Charles Sr. enjoyed his chosen profession and believed real estate to be one of the best investments available, particularly when buying and selling ranch land. These endeavors were to be prophetic to his young son's life as well.

When young Charles was six years old, he developed tuberculosis of the hip, a disease that would leave him on crutches during his formative years, resulting in pain and spinal issues throughout his life. In spite of his son's disease, Charles Sr. instilled in him a love of the outdoors and taught his son pursuits dear to his own heart: fishing, hunting and golf. From an

Charles Leavell Sr. fly-fishing, 1917. *From the collection of the Leavell family.*

early age, Charles Jr. was taken fishing on the Rio Grande, and fly-fishing became a lifelong passion, one he would share with his own children and grandchildren in years to come.

Charles Jr. attended Stanford University, majoring in engineering. When the Depression hit, money was scarce, so Charles wrote to his parents that he would return to El Paso to help the family. His mother, Mabel, replied that he was to stay at Stanford and figure out how to pay for schooling on his own. Undaunted, he took odd jobs, stayed in school and graduated in 1933 with a degree in civil engineering.

Three years later, in 1936, tragedy struck the family: Charles Sr. died of a brain tumor. Devastated, twenty-four-year-old Charles turned to his father's brother John for guidance. Like Charles Sr., John Leavell was a great outdoorsman but also a successful oil man who spent much time in the Middle East. While it was Charles's father who gave him a love of the outdoors, his Uncle John gave him an intrepid world view and an appreciation for international business relations.

Shirley Terrell was born in El Paso, Texas, on September 1, 1917, to Dr. Scurry Terrell and his wife, Homer. Dr. Terrell was a personal physician

Charles Leavell Jr. fly-fishing, circa 1917. *From the collection of the Leavell family.*

to former president Teddy Roosevelt, and it was he who was present when Roosevelt was shot in the chest by an assailant preceding a campaign speech in Milwaukee, Wisconsin. Shirley's mother, Homer, succumbed to tuberculosis when Shirley was four years old, so Dr. Terrell sent Shirley to live with his sister in Beverly Hills, where Shirley grew up among the Hollywood stars of the time. When Shirley was a teenager, she went to Hockaday private school in Dallas, then to Brillantmont finishing school in Lausanne, Switzerland. As Hitler was gaining popularity in Europe, her father was concerned about her being overseas, so Shirley returned to the United States and attended Pine Manor College in Massachusetts. In 1937, she returned to El Paso to visit her father during a break from college. While there, she met Charles Leavell, and it was love at first sight. By 1938, they were married. The couple welcomed daughter Mary Lee in 1939, and son Charles Scurry "Pete" in 1942.

As World War II gripped the nation, Charles attempted to enlist in the armed forces, but he was ineligible because of his ill-formed hip. Not to be daunted, in 1939, Charles formed his own construction company and quickly made a name for himself with many federal contacts in support of the war effort. From those small beginnings, Charles built the C.H. Leavell Company. By the 1960s, it was one of the largest construction firms in the United States and specialized in large-scale projects both domestic and international—undertaking projects in the Sudan and Thailand, among other countries. Leavell's work in Thailand led him to be awarded the title of honorary counsel general to Thailand for the State of Texas.

In the summer of 1946, Charles and Shirley took their children, Mary Lee and Pete, to the Wagon Wheel Ranch outside of Creede, Colorado. Located along the Rio Grande River, it was a favorite vacation spot for Texans who could spend time fly-fishing and relaxing in the Rocky Mountains—enjoying a climate cooler than that of Texas. Here Charles first visited the property that twenty-five years later he and Shirley would own.

Charles and Shirley were devoted to each other, their family and their beloved community of El Paso, forming great friendships and bonds that lasted their entire lives. They were extremely close to Charles's younger sister Josephine, who had married James H. Polk, a dashing young lieutenant in the U.S. Army. A great horseman and superb leader, Polk was later a decorated war hero in World War II while serving in the Third Armored Cavalry under General George Patton. By the end of his career, he was a four-star general and commander of the 7th Army and United States Armed

Pete and Mary Lee Leavell on the porch of the Holy Moses cabin at the Wagon Wheel Ranch, 1946. *From the collection of the Leavell family.*

Forces Europe. They retired to El Paso and were frequent guests of the Leavells at the 4UR Ranch.

From early in their marriage, the Leavells were also dear friends with Tom Lea and his wife, Sarah. Tom was a great artist in Texas. A painter and author of six novels, Lea had served as a war correspondent for *Life* magazine, landing on the beaches of Peleliu, painting and drawing the action of war as it happened. Charles and Shirley were not only great friends but also patrons and collectors of his work. The Leavells and Leas traveled together and twice took fishing trips by horseback through the Wind River Mountains of Wyoming. However, some of the favorite times together were those spent on Goose Creek at the 4UR. Tom so loved the ranch that he painted a map of the fishing stations along Goose Creek as a gift and presented to his dear friends.

Ensuring their children received a great education was a priority for Shirley and Charles, and they determined to send Mary Lee and Pete to private high schools in the East. In 1953, they put Mary Lee on a DC-3 bound for Philadelphia to attend Shipley School in Bryn Mawr,

Pennsylvania. She graduated in 1956. By September of that same year, she matriculated at Stanford University, pursuing a degree in psychology. She later graduated in 1960.

While attending Stanford, Mary Lee met and married David Winston, a fellow Texan whose family lived in Houston. The Leavells got along well with their son-in-law, and Charles and David turned out to be well suited to the pursuit of buying and selling ranches together, an endeavor for which Mary Lee was a perfect fit. The Winstons' first son, Matthew, was born in 1958, and after the birth of their second son, Frederick, in 1960, Mary Lee and David joined Charles in forming the Leavell Cattle Company. Working out of El Paso, the Leavell Cattle Company and later the Winston-Leavell Cattle Company went into full swing and purchased, managed and sold ranches for the next decade.

In 1972, Charles was offered the 4UR guest ranch he and Shirley had first visited decades before. Charles and Shirley were well acquainted with Allan and Clara Phipps, who owned both the La Garita Ranch and the 4UR Ranch along the Rio Grande. Allan knew of Charles's familiarity with the property and asked ranch manager Chuck Davlin to contact him to see if he was interested. Charles thanked Chuck but turned down the offer. Chuck suggested that Charles sleep on it. The next morning, Chuck received a phone call from Charles, and the first thing Charles said was, "Damn you, Chuck! I didn't sleep a wink last night and I'll take it!" Later, Charles would tell the story that he and Allan made the deal on the back of a napkin in the bar at the ranch.

The price of the 4UR was a bit steep for Charles, so he asked his friend Willie Farah to come along as a partner. Farah was CEO of Farah Inc., one of the largest clothing manufacturers in the country. His keen business mind was a good match for Charles, and they purchased the guest ranch together with plans to develop the Goose Creek valley. However, within a couple of years, Farah's company became embroiled in a labor dispute. The strike, which was billed as the second largest of its kind after the California grape strike, lasted twenty-two months and caused Farah such significant financial difficulties that he asked Charles to buy him out. Charles was still in favor of having a partner, however, and approached the owner of the neighboring Humphreys Ranch, Ruth Brown. Access to the Humphreys Ranch went directly through 4UR property, and Ruth was more than happy to become Charles's partner and protect the valley from any development. Charles and Shirley quickly became great friends with Ruth and her husband, Darcy.

Shirley and Charles Leavell, on the porch of the lodge at the 4UR, circa 1986. *From the collection of the Leavell family.*

The first operating season of the 4UR resort for Charles and Shirley was the summer of 1973. They hired a couple from El Paso, Joe and Katus Walton, to manage the guest operations. Joe had been a colonel with the Military Police, now retired, and Katus was a beautiful Hungarian who, as a refugee during World War II, had walked for days to get out of Hungary and into Austria. She and Joe met at a refugee camp where he was commander of the Military Police. They married soon after, and when Joe retired, they moved to El Paso, where he had been stationed at Fort Bliss.

While managing the 4UR, Katus was the consummate hostess, where Joe was everything one would expect from an ex-military policeman. He was a by-the-book type of man used to giving orders and having them followed. Joe and Katus were a great team and managed the ranch for Charles and Shirley until 1988, when they retired and moved back to El Paso.

In 1986, after thirteen seasons of supplementing the income of guest operations at the 4UR, owners Ruth Brown and Charles Leavell decided to come to a different arrangement in their partnership. They agreed that Charles and Shirley would own the business and lease Ruth's half of the land. Charles and Shirley were then free to handle the business as sole proprietors. This was a challenge, as the ranch lost money most years and was managed as a labor of love. By 1988, Charles wanted to retire and worked out a plan whereby his children, Mary Lee and Pete, could purchase the ranch, which would take it out of the Leavells' estate. Once this was accomplished, Charles approached Pete to take over his duties overseeing the management of the ranch. This was a considerable concern for both Pete and Mary Lee because they were not financially capable of subsidizing the business as their father had done. Pete agreed to take over Charles's responsibilities, but some tough decisions would need to be made to get things on sound financial footing. Given that the ranch finances consisted of twelve months of bills and only four months of income, this was something that Charles did not believe possible, but Pete was determined and persevered in his vision over the next three decades.

Charles stayed active with the ranch, working in partnership with Pete as a strong patriarch, infusing the ranch with his enthusiasm and personality for almost thirty years. In January 2000, he passed away at the age of eighty-eight. This was poignant time for the family and a time of transition in the legacy of the 4UR Ranch.

In September 2007, the Leavells held an extended family gathering in honor of Shirley Leavell's ninetieth birthday. It was a wonderful event for the family matriarch but sadly was to be the last visit she would make to the ranch. From that time on, she remained in El Paso with caregivers until her passing on March 4, 2013.

PETE LEAVELL

In 1957, at the age of fifteen, Pete boarded a train and began a two-day trip to the Phillips Academy in Andover, Massachusetts. Pete discovered a new world of classic literature, art and history while experiencing a part of the United States that had little resemblance to the rough-and-tumble West Texas border town in which he had been raised. He graduated in 1960, and then, like Mary Lee and his father, attended Stanford University, graduating with a degree in history in 1965.

It was the height of the Vietnam War, and Pete received his draft notice shortly thereafter. Knowing he was to report for duty in September, he enrolled in Officer Candidate School, receiving his commission in 1966. Returning to El Paso, Pete reunited with his longtime girlfriend Pam MacGuire, and they were married the following December. In 1967, Pete and his new wife were stationed in Germany, where, as a first lieutenant, Pete commanded a 155mm mechanized artillery battery in the Third Armored Division. By 1969, Pete, now a captain, had fulfilled his commitment to the army and received an honorable discharge.

Once back in El Paso, Pete and Pam settled into civilian life and welcomed daughter Jennifer in June 1970. Pete began working at the Leavell Company, but by the following year, he and Pam decided to make a life for themselves elsewhere.

The family moved to Colorado, where their future took a surprising turn. Through a series of unexpected introductions, Pete and a good friend formed a film company and were hired by Phillip Morris to shoot a documentary about the 1973 European Formula One Grand Prix racing season. The family moved to London for a year, shot the movie (now titled *One by One)* and, upon returning to the United States, settled in Los Angeles, where Pete and Pam subsequently divorced.

In 1975, Pete met Lindsey Moore, who was an assistant to a prominent Hollywood talent agent. They dated for two years and were married in 1977. In 1978, Pete and Lindsey moved to Boulder, Colorado, and by 1979, they had welcomed a son, Brian. Pete's daughter, Jennifer (now eight years old), came to live with them, and the family settled into their adopted state of Colorado.

Over the next ten years, Pete formed a company that worked in land development, oil and gas leases and ownership of five renaissance fairs throughout the country. Lindsey studied painting in the Fine Arts department of the University of Colorado and then set out on an art career of her own. Lindsey's paintings were shown in galleries in Colorado and New Mexico and appeared on the album covers of recording artists, magazines and book covers.

THE RANCH

When Pete began overseeing the business of the 4UR, he implemented new practices, including better financial reporting procedures and higher standards of guest services. On the recommendation of friends, Pete hired Rock and Kristen Swenson as general managers to fill the position left by the Waltons. The Swensons had worked at the A-Bar-A Ranch in Wyoming and had a good deal of experience in the guest ranch business, especially understanding the importance of nurturing relationships with longtime returning guests.

Ed Wintz and his wife, Bea Jean, chose to stay on as ranch foreman and head housekeeper, respectively, after the Waltons retired. Ed had been a fixture at the 4UR since being brought on by Arthur Sharp in the 1950s. He ran the guest horse operation, oversaw the cattle operation and was responsible for maintenance of the pastures, grounds, buildings, water and waste treatment. He and Bea Jean raised their two children, daughter Lisa and son Kim, on the ranch, and both grew up wrangling horses during their summers as teens.

The day after Pete took the reins from Charles, and in what could only be described as "baptism by fire," Pete received a letter from the State of Colorado containing a cease and desist order for noncompliance with sewage treatment. With a steep learning curve and guests scheduled to arrive in a couple of months, Pete scrambled to get an extension from the state, pulled the family together to bring cash to the table and began immediate construction to fix the problem. It was this event that signaled to Pete he needed to reevaluate every system within the operation and make a long-range plan for upgrades and sustainability. As a result, Pete and his father inspected and assessed every aspect of the ranch, from buildings, to food, to the horses and, of key importance: Goose Creek and the fishing.

As part of Pete's new administrative approach, the ranch managers would be living on site year-round instead of just in the summer months. This decision required providing adequate housing for full-time occupancy, instead of the previous accommodations found in a temporary double-wide trailer. The new home was built along the west bank of Goose Creek on Staff Row. Over the next few years, all of the staff living quarters were addressed and upgraded either by remodeling or building new seasonal employee dormitories from the ground up. Goose Hall, Bird's Nest and Spruce Tree were each remodeled, while Willows and Creekside were new construction.

Pete also took issue with overfishing of Goose Creek by the summer guests. Throughout the entire history of the ranch, overfishing had been of concern. It had been common practice to stock and restock Goose Creek throughout the season to accommodate the amount of fish taken by guests during their stay. Pete felt the time was right to institute a catch-and-release policy. There was much concern and anticipation about the effect this would have on the business. Fortunately, the guests were on board with the changes, and rebuilding the Goose Creek fishery was underway.

Along with a revision in fishing policies came a good hard look at the condition of the stream itself. What was the state of the fish habitat along the seven miles of stream? What effect did the cattle grazing have along the riparian zones of the stream banks? Pete brought in stream experts, and it was determined that Goose Creek did in fact need help. Over the next few years, contractors were hired to secure the banks, position boulders, place logs to slow the current and create conditions that would provide rest and shade for the trout.

One major concern presented to Pete was the impact of pasturing cattle. Because the cattle had free access to the stream for water, they had damaged the stream banks and trampled the riparian zones, greatly restricting the bug life and grasses necessary for a healthy fish environment. This was a difficult and sensitive topic to discuss with the ranch foreman, Ed Wintz, who had been running cattle on the property since coming to work for Arthur Sharp in the 1940s. However, the evidence was so compelling that the presence of cattle was detrimental to the ecology of the stream that in the end the cattle were taken out of 4UR operations. This resulted in a resurgence of plant and insect life in the riparian zone and greatly improved the trout habitat. The renewed priority of fishing became the guiding focus of the future.

No longer able to run cattle at the 4UR, Ed and Bea Jean decided to build a home and run their own cattle operation on family land in the nearby Trout Creek drainage. They continued to welcome longtime guests of the ranch who had become lifelong friends and who loved to ride the mountains with their favorite horseman—Ed. The family was sad to see them go and knew that filling the shoes they left behind would be no easy task.

Although many changes were instituted at the 4UR, those long-standing traditions and favorites of the guest endure, including the weekly fish fry on Fridays, ice delivered every evening to the porches and the ringing of ranch bells for the guests as their departure.

The Swensons began looking for a couple in which the husband could take over the horse operation as well as the property and the wife could take over Bea Jean's department of housekeeping. Soon the ranch was contacted by Kathy and Jimmy Adelman, a couple from Kansas expressing interest in the job. Jimmy and Kathy Adelman had spent a couple of summers in Mineral County working cattle in the high country for the San Luis Valley Park Association. Jimmy was a good cowboy with a degree in animal science and Kathy was a bright, talented and willing team member. They were hired and moved to the 4UR with their two young sons, Cody (eleven) and Casey (nine). By 1995, Kathy had moved into the newly formed position of office manager, while Jimmy left his position at 4UR to work for a local home builder in the area. Their son Cody grew up and became a fishing guide in Alaska and later a registered nurse in nearby Alamosa. Casey spent summers working for the Brown family at the neighboring Humphreys Ranch and was hired as permanent foreman in 2016. In 2017, to the admiration of family and staff, Kathy celebrated her twenty-fifth year of working with the 4UR, and Jimmy continues his relationship with the ranch by taking guests up to the Lost Lakes for a day of fishing and a bit of history along the way.

After twelve years at the helm as general managers of the 4UR, Rock and Kristen Swenson, now parents of twin boys, decided to return home to family and took a job with another ranch in Montana. Fortunately for Pete and Lindsey, Aaron and Robin Christensen, who were assistant managers of the Vista Verde Ranch, a high-end resort near Steamboat Springs, were at that time looking for a general manager position of a guest ranch. This was a great fit for the Leavell and Christensen families. Aaron had been raised in Colorado, was an expert fishing guide and graduated with a business degree from New Mexico State University (NMSU). Robin had been raised on a large cattle ranch in New Mexico, was an expert wrangler, a former New Mexico state champion barrel racer and also a graduate of NMSU with a degree in hospitality. The Christensens became general managers in 1999.

In their first year of management, Robin and Aaron hired a young ranch hand, Damon Gibbons, from Wyoming. Damon would go on to be the head wrangler at the ranch for the next twenty years. During that time, he married his wife, Kierra, and they welcomed three children: daughters Adelaide and Nemonie and son Liam, all born at their 4UR home, the former Palmer fish hatchery. In 2019, Damon resigned from his position to seek opportunities elsewhere.

In 1999, it also became obvious that the original Holy Moses cabin at the western end of the compound was in desperate need of repair and could not be put off. With the 4UR workload piling up, Lindsey decided to take a hiatus from painting to concentrate on overseeing new construction projects, remodels and marketing.

A longtime guest and friend of the family, Robert Clark, was a prominent architect from Dallas with his firm Robert Clark and Associates. He counseled the family not to demolish the Holy Moses guest cottage because the historical importance was too significant to be lost. He urged that the building be renovated instead. The family agreed and committed that going forward, all renovations and new construction would mirror the original 1906 materials and style as much as possible, including matching the pitch of all roofs on the compound to the historic lines. A contractor was found who could lift the entire structure, build a foundation and set it back in place. It was then replumbed, redecorated and once again ready to welcome guests by the summer season.

Things were going well for the new managers until 2002, when Colorado experienced the driest year on record to date and the entire southern region was a tinderbox. On July 19, a fire spontaneously broke out thirteen miles to the southeast, destroying homes and becoming one of the most devastating fires in southern Colorado in one hundred years. The 4UR was put on notice of possible evacuation, but the fire moved east, no longer threatening the ranch. However, by August of that year, Pierce Creek—the potable water source for the ranch—dried up. Management scrambled to provide for guests, bringing in water trucks and cases of bottled water to finish out the season. This crisis was a wake-up call and resulted in the drilling of a domestic water well and installing a state-of-the-art water treatment facility.

With a property so historically important, the Leavell family renewed their commitment to the ranch, investing in maintenance, construction, renovations and remodeling. Robert Clark and his firm continued their professional relationship with the Leavells, designing a seasonal staff women's dormitory called the Willows and a new home designated North Star for Pete and Lindsey Leavell and their family. In 2012, in conjunction with Avery Augur of Creede America, Clark designed a new swimming pool and spa building called Little Medicine. Guest cabins throughout the compound had always been named after historical silver mines in the area; Commodore, Holy Moses and Amethyst. However, the new pool and hot springs area was named Little Medicine. This was the designation the Ute tribe gave to the property's hot springs to distinguish them from Big Medicine springs located in Pagosa Springs on the other side of Wolf Creek Pass. (For many years, the trail between the two was still visible at the southern end of the property.)

Following the success of Little Medicine, Avery Augur then redesigned the offices of the main lodge as well as a new deck with fire pit along on the south side of Maude's Bar. All dining room furniture and fixtures were replaced, and new porch furniture appeared throughout the ranch. In 2016, Augur designed and sited a beautiful new guest cabin on the western edge of the compound next to Pierce Creek christened the Molly Ess. With new furnishings and individual screened-in porches, this quickly became a favorite of guests.

June 2013 turned out to be another catastrophically dry year. A fire began with a lightning strike south of the 4UR on the opposite side of the Continental Divide near Wolf Creek Pass. The fire, called West Fork Complex, slowly spread north and east, where it threatened the small town of South Fork. The dry winds quickly increased, whipping embers across the tundra above timberline and, to the amazement of all, sent flaming pinecones across the Continental Divide. After two weeks, the fire was approaching from the south, and 4UR was ordered by Fred Hosselkus, the Mineral County sheriff, to evacuate. The 4UR staff had prepared an evacuation plan that was put into effect immediately, and 50 guests, 35 staff, 50 horses, 7 vehicles, 5 dogs, 4 goats, 4 pigs, 6 cats, artwork, documents, and computers were all evacuated in 2 hours. By the time of evacuation, the fire was massive and ultimately covered 124,000 acres, making it the second-largest conflagration in Colorado history. Over 1,200 firefighters were involved along with 7 helicopters, 2 slurry bombers and innumerable fire trucks—at a cost of over $12 million. Several command posts were established, including one on the 4UR property itself. A Nature Conservancy hot shot team protected the Humphreys Ranch property above the 4UR Ranch. Though forty-mile-per-hour winds whipped the fire onto the southern end of the ranch, the wind miraculously shifted, carrying the flames to the east and away from the 4UR. After six weeks, the fire was pronounced contained—without the loss of a single home or reported injuries.

The Leavell family, and their land partners the Browns, have long been advocates of conservation. After years of diligence, they concluded the process of placing a series of conservation easements on the southern 1,400 acres of the ranch, protecting the beauty and pristine nature of the valley. Working with the Rio Grande Headwaters Land Trust and dividing the effort into two phases, the process was completed in 2015, enabling the Leavells to transfer their ranch ownership to the next generation, thus keeping it within the family for three generations.

HISTORY Colorado

This is to certify that the

Wagon Wheel Gap Hot Springs Resort

has been listed in the

National Register of Historic Places

by the

United States Department of the Interior

on

September 26, 2019

Holly K. Norton, Ph.D.

Deputy State Historic Preservation Officer

Certificate of listing of the Wagon Wheel Gap Hot Springs Resort in the National Register of Historic Places, 2019. *Courtesy of the 4UR Ranch.*

In 2018, the Leavell family celebrated twenty years of working with Aaron and Robin Christensen. During that time, Robin gave birth to four children: Cole (2001), Kylee (2003), Luke (2005) and Laci (2007), who have all grown up on the ranch and are an integral part of the 4UR family. Robin and Aaron and their children have become fixtures at the 4UR, and to date, their tenure as general managers is the longest in the history of the ranch.

After forty-seven years of ownership, the Leavells initiated an effort to have the Wagon Wheel Gap Fluorspar Mine and Mill and the Wagon Wheel Resort (now 4UR Ranch) both placed in the National Register of Historic Places. In 2019, with the help of History Colorado, this honor was awarded to the ranch. The Leavell family, now approaching its fiftieth year of stewardship, looks forward to protecting the legacy of 4UR Ranch and the Goose Creek Valley for years to come.

EPILOGUE

There is the "history of art" and "the art of history."

Years ago, our neighbor Doug Davlin gave us a photocopy of a beautiful engraving of the Wagon Wheel Gap dating from the 1880s. The detail was extraordinary, showing the massive cliff formation, the terminus of the rail line at the depot and riders coming back from what we knew to be the hot springs.

We appreciated the gift and put it in our file of ranch memorabilia for safekeeping. A few years later, a friend told us about a painting of the Wagon Wheel Gap being sold by a dealer of regional art in Denver. We were in that city at the time, so we drove over and purchased the painting, which looked remarkably familiar.

When we returned to the ranch, we placed our new purchase next to the small print from Doug and discovered we had a mystery on our hands. One had definitely been taken from the other, but the engraving was the better perspective and drawn by a more skilled hand. Through research, we believed the engraving to be done by John Karst (1836–1922), and though we put much effort into attempting to unlock our mystery, we had no luck.

About five years later, a dinner guest presented us with a special gift he found in a vintage print shop. It was the same image of Wagon Wheel Gap as the print that Doug had given us. This one had been an illustration in *The Crest of the Continent*, a railroad travelogue written in the early 1880s. Luckily, we were able to obtain an original copy of this publication and were amazed

Wagon Wheel Gap depot and stage station with Rio Grande bridge, circa 1883. Karst engraving of a Moran drawing published in *The Crest of the Continent* by Ernest Ingersoll, 1885. *Courtesy of the 4UR Ranch.*

to discover the author had devoted six pages to the hotel and hot springs of Wagon Wheel Gap—the same property owned by our family for almost half a century.

At this point, we felt the mystery of the print was solved. We now knew it to be a John Karst engraving of an original Thomas Moran drawing, as confirmed by Joni Louise Kinsey, author of *Thomas Moran and the Surveying of the American West.*[532]

Though to date we have not yet solved the mystery of the oil painting, the journey to discover the origins of the Karst engraving sparked our interest in the greater history of the 4UR Ranch, which ultimately led to the writing of this book. By learning of all those who have left their mark on the ranch, we know the journey continues, time marches on and today we are the history of tomorrow.

Thank you for sharing your time in reading our history. We'll leave you with a favorite quote by Leonardo da Vinci on which we reflect when fishing Goose Creek or the Rio Grande. "In rivers, the water that you touch is the last of what has passed and the first of that which comes: and so, with present time."

Lindsey Leavell, August 2019

GEOLOGY GLOSSARY

alluvial (**alluvium**). Deposit of clay, silt, sand and gravel left by a river or other stream in a valley.

andesite. An intermediate extrusive volcanic rock type or magma with silica content falling somewhere between basalt and dacite. Typically contains phenocrysts.

ash. Volcanic particles less than two millimeters in diameter.

basalt. A dark-colored extrusive volcanic rock with high iron and magnesium content and low silica content. Formed by the solidification of lava rich in iron and magnesium.

breccia. Composed of broken pieces of older rocks. Pieces are relatively course and greater than two millimeters.

caldera. A volcanic landform that represents a large collapse depression resulting from a catastrophic eruption that caused the roof of a magma reservoir to collapse. May contain a central peak or resurgent dome. Largest calderas known as supervolcanoes.

colluvial (**colluvium**). Loose, unconsolidated sediments that are deposited at the bottom of a hillslope by the downward pull of gravity.

conduit. A pathway used by magma to ascend to Earth's surface from a magma reservoir.

dacite. An intermediate, extrusive rock or magma with silica content falling somewhere between andesite and rhyolite. Typically contains phenocrysts.

dike. A discordant sheet-like body of magma that rises vertically through fractures in the surrounding rock around a magma chamber. Once cooled, it solidifies and is a visual representation of how magma intrudes into older sediments.

effusive. A type of eruption involving passive discharge of lava from a volcanic vent. Viscosity of lava is relatively low.

felsic. Property of volcanic rocks, usually light in color, that are rich in silica and elements that form feldspars and quartz.

frost action. The mechanical weathering process due to repeated freezing and thawing of water in fractures, cracks and other openings—causing the expansion of such openings.

geothermal. Naturally occurring thermal water in the Earth's crust, usually due to an underlying hydrovolcanic system.

granitic. Pertaining to or composed of granite—an intrusive igneous rock largely composed of quartz and feldspars.

hoodoo/goblin/spire. A column or pillar of rock produced by differential weathering of less cohesive and less resistant layers within a formation. Often found in eccentric or grotesque forms.

hydrothermal. A groundwater system that has a heat source, such as the mantle—also known as magmatic hydrothermal system.

hydrovolcanic. A term to describe magma-water interactions.

igneous. Refers to volcanic rocks solidified from lava or magma.

ignimbrite. Deposit of pumice-laden layer. Typically, largely composed of tuff that contains volcanic ash, pumice and rock fragments.

latite. An extrusive volcanic rock which has an intermediate composition between andesites and trachytes.

mafic. Property of volcanic rocks describing a high content of iron and magnesium, and very little silica and aluminum.

magma. High-temperature silica mixture of solids, gas and liquid rock found underneath the Earth's surface.

mantle. The largest layer of the Earth between the crust and the outer core. Temperatures and pressures vary throughout the mantle.

Miocene epoch. Early Tertiary period, about 23 million to 5.3 million years ago.

Oligocene epoch. Early Tertiary period, about 33.9 million to 23 million years ago.

oxidation. The process of combining oxygen with one or more metallic elements, such as iron, zinc, manganese and son on.

phenocryst. Large crystals surrounded by fine-grained matrix in volcanic rocks.

pumice. Volcanic glass that is vesicular due to the presence of water and gas bubbles trapped in the rock during explosion.

rhyolite. An extrusive volcanic rock of felsic composition. Usually of very high silica content.

sill. A concordant sheet-like body of magma that spreads out horizontally along fractures in the surrounding rock around a magma chamber.

stratovolcano. Also known as a composite volcano, a conical-shaped volcano constructed of layers of lava and tephra ejected during a volcanic explosion.

talus. A sloping mass of broken rock fragments at the foot of a cliff.

tephra. Greek for "ash," used to describe explosively ejected material from a volcano—likely a stratovolcano, also known as a composite volcano.

Tertiary period. The first period of the Cenozoic era (aka Age of Mammals), covering the span between 65 million and 2 million years ago, and divided into five epochs: Paleocene, Eocene, Oligocene, Miocene and Pliocene.

welding. Process of heating and then slowly cooling hot ductile volcanic ejecta. This process typically compacts and reduces porosity of material.

NOTES

Chapter 1

1. Gonzales and Karlstrom, "Legacy of Mountains," 3–16.
2. Ibid.
3. Cather, *Laramide Orogeny.*
4. Ibid.
5. Steven and Lipman, *Calderas.*
6. Ibid.
7. Blair and Gillam, "Geomorphic History," 61–78.
8. Blair, Dixon, Miskell-Gerhardt, Gillam and White, "Eastern San Juan Mountains," 243–98.
9. Larsen and Lipman, "Exploring the Ancient."
10. Hulen, *Field Geologic Summaries.*
11. Williams and Chronic, *Roadside Geology.*
12. Larsen and Lipman, "Exploring the Ancient."
13. Colorado Geological Survey, *Calderas.*
14. Williams and Chronic, *Roadside Geology.*
15. Cappa and Wallace, *RS-44 Geology.*
16. Blair and Gillam, "Geomorphic History," 61–78.
17. Cappa and Wallace, *RS-44 Geology.*
18. Lipman, *Geologic Map.*
19. Lipman, "Central San Juan Caldera Cluster," 9–71.
20. Caine and Wilson, "Hydrogeology," 79–98.
21. Bethke, "Mineralization," 39–60.
22. Aurand, *Fluorspar Deposits of Colorado.*
23. Bethke, "Mineralization," 39–60.
24. Ibid.

Chapter 2

25. Howard, *Diary of San Juan Travels.*
26. Bureau of Land Management, General Land Office Records.
27. *Colorado Daily Chieftain*, August 19, 1875.
28. Hall, *History of the State of Colorado.*
29. *Creede Candle*, January 5, 1922.
30. Hafen and Hafen, *Fremont's Fourth Expedition.*
31. *Daily News* (Denver, CO), July 21, 1901.
32. Hall, *History of the State of Colorado.*
33. Nossaman, *Many More Mountains, Volume 1: Silverton's Roots.*
34. Ibid.
35. Ibid.
36. Ibid.
37. Ridgeway, "Stony Pass Road."
38. Bellamy, "Wagon Wheel Gap."
39. Ruffner, *Report of a Reconnaissance*.
40. *Golden Weekly Globe*, June 21, 1873.
41. *Colorado Daily Chieftain*, September 4, 1875.
42. Ruffner, *Report of a Reconnaissance*.
43. *Pueblo Chieftain*, June 22, 2008.
44. U.S. Forest Service, "History and Culture."
45. Nossaman, *Many More Mountains, Volume 1: Silverton's Roots.*
46. Ruffner, *Report of a Reconnaissance*.

Chapter 3

47. Hinshaw, *Crusaders for Wildlife*.
48. Hart, *Appraisal Confederated Ute Indian Lands.*
49. Delaney, *Southern Ute People.*
50. Baker and Hafen, *History of Colorado*, 1:278.
51. Carrillo, "Spanish Exploration."
52. Hinshaw, *Crusaders for Wildlife*.
53. Fowler, *Journal of Jacob Fowler*, 124–25.
54. Ibid.
55. Ibid., 173.
56. History.com, "Treaty of Guadalupe Hidalgo."
57. Richmond, *Trail to Disaster*.
58. Nossaman, *Many More Mountains, Volume 1: Silverton's Roots.*
59. Weiser, "Chief Ouray."
60. Nossaman, *Many More Mountains, Volume 1: Silverton's Roots.*
61. Weiser, "Navajo Long Walk."
62. Weiser, "Chief Ouray."

63. Horn, *National Register of Historic Places for the Ute-Ulay Mine and Mill.*
64. Ruffner, *Report of a Reconnaissance.*
65. Horn, "Brunot Agreement."
66. Richmond, "La Loma Settlements"; U.S. Forest Service, "History and Culture."
67. Richmond, *La Loma de San Jose.*
68. *Colorado Daily Chieftain*, December 11, 1872.
69. Wagner and Wetherill, *Hidden History of the Upper Rio Grande.*
70. Colville, "Timeline."
71. Horn, "Brunot Agreement."
72. Hubbard, "Letter from Arthur Hubbard."
73. Ibid.
74. *Colorado Weekly Journal*, October 18, 1877.
75. Hubbard, "Letter from Arthur Hubbard."
76. Ibid.
77. Fossett, *Colorado.*
78. Espinosa, "Del Norte."
79. Ibid.
80. Colville, "Timeline."
81. *San Juan Prospector*, July 1, 1876.
82. *Colorado Daily Chieftain*, July 15, 1877.
83. Ralston, "William Jackson Palmer."
84. Hubbard, "Letter from Arthur Hubbard."
85. *Saguache Chronicle*, July 13, 1883.
86. Creede Railroad.
87. *Creede Candle*, October 7, 1911.
88. *Colorado Daily Chieftain*, August 2, 1884.
89. Carter, *Denver & Rio Grande Western Depots.*
90. National Historic Register Program designation for the Thornton Depot.

Chapter 4

91. Licht, *Medical Hydrology.*
92. Crook, *Mineral Waters.*
93. Ryan, *Forgotten Plague.*
94. Ibid.
95. Ibid.
96. Niemeyer, *Clinical Lectures.*
97. Denison, *Rocky Mountain Health Resorts.*
98. WebMD, "Understanding Rheumatic Fever."
99. Hall, *History of the State of Colorado.*
100. *Fort Collins Standard*, August 5, 1874.
101. Wheeler, *Geographical and Geological Explorations.*
102. Denison, *Rocky Mountain Health Resorts.*
103. Wheeler, *Geographical and Geological Explorations.*

104. *Pantagraph* (Bloomington, IL), December 18, 1878, 4.
105. *Denver Mirror*, November 29, 1874.
106. Aclara, "Water Heater Temperature Safety."
107. Wagner and Wetheril, *Hidden History of the Upper Rio Grande.*
108. *Saguache Chronicle*, November 25, 1876.
109. Nesdale, "5 Therapeutic Benefits."
110. Colorado College, *Analysis of Wagon Wheel Gap Waters.*
111. Columbia University, "Glauber's Salt."
112. Basch, *Indications.*
113. Barrett and Pearl, *Hydrogeological Data.*
114. Warmflash, "Could Small Amounts of Radiation Be Good For You?"
115. Frame, *Radioactive Curative Devices.*
116. Ibid.
117. Ibid.
118. Ibid.
119. Ibid.
120. *Rocky Mountain News*, October 19, 1877, 4.
121. *Castle Rock Journal*, March 14, 1902.
122. Croffut, *Croffut's Grip-sack Guide to Colorado*.
123. *Walnut Valley Times* (El Dorado, KS), July 30, 1903, 7.
124. McClaren, *Blueprints for Modernization of Wagon Wheel Gap*.
125. Emmons and Larsen, "Hot Springs and the Mineral Deposits."
126. Basch, *Indications.*
127. *Rocky Mountain News*, January 1, 1881.
128. *Rocky Mountain Presbyterian*, October 1, 1877, 1.
129. *Creede Candle*, May 20, 1892, 4.
130. Ibid., May 18, 1907.
131. Basch, *Indications.*
132. *Creede Candle*, January 19, 1894.
133. Ibid., December 23, 1892.
134. Ibid., January 19, 1894.
135. *Whitehorn News*, January 27, 1899.
136. Bennett, *History of the Louisiana Purchase Exposition.*
137. Poland Spring, www.polandspring.com.
138. Emmons and Larsen, "Hot Springs and the Mineral Deposits."
139. Ibid.
140. Barrett and Pearl, *Hydrogeological Data.*
141. Ibid.
142. Fowler, *Journal of Jacob Fowler*; Wheeler, *Geographical and Geological Explorations*.
143. Caine and Wilson, "Hydrogeology."
144. How, personal communication.
145. U.S. Census.
146. *Montezuma Millrun*, September 2, 1882; *Denver Republican*, August 27, 1882.
147. *Colorado Daily Chieftain*, November 12, 1882.

148. *Creede Candle*, October 22, 1921.
149. Root-Bernstein and Root-Bernstein, *Honey, Mud, Maggots*.
150. *Sierra Journal* (Rosita, CO), January 10, 1884.

Chapter 5

151. Cunningham, "Western Hospitality Meets Laid-back Fun."
152. *Colorado Daily Chieftain*, July 21, 1875.
153. *Colorado Weekly Chieftain*, August 15, 1895.
154. Hinshaw, *Crusaders for Wildlife*.
155. Ibid.
156. Ibid.
157. Wagner and Wetheril, *Hidden History of the Upper Rio Grande*.
158. Ibid.
159. *San Luis Valley Courier*, January 22, 1890.
160. Hogan, "Brook Trout Life Cycle."
161. Wagner and Wetheril, *Hidden History of the Upper Rio Grande*.
162. Hinshaw, *Crusaders for Wildlife*.
163. *Herald Democrat*, September 15, 1906.
164. *Telluride Journal*, July 12, 1906.
165. *Creede Candle*, September 24, 1910.
166. Ibid., September 16, 1911.
167. *Pueblo Chieftain*, May 5, 1918.
168. Getz, personal communication.
169. Fraser, *State of Colorado Game and Fish Regulations*.
170. Colorado Parks and Wildlife, 2019 Colorado Fishing.
171. Dawes, *Notes as Vice President*, 87.
172. *Creede Candle*, August 30, 1919.
173. *Longmont Daily Times*, January 30, 1925.
174. *Salida Mail*, August 11, 1922.
175. Izaak Walton League of America, "History & Mission."
176. Walton, *Compleat Angler*.
177. Ibid.
178. Hinshaw, *Crusaders for Wildlife*.
179. Dunlap, *Charles Gates Dawes: A Life*.
180. *Daily Times* (Longmont, CO), July 29, 1925.
181. Ibid., July 3, 1926.
182. Ibid., August 10, 1926.
183. 4UR Anglers Advisory, 2018.
184. *Craig Empire Courier*, August 7, 1940.
185. *Colorado Daily Chieftain*, September 7, 1875.

Chapter 6

186. Ibid., July 25, 1877.
187. Bureau of Land Management, General Land Office Records.
188. Heritage Quest.
189. Nossaman, *Many More Mountains, Volume 2: Ruts into Silverton.*
190. *Colorado Daily Chieftain*, August 21, 1875.
191. Ibid., July 28, 1876.
192. Ibid., March 30, 1877.
193. Mineral County Courthouse Records.
194. Pangborn, *Rocky Mountain Tourist.*
195. *Saguache Chronicle*, October 29, 1880.
196. Heritage Quest.
197. Mineral County Records, Book 1, pages 3 and 4.
198. *Silver World*, May 7, 1881, 3.
199. *Leadville Daily Herald*, January 12, 1883.
200. *Wichita Daily Eagle*, July 1, 1887; August 5, 1887.
201. *Creede Candle*, May 20, 1892, 4.
202. Rasmussen, *Rio Grande's La Veta Pass Route.*
203. D&RG, *Tourist's Handbook*.
204. Ellis, "Postmasters in Mineral County."
205. Bauer, Ozment and Willard, *Colorado Post Offices.*
206. Carter, *Denver & Rio Grande Western Depots*.
207. *Alamosa Journal*, April 2, 1945.
208. Ellis, "Postmasters in Mineral County"; Bauer, Ozment and Willard, *Colorado Post Offices.*

Chapter 7

209. *Lake City Silver Thread*, September 20, 1991.
210. Bureau of Land Management, General Land Office Records.
211. Hall, *History of the State of Colorado*.
212. Bureau of Land Management, General Land Office Records.
213. *Pittsburgh Weekly Gazette*, August 7, 1875
214. Toll, "Letter from Wagon Wheel Gap."
215. Wheeler, *Geographical and Geological Explorations*; *San Juan Prospector*, July 1, 1976.
216. *Colorado Daily Chieftain*, March 20, 1877.
217. *Colorado Springs Gazette*, November 3, 1877.
218. Colorado State Archives, Wagon Wheel Gap Hot Springs Company.
219. Horn, *National Register of Historic Places for the Ute-Ulay Mine and Mill.*
220. Ibid.
221. *Silver World*, December 2, 1876.
222. Prabook, "Adair Wilson."
223. Stone, *History of Colorado*.

224. *Colorado Daily Chieftain*, August 13, 1875.
225. *Rocky Mountain News*, October 19, 1877, 4.
226. *Colorado Springs Gazette*, June 29, 1878.
227. Pangborn, *Rocky Mountain Tourist.*
228. *Colorado Transcript*, November 6, 1878.
229. Heritage Quest.
230. *Colorado Daily Chieftain*, December 5, 1878.
231. Ibid., August 6, 1880.
232. Ibid., June 29, 1881.
233. *Colorado Daily Chieftain*, June 29, 1881.
234. Pangborn, *Rocky Mountain Tourist.*
235. Ibid., *Picturesque B. and O.*
236. Hafen and Hafen, *Diaries of William Henry Jackson.*
237. Strochlic, "We Have a Painter to Thank for Yellowstone."
238. Hafen and Hafen, *Diaries of William Henry Jackson.*
239. Ingersoll, *Crest of the Continent.*
240. Wilkins, *Thomas Moran.*
241. *Rocky Mountain News*, April 20, 1884.
242. *Alamosa Journal*, July 31, 1884.
243. *Castle Rock Journal*, August 26, 1885.
244. Ladoo, *Fluorspar.*
245. *Creede Candle*, December 23, 1892.
246. *Rocky Mountain News*, January 21, 1897; April 16, 1898, 7.
247. *Colorado Daily Chieftain*, August 31, 1899.
248. *Alamosa Journal*, December 25, 1902.
249. Ibid., June 4, 1903.
250. *Durango Democrat*, February 24, 1903.
251. Mineral County Records.
252. *Denver Post*, November 10, 1902, 1.
253. *Creede Candle*, April 2, 1904.
254. Heritage Quest.

Chapter 8

255. Scamehorn, *A.E. Humphreys and Sons.*
256. Walsh, *Grande Dame of Quality Hill.*
257. Dooley, personal communication.
258. *Denver Post*, January 9, 2011.
259. Parrish, *WASP in Their Own Words.*
260. Dooley, personal communication.
261. *Denver Rocky Mountain News*, May 28, 1922; LaFont, *Homesteaders of the Upper Rio Grande.*
262. Hinshaw, *Crusaders for Wildlife.*
263. *Creede Candle*, April 2, 1904.

264. Ibid., September 20, 1919.
265. *Colorado Springs Gazette*, May 28, 1922.
266. Walsh, *Grande Dame of Quality Hill.*
267. *Creede Candle*, December 30, 1922.
268. Ibid., July 21, 1923.
269. Ibid., August 4, 1923.
270. McCartney, *Teapot Dome Scandal.*
271. *Daily Times* (Longmont, CO), May 9, 1927.
272. *Denver Post*, January 9, 2011.
273. Jacobs, *Ribs of Silver.*
274. Ibid.
275. *Aspen Times*, January 1, 2011.
276. *Creede Candle*, December 29, 1923.
277. *Aspen Times*, October 30, 2009.
278. Adelman, personal communication.
279. *Creede Candle*, February 4, 1922.
280. *Rocky Mountain News*, March 31, 1903, 3.
281. Bureau of Land Management, General Land Office Records.
282. *Denver Post*, September 29, 1899, 9.
283. Aldrich, *Annals of Iowa*.
284. Ibid.
285. *Rocky Mountain News*, February 16, 1915, 7.
286. *Creede Candle*, August 10, 1907.
287. LaFont, *Homesteaders of the Upper Rio Grande.*
288. Britain, personal communication.
289. Ibid.
290. *Creede Candle*, June 29 and July 6, 1918.
291. Ibid., October 8, 1921.
292. Ibid., March 10, 1923.
293. Rasmussen, *Katherine Speaks Out.*
294. Jacobs, *Ribs of Silver.*
295. Britain, personal communication.
296. Bureau of Land Management, General Land Office Records.
297. Jacobs, *Ribs of Silver.*
298. *Creede Candle*, December 10, 1921.
299. Elliott, personal communication.
300. Gjellum, personal communication.
301. *Denver Post*, December 22, 1918, 56.
302. *Rocky Mountain News*, February 14, 1919, 2.
303. Gjellum, personal communication.
304. Ibid.
305. Heritage Quest.
306. Wyley, personal communication.
307. Dooley, "2009 Creede People of the Year."

308. Wyley, personal communication.
309. Wyley, "Cottonwood Cove," unpublished memoir.
310. Dooley, "2009 Creede People of the Year."
311. Jacobs, *Ribs of Silver*.
312. Dooley, "2009 Creede People of the Year."
313. Phipps and Phipps, "La Garita Club."
314. Heritage Quest.
315. *Colorado Springs Gazette*, September 20, 1915.
316. Bureau of Land Management, General Land Office Records.
317. *Denver Post*, March 3, 1908.
318. *Colorado Springs Gazette*, October 16, 1904.
319. Ibid., August 1, 1905.
320. *Denver Post*, June 10, 1909, 4.
321. Hinshaw, *Crusaders for Wildlife*.
322. *New York Times*, "Lawrence C. Phipps, Ex-Senator, Dies; Colorado G.O.P. Leader, 95; Was Carnegie Executive Before U.S. Steel Merger," March 3, 1958.
323. Smith, "In Search of 'Black Jack' Pershing."
324. *Aspen Daily Times*, October 22, 1936.
325. T. Phipps, personal communication.
326. Lands of America, "1,880 Acres in Mineral County."
327. Wright, *Rocky Mountain Divide*.
328. G. Phipps, personal communication.
329. Weisse, "Phipps La Garita Ranch."

Chapter 9

330. Ralston, "William Jackson Palmer."
331. May, *Kingdom of Their Own*.
332. Ralston, "William Jackson Palmer."
333. Richards, *Britannia's Children*.
334. Ibid.
335. Gazetteer for Scotland. "Sir James Key Caird."
336. *Colorado Daily Chieftain*, November 18, 1877.
337. Ralston, "William Jackson Palmer."
338. Rio Grande County Courthouse, Warranty Deed, No. 5068, book 7, page 631.
339. Ibid., Warranty Deed, No. 6304, book 12, page 216.
340. *Denver Republican*, July 9, 1883, 8.
341. *Silver World*, March 5, 1881, 3.
342. *Denver Rocky Mountain News*, April 17, 1885, 5.
343. *Colorado Daily Chieftain*, August 20, 1885.
344. Ibid., September 19, 1886.
345. *Silver Cliff Rustler*, October 20, 1887.
346. *Colorado Weekly Chieftain*, August 3, 1876.
347. *Colorado Daily Chieftain*, February 4, 1873.

348. *Colorado Transcript*, June 16, 1921.
349. *Colorado Springs Gazette*, January 27, 1877.
350. *Gunnison Daily News-Democrat*, January 25, 1882.
351. *Colorado Republican*, December 14, 1905.
352. *Aspen Democrat*, June 5, 1909.
353. *Colorado Daily Chieftain*, April 1, 1890.
354. San *Juan Prospector*, May 16, 1891.
355. *Colorado Daily Chieftain*, May 22, 1891.
356. Ibid., July 18, 1889.
357. Ibid., July 30, 1889.
358. *San Juan Prospector*, April 11, 1891.
359. *Rocky Mountain News*, June 15, 1892, 2; *Creede Candle*, July 1, 1892, 1.
360. *Creede Candle*, June 9, 1893, 4.
361. Ibid., June 8, 1894.
362. *Colorado Daily Chieftain*, January 21, 1895.
363. Ralston, "William Jackson Palmer."
364. *Salida Mail*, June 24, 1898.
365. *Rocky Mountain News*, June 24, 1901, 1.
366. Ralston, "William Jackson Palmer."
367. Glen Eyrie.
368. Mineral County Records.
369. Thomas MacLaren School.
370. *Colorado Springs Weekly Gazette*, April 10, 1902.
371. *San Juan Prospector*, February 22, 1902.
372. *Western Field: Sportsman's Magazine of the West* 8, no. 1 (February 1906).
373. *Alamosa Journal*, September 11, 1902.
374. Jacobs, *Ribs of Silver.*
375. *Walnut Valley Times* (El Dorado, KS), July 30, 1903, 7.
376. *Colorado Springs Gazette*, May 17, 1903, 3.
377. Ibid., May 14, 1905, 15.
378. *Fowler Tribune*, October 2, 1903; *Durango Democrat*, February 24, 1903.
379. *Denver Times*, May 7, 1902, 8.
380. *Alamosa Courier*, March 18, 1905.
381. *Creede Candle*, July 14, 1906.
382. Ibid., November 27, 1909.
383. Notice on bridge at Wagon Wheel Gap, August 1908, Steen and Evaskovich.
384. *Alamosa Journal*, December 1, 1905; *Creede Candle*, July 14, 1906, 8; *Colorado Transcript*, January 25, 1906.
385. *Creede Candle*, March 3, 1906, 1; *Whitehorn News*, June 22, 1906.
386. *San Juan Prospector*, September 22, 1906.
387. *Sportsman's Magazine of the West.*
388. *Creede Candle*, August 18, 1906.
389. *Herald Democrat*, October 28, 1906.
390. *Brush Tribune*, March 1, 1907.

391. Gaddy, "Will $150,000 Buy You the Best Sleep You've Ever Had?"
392. *Creede Candle*, May 18, 1907.
393. *Tiger*, January 31, 1908.
394. *Aspen Daily Times*, March 14, 1909.
395. *Salida Record*, January 22, 1909.
396. *Routt County Courier*, March 25, 1909.
397. *Colorado Transcript*, May 6, 1926; *Record Journal of Douglas*, July 15, 1938.
398. Mineral County Records, 12082.
399. *Creede Candle*, November 20, 1909.
400. Ibid., March 19, 1910.
401. Ibid., July 23, 1910.
402. Ibid., January 11, 1913.
403. *Rocky Mountain News*, September 1, 1914.
404. *Walsenburg World*, June 11, 1914.
405. *Routt County Sentinel*, November 13, 1914.
406. *Creede Candle*, August 28, 1915.
407. *San Juan Prospector*, May 20, 1916; September 21, 1917.

Chapter 10

408. Burchard, *Fluorspar Deposits.*
409. Copeland and Vendl, "Wagon Wheel Gap Fluorspar Mine."
410. Ibid.
411. Colorado State Archives, Incorporation Records.
412. Emmons and Larsen, "Hot Springs and the Mineral Deposits"; Copeland and Vendl, "Wagon Wheel Gap Fluorspar Mine"; Seyfarth, *National Register of Historic Places for the Wagon Wheel Gap Fluorspar Mine.*
413. Colorado State Archives, Incorporation Records.
414. Seyfarth, *National Register of Historic Places for the Wagon Wheel Gap Fluorspar Mine.*
415. Copeland and Vendl, "Wagon Wheel Gap Fluorspar Mine."
416. *Creede Candle*, August 20, 1921.
417. Ibid., April 20, 1918.
418. *Colorado Springs Gazette*, February 6, 1921.
419. *Creede Candle*, November 27, 1920.
420. *Colorado Springs Gazette*, April 2, 1921; May 10, 1921.
421. *Creede Candle*, February 5, 1921.
422. Obermeier et al., "Diseases of Lettuce and Tomato."
423. McGinty, *Head Lettuce in Colorado.*
424. *Creede Candle*, December 10, 1921.
425. Ibid., July 22, 1922.
426. Ibid., May 6, 1922.
427. *Aspen Daily Times*, August 20, 1924
428. *Denver Post*, July 29, 1924.

429. Whiteside, *Regulating Danger*, 7.
430. *Colorado Daily Chieftain*, December 9, 1880.
431. Scamehorn, *Pioneer Steelmaker in the West.*
432. Copeland and Vendl, "Wagon Wheel Gap Fluorspar Mine."
433. Ibid.
434. Evans, et al., "Orient Mine."
435. Seyfarth, *National Register of Historic Places for the Wagon Wheel Gap Fluorspar Mine.*
436. Cook, personal communication.
437. Korzeb, "Wagon Wheel Gap Fluorspar Mine."
438. *Steamboat Pilot*, July 20, 1950.
439. Rio Grande Courthouse Records.
440. Seyfarth, *National Register of Historic Places for the Wagon Wheel Gap Fluorspar Mine.*
441. Chapman, personal communication.
442. Korzeb, "Wagon Wheel Gap Fluorspar Mine."
443. Kirkham, personal communication.
444. Ibid.
445. Burchard, "Fluorspar Deposits."
446. Ladoo, *Fluorspar*.
447. Ibid.
448. Kirkham, personal communication.
449. Burchard, "Fluorspar Deposits."
450. Ladoo, *Fluorspar*.
451. Wyley, *CF&I Fluorspar Mill Tour.*
452. Berquist, "CF&I Fluorspar Mill."
453. Ibid.
454. Ibid.
455. Wyley, *CF&I Fluorspar Mill Tour.*

Chapter 11

456. Ryan, *Forgotten Plague*; Murray, "Thousand Years of Pulmonary Medicine."
457. Ryan, *Forgotten Plague*.
458. Murray, "Thousand Years of Pulmonary Medicine."
459. Halpin, "History of T.B."
460. *Colorado Springs Gazette*, June 23, 1915.
461. Ibid., June 21, 1916; July 15, 1917.
462. *Pueblo Chieftain*, July 18, 1918, 7.
463. Cook, personal communication.
464. *Colorado Springs Gazette*, May 11, 1919.
465. Bergey, letter, April 15, 1935.
466. Colorado Hotel and Motel Red Book, "Wagon Wheel Gap."
467. Bergy, letter to son Bill, May 17, 1938.
468. *Denver Post*, June 16, 1943.
469. LaFont, *Homesteaders of the Upper Rio Grande.*

470. *Princeton Alumni Weekly* 55 (1954): 88.
471. Myers, personal communication.
472. Ibid.
473. Wartman and Cochran, personal communication.
474. Cook, personal communication.
475. Colorado Hotel and Motel Red Book, "Wagon Wheel Gap."
476. Cook, personal communication.
477. Ibid.
478. Francis, personal communication.
479. Myers, personal communication.
480. Cook, personal communication.
481. Ibid.
482. Colorado State Board of Stock Inspection Commissioners.
483. Wintz, personal communication.
484. *Princeton Alumni Weekly* 5, no. 1 (Fall 1950): 21.
485. San Luis Valley Rural Electric Cooperative, "4UR Guest Ranch."
486. *University of Denver Magazine*, "Phipps Legacy."
487. Ibid.
488. Heritage Quest.
489. *University of Denver Magazine*, "Phipps Legacy."
490. Ibid.
491. Colorado Business Hall of Fame, "Allan and Gerald Phipps."
492. *University of Denver Magazine*, "Phipps Legacy."
493. Shrake, "Love Affair with a Loser."
494. Heritage Quest.
495. G. Phipps, personal communication.
496. Heritage Quest.
497. Clara Phipps obituary.
498. Colorado Business Hall of Fame, "Allan and Gerald Phipps."
499. Phipps 4UR brochure, 1963.
500. G. Phipps, personal communication.
501. IMDb, "Lauritz Melchior."
502. San Luis Valley Rural Electric Cooperative, "4UR Guest Ranch."
503. *Rocky Mountain News*, September 9, 1972.

Chapter 12

504. Wagner and Wetheril, *Hidden History of the Upper Rio Grande.*
505. Rasmussen, *Katherine Speaks Out on Her History.*
506. Colorado School of Mines communication.
507. Rasmussen, *Katherine Speaks Out on Her History.*
508. Bureau of Land Management, General Land Office Records.
509. *Aspen Daily Times*, July 29, 1900.
510. *Salida Record*, January 3, 1902.

511. Hinshaw, *Crusaders for Wildlife*.
512. Ibid.
513. Ibid.
514. Copeland and Vendl, "Wagon Wheel Gap Fluorspar Mine."
515. *Creede Candle*, April 20, 1918.
516. Haskell, *Lost Lakes Chain of Title.*
517. *Denver Post*, July 29, 1924.
518. Hinshaw, *Crusaders for Wildlife*.
519. Ibid.
520. Ibid.
521. Wagner and Wetheril, *Hidden History of the Upper Rio Grande.*
522. Rasmussen, *Katherine Speaks Out on Her History.*
523. Haskell, *Lost Lakes Chain of Title.*
524. Davis, *Inspection of Lower Lost Lake Reservoir Dam.*
525. Leavell, Memorandum to Ed Wintz.
526. Ibid., letter to the Office of the State Engineer.
527. Ibid., letter to Don Taranto.
528. Ibid., letter to Thomas Lonberger.
529. Bureau of Land Management, General Land Office Records.
530. Vandiver, letter to San Luis Valley Irrigation District.
531. Ogburn, *Charles Leavell v. San Luis Valley Irrigation District and State Water Engineer.*

Epilogue

532. Kinsey, *Thomas Moran.*

BIBLIOGRAPHY

4UR Anglers Advisory, 2018. From the Leavell Family collection.

Aclara Technologies, LLC. "Water Heater Temperature Safety". www.energyguide.com.

Adelman, Casey. Humphreys Ranch manager. Personal communication, 2019.

Aldrich, Charles. *Annals of Iowa, A Historical Quarterly* 8, no. 4 (January 1908).

Atwood, Wallace W., and Kirtley F. Mather. *Physiography and Quaternary Geology of the San Juan Mountains, Colorado.* Washington, D.C.: U.S. Government Printing Office, 1932.

Aurand, H. *Fluorspar Deposits of Colorado.* Denver: Colorado Geological Survey, 1920.

Baer, Steve. Personal communication, 2019.

Baker, James Hutchins, and LeRoy Reuben Hafen. *History of Colorado*. Denver, C: Linderman Company, 1927.

Barrett, James K., and Richard Howard Pearl. *Hydrogeological Data of Thermal Springs and Wells in Colorado.* Denver: Colorado Geological Survey Department of Natural Resources, 1976.

Basch, Seymour, MD. *Indications for the Drinking of Mineral Waters in Gastrointestinal Diseases*. New York: A.R. Elliott Publishing, 1909.

Bauer, William H., James L. Ozment and John H. Willard. *Colorado Post Offices 1859–1989.* Golden: Colorado Railroad Museum, 1990.

Bellamy, Lauretta Moloney. "Wagon Wheel Gap." *San Luis Valley Historian* 7, no. 1 (1975): 39.

Bennett, Mark, ed. *History of the Louisiana Purchase Exposition: The St. Louis World's Fair of 1904.* St. Louis, MO: Universal Exposition Publishing, 1905.

Bergey, Ellwood. Letter to Son Bill at the New Mexico Military Institute, April 15, 1935.

———. Letter to Son Bill at the New Mexico Military Institute, May 17, 1938.

Berquist, Robert. "CF&I Fluorspar Mill and Mine Complex at Wagon Wheel Gap." Personal communication, 2017.

Bethke, P.M. "Mineralization in the Eastern San Juan Mountains." In *The Eastern San Juan Mountains: Their Geology, Ecology, and Human History*, edited by R. Blair and G. Bracksieck, 39–60. Boulder: University Press of Colorado, 2011.

Blair, R., and M. Gillam. "Geomorphic History of the San Juan Mountains." In *The Eastern San Juan Mountains: Their Geology, Ecology, and Human History*, edited by R. Blair and G. Bracksieck, 61–78. Boulder: University Press of Colorado, 2011.

Blair, R., H. Dixon, K. Miskell-Gerhardt, M. Gillam and S. White. "Eastern San Juan Mountains Points of Interest Guide." In *The Eastern San Juan Mountains: Their Geology, Ecology, and Human History*, edited by R. Blair and G. Bracksieck, 243–98. Boulder: University Press of Colorado, 2011.

Bosa, Ashley. Geologist, personal communication, 2019.

Britain, Howard, son of Ad Britain. Personal communication, 2019.

Burchard, E.F. "Fluorspar Deposits in Western United States." *American Institute of Mining and Metallurgy Engineers Technical Publication* no. 500 (1933).

Bureau of Land Management. General Land Office Records. U.S. Dept. of the Interior. www.glorecords.blm.gov.

Caine, J.S., and A.B. Wilson. "The Hydrogeology of the San Juan Mountains." In *The Eastern San Juan Mountains: Their Geology, Ecology, and Human History*, edited by R. Blair and G. Bracksieck, 79–98. Boulder: University Press of Colorado, 2011.

Cappa, J., and C.A. Wallace. *RS-44 Geology and Mineral Resources of Saguache County, Colorado.* Denver: Colorado Geological Survey, Division of Minerals and Geology, Department of Natural Resources, 2007.

Carrillo, Richard. "Spanish Exploration in Southeastern Colorado, 1590–1790." Colorado Encyclopedia, coloradoencyclopedia.org.

Carter, Clive. *Denver & Rio Grande Western Depots.* Vol. 2. N.p.: self-published, 2013.

Cather, S. "Laramide Orogeny in Central and Northern New Mexico and Southern Colorado." In *The Geology of New Mexico: A Geologic History*, edited by G.H. Mack and K.A. Giles, 203–48. Canada: New Mexico Geological Society, 2004.

Chapman, Mary Mortimer. Personal communication, 2019.

Clara Phipps obituary. www.legacy.com.

Cochran, Chad. Wagon Wheel Gap area grazing lease holder. Personal communication, 2019.

Colorado Business Hall of Fame. "Allan and Gerald Phipps." coloradobusinesshalloffame.org.

Colorado College. *Analysis of Wagon Wheel Gap Waters, 1904.* From the Leavell Family collection.

Colorado Encyclopedia. "Creede Railroad." coloradoencyclopedia.org.

Colorado Geological Survey. "Calderas." coloradogeologicalsurvey.org.

Colorado Historic Newspapers Collection. coloradohistoricnewspapers.org.

Colorado Hotel and Motel Red Book and Directory. "Wagon Wheel Gap." Mineral Co. Wagon Wheel Ranch, Arthur & Geneva Sharp, Owners & Mgrs. (Mid-June through September).

Colorado Parks and Wildlife. "2019 Colorado Fishing." cpw.state.co.us.

Colorado School of Mines Registrar's Office. Personal communication, May 2019.

Colorado State Archives, Incorporation Records. 1313 Sherman St., Room 1B-20, Denver, Colorado, 80203.

———. Wagon Wheel Gap Hot Springs Company, October 7, 1877. Certificate of Incorporation, October 20, 1877.

Colorado State Board of Stock Inspection Commissioners, Denver. *Colorado Brand Book*, November 10, 1948.

Colorado State Business Directory, Sixth Annual Volume. Denver, CO: J.A. Blake, 1880.

Columbia University. "Glauber's Salt." encyclopedia.com.

Colville, R.M. "Timeline." *San Luis Valley Historian* 1, no. 1 (January 1969): 16–17.

Cook, Edward Han, 4UR guest from Oklahoma since 1945. Transcribed interview, 1990s. From the Leavell Family Collection.

Copeland, James B., and Mark A. Vendl. "The Wagon Wheel Gap Fluorspar Mine." *Mining History Journal* 18 (2011): 49–65.

Croffut, George A. *Croffut's Grip-sack Guide to Colorado*. Vol. 2. Omaha, NE: Overland Publishing, 1885.

Crook, James K., AM, MD. *The Mineral Waters of the United States and Their Therapeutic Uses.* New York: Lea Brothers & Company, 1899.

Cunningham, Sandy. "Western Hospitality Meets Laid-Back Fun." Outside GO, outsidego.com.

Davis, Paul B. *Inspection of Lower Lost Lake Reservoir Dam*. Davis Engineering, May 17, 1987.

Davlin, Doug. Personal communication, 2019.

Dawes, Charles G. *Notes as Vice President, 1928–1929*. Boston: Little, Brown and Company, 1935.

Delaney, Robert W. *The Southern Ute People*. Phoenix, AZ: Indian Tribal Series, 1974.

Denison, Charles. *Rocky Mountain Health Resorts; An Analytical Study of High Altitudes in Relation to the Arrest of Chronic Pulmonary Disease.* Boston: Houghton, Osgood and Company, 1880.

Denver and Rio Grande Railroad. *Tourist's Handbook, Descriptive of Colorado, New Mexico and Utah*. Washington, D.C.: Office of the Librarian, 1896.

Dooley, Kirk. "2009 Creede People of the Year: Nell and Ed." *Creede Magazine*, Spring 2009, 12–15.

Dooley, William "Bill." Personal communication, Creede, Colorado, 2018.

Dunlap, Annette B. *Charles Gates Dawes: A Life*. Evanston, IL: Northwestern University Press, 2016.

Eberhardt, Perry. *Guide to the Colorado Ghost Towns and Mining Camps*. 4th edition. Athens, OH: Swallow Press, 1981.

Elliott, Thad. Grandson of Thaddeus Elliott. Personal communication, 2019.

Ellis, Erl H. "Early-Day Hinsdale County Post Offices and Managers." Personal communication with Erl H. Ellis, February 14, 1975. Letter.

———. "Postmasters in Mineral County, after 1892." Personal communication with Erl H. Ellis, April 19, 1975. Letter.

Emmons, William Harvey, and E.S. Larsen. "The Hot Springs and the Mineral Deposits of Wagon Wheel Gap, Colorado." *Economic Geology* 8, no. 3 (April 1913): 235–46.

Espinosa, Fred. "Del Norte—Its Past and Present." *Colorado Magazine* 1, no. 3 (June 1928): 95–102.

Evans, Marjorie Woodard, J. Robert Outerbridge, Elaine Woodard and John Marold Woodard. "The Orient Mine and the Big Cave-In." *San Luis Valley Historian* 20, no. 2 (1988).

Fossett, Frank. *Colorado, Its Gold and Silver Mines, Farms and Stock Ranges, and Health and Pleasure Resort, 1876–1880: Tourist's Guide to the Rocky Mountains*. New York: C.G. Crawford, 1880.

Fowler, Jacob. *The Journal of Jacob Fowler: Narrating an Adventure from Arkansas through the Indian Territory, Oklahoma, Kansas, Colorado, and New Mexico, to the Sources of Rio Grande del Norte, 1821–22*. Edited, with notes, by Elliott Coues. New York: F.P. Harper, 1898.

Frame, Paul W. "Radioactive Curative Devices and Spas." *Oak Ridger*, November 5, 1989.

Francis, Jim. Longtime guest at the 4UR, personal communication, 2019.

Fraser, W.B. *State of Colorado Game and Fish Regulations*. Colorado State Game and Fish Commissioner, April 11, 1917, Colorado Parks and Wildlife.

Gaddy, James. "Will $150,000 Buy You the Best Sleep You've Ever Had?" *Bloomberg*, December 2, 2016. bloomberg.com.

Gazetteer for Scotland. "Sir James Key Caird, 1837–1916." scottish-places.info.

Getz, William. Personal communication. Various, 2018 and 2019.

Gjellum, Dr. George Robert. Son of Dr. Arthur B. Gjellum. Personal communication, October 30, 2018.

Gonzales, D.A., and K.E. Karlstrom. "A Legacy of Mountains Past and Present in the San Juan Region." In *The Eastern San Juan Mountains: Their Geology, Ecology, and Human History*, edited by R. Blair and G. Bracksieck, 3–16. Boulder: University Press of Colorado, 2011.

Hafen, LeRoy R., and Ann W. Hafen, eds. *The Diaries of William Henry Jackson, Frontier Photographer: With the Hayden Surveys to the Central Rockies, 1873, and to the Utes and Cliff Dwellings, 1874*. Glendale, CA: A.H. Clark Company, 1959.

———. *Fremont's Fourth Expedition: A Documentary Account of the Disaster of 1848–1849, with Diaries, Letters, and Reports by Participants in the Tragedy, v. 11*. Glendale, CA: A.H. Clark Company, 1960.

Hall, Frank. *History of the State of Colorado from Prehistory to 1890*. N.p.: Rocky Mountain Historical Co., 1895.

Halpin, Evelyn H. "The History of TB in the U.S., Tuberculosis Mortality in the United States, 1946." *Public Health Reports (1896–1970)* 63, no. 32 (August 1948): 1029–45.

Hargraves, Orin. "All About My Mother." www.orinhargraves.com.

Hart, Gerald T. *Appraisal Confederated Ute Indian Lands, Indian Claims Commission Dockett, #327*. MAI Valuation Consultant, Denver, Colorado, April 29, 1874.

Haskell, Alena. *Lost Lakes Chain of Title.* Hinsdale Title Company, January 2, 2019.

Heritage Quest. ancestryheritagequest.com. HeritageQuest® Online is a registered trademark of ProQuest, LLC.

Hinsdale County Records, Lake City, Colorado.

Hinshaw, Glen A. *Crusaders for Wildlife*. Ouray, CO: Western Reflections Publishing, 2000.

History.com. "Treaty of Guadalupe Hidalgo." A&E Television Networks, November 9, 2009. www.history.com.

Hogan, Mary. "Brook Trout Life Cycle." https://sites.google.com/site/tictroutintheclassroom/brook-trout-life-cycle.

Horn, Jon. "Brunot Agreement." Colorado Encyclopedia, coloradoencyclopedia.org.

———. *National Register of Historic Places for the Ute-Ulay Mine and Mill.* United States Department of the Interior, 2017.

Howard, George. *Diary of San Juan Travels, 1872*. Transcription by Frances Jacobs, Creede Historical Society, 1987.

Hubbard, Arthur. "Letter from Arthur Hubbard [Alonzo Hubbard's son]." *San Luis Valley Historian* 8, no. 2 (1976): 18.

Hulen, J. Field Geologic Summaries for Core Holes CCM-2 (Airport 1-6) and CCM-1 (Josselkus 1-10). *Creede Scientific Drilling Project Report ESL-920111-TR*, 1992.

Ingersoll, Earnest. *The Crest of the Continent*. Glorieta, NM: Rio Grande Press, 1883.

Internet Movie Database. "Lauritz Melchior." www.imdb.com.

Izaak Walton League of America. "History & Mission." www.iwla.org.

Jacobs, Janis. *Ribs of Silver; Hearts of Gold.* Vol. 2. 1st ed. Creede, CO: Creede Historical Society, 1994.

Kinsey, Joni. *Thomas Moran and the Surveying of the American West.* Washington, D.C.: Smithsonian Institution Press, 2012.

Kirkham, Robert M. Personal communication regarding fluorspar mine reclamation, April 2019. Robert M. Kirkham, PG, CPG, GeoLogical Solutions, Alamosa, Colorado.

Kirkus Reviews. "*Wild Animals of the Five Rivers Country*, by George Cory Franklin." www.kirkusreviews.com.

Korzeb, Stanley L. "The Wagon Wheel Gap Fluorspar Mine, Mineral County, Colorado." *Mineralogical Record* 24, no. 1 (January–February 1993): 23–29.

Ladoo, Raymond B. *Fluorspar: Its Mining, Milling, and Utilization*. Washington, D.C.: Department of Commerce, Bureau of Mines, Government Printing Office, 1927.

LaFont, John. *The Homesteaders of the Upper Rio Grande.* Birmingham, AL: Oxmoor Press, 1971.

LaMorte, Wayne, MD, PhD, MPH. *Annual Mortality from Pulmonary Tuberculosis in England and Wales.* Boston University School of Public Health, May 5, 2017. Used with permission.

Lands of America. "1,880 Acres in Mineral County, Colorado."

Larsen, D., and P. Lipman. "Exploring the Ancient Volcanic and Lacustrine Environments of the Oligocene Creede Caldera and Environs, San Juan

Mountains, Colorado." In S. Keller & M. Morgan, *Unfolding the Geology of the West*, edited by S. Keller and M. Morgon, 1–40. Boulder, CO: Geological Society of American Field Guide, 2016.

Leavell, Charles H. Letter to Don Taranto, regarding Lower Lost Lakes dam repair. October 22, 1987. From the Leavell Family Collection.

———. Letter to the Office of the State Engineer, Division of Water Resources regarding the Lower Lost Lakes dam. August 31, 1987. From the Leavell Family Collection.

———. Letter to Thomas Lonberger, USFS Special Use Permit for Lower Lost Lakes Dam repair. September 18, 1987. From the Leavell Family Collection.

———. Memorandum to Ed Wintz, Lower Lost Lakes Dam. July 1, 1987. From the Leavell Family Collection.

Licht, Sidney Herman. *Medical Hydrology*. New Haven, CT: Elizabeth Licht, 1963.

Lipman, P.W. "The Central San Juan Caldera Cluster: Regional Volcanic Framework." In *Ancient Lake Creede: Its Volcano-Tectonic Setting, History of Sedimentation, and Relation of Mineralization in the Creede Mining District*, edited by P. Bethke and R.E. Hay, 9–71. Geological Society of America Special Paper 356, 2000.

———. *Geologic Map of the Central San Juan Caldera Cluster, Southwestern Colorado*. U.S. Geological Survey, 2006.

Lund, John W. *Balneological Use of Thermal Waters*. Klamath Falls: Geo-Heat Center, Oregon Institute of Technology, n.d.

May, Stephen J. *A Kingdom of Their Own. The Story of the Palmers of Glen Eyrie.* Boulder, CO: Johnson Books, 2016.

McCartney, Laton. *The Teapot Dome Scandal*. New York: Random House, 2008.

McClaren, Thomas. *Blueprints for Modernization of Wagon Wheel Gap: Barn and Springs*. 1902. From the Leavell Family Collection.

McGinty, R.A. *Head Lettuce in Colorado.* The Colorado Experiment Station, Agricultural Division, Bulletin 283, March 1923.

Mineral County Records, Mineral County Courthouse, Creede, Colorado.

Murray, John F. "A Thousand Years of Pulmonary Medicine: Good News and Bad." *European Respiratory Journal* 17 (2001): 558–65.

Myers, Kate. Granddaughter of Arthur Sharp Jr. Personal communication, 2019.

National Historic Register Program designation for the Thornton Depot. https://npgallery.nps.gov.

Nesdale, Sheldon. "5 Therapeutic Benefits From Hot Spring Pools You Didn't Know You Were Getting" nzhotpools.co.nz.

Niemeyer, Felix von. *Clinical Lectures on Pulmonary Phthisis* (1868). Whitefish, MT: Kessinger Legacy Reprints, 2010.

Nossaman, Allen. *Many More Mountains, Volume 1: Silverton's Roots.* Denver, CO: Sundance Publications, 1989.

———. *Many More Mountains, Volume 2: Ruts into Silverton.* Denver, COL Sundance Books, 1993.

Obermeier, C.J. Sears, H. Y. Liu, K. Schlueter, E. Ryder, J. Duffus, S. Koike and G. Wisler. "Diseases of Lettuce and Tomato Caused by Tombusviruses in the Western United States." *Phytopathology* 91, no. 8 (August 2001): 797–806.

Ogburn, Robert W. Judgement and Decree: *Charles Leavell vs. San Luis Valley Irrigation District and State Water Engineer.* District Court, Water Division No. 3, State of Colorado. February 28, 1992. From the Leavell Family Collection.

Pangborn, J.G. *Picturesque B. and O. Baltimore and Ohio Railroad Company*. Chicago: Knight and Leonard, 1882.

———. *The Rocky Mountain Tourist: Arkansas Valley and San Juan Guide.* Chicago: Knight and Leonard, 1878.

Parrish, Nancy. *WASP in Their Own Words: An Illustrated History*. Waco, TX: Wings Across America Publications, 2010.

Phipps 4UR brochure, 1963. From the Leavell Family Collection.

Phipps, Graham. Grandson of Lawrence C. Phipps. Personal communication, 2019.

Phipps, Graham, and Tony Phipps. "The La Garita Club—How It All Began." Presentation to the Creede Historical Society, 2008.

Phipps, Tony. Grandson of Lawrence C. Phipps. Personal communication, November 6, 2018.

Poland Spring. polandspring.com.

Prabook. "Adair Wilson." prabook.com.

Ralston, Larry. "William Jackson Palmer." Presentation to the Longmont, Colorado Senior Center, 2013. historicdenver.org.

Rasmussen, Katherine. Eldest daughter of Shrive Collins. *Katherine Speaks Out on Her History.* 1981. From the Leavell Family Collection.

Rasmussen, Stephen. *The Rio Grande's La Veta Pass Route.* Burlington, VT: Evergreen Press, 2000.

Richards, Eric. *Britannia's Children: Emigration from England, Scotland, Wales and Ireland, since 1600.* London: Hambledon, 2004

Richmond, Pat. "The La Loma Settlements." *San Luis Valley Historian* 5, nos. 2, 3 (1973).

———. *The Story of La Loma de San Jose, Rio Grande County's First Settlement: A Description of the Site Excavation and the Story of the Fourteen Founding Families as Revealed through the Diary of Juan Bautista Silva.* Crestone, CO: P.J. Richmond, 1997.

———. *Trail to Disaster*. Denver: Colorado Historical Society, 1990.

Ridgeway, Arthur. "The Stony Pass Road." *Colorado Magazine* 16 (March 1939).

Rio Grande County Courthouse. Warranty Deed, No. 5068, book 7, page 631, September 24, 1881. Rio Grande County Courthouse, Del Norte, Colorado.

———. Warranty Deed, No. 6304, book 12, page 216, January 2, 1883. Rio Grande County Courthouse, Del Norte, Colorado.

Rio Grande Water Conservancy District and Wagon Wheel Gap Reservoir, meeting minutes, December 1, 1941. Committee for Wagon Wheel Gap Reservoir, Monte Vista, Colorado.

Root-Bernstein, Robert, and Michèle Root-Bernstein. *Honey, Mud, Maggots and Other Medical Marvels.* Boston: Houghton Mifflin, 1997.

Ruffner, Lieutenant E.H. *Report of a Reconnaissance of the Ute Country Made in the Year 1873*. Washington, D.C.: Government Printing Office, 1874.

Ryan, Frank, MD. *The Forgotten Plague: How the Battle Against Tuberculosis Was Won—And Lost.* Boston: Little Brown and Company, 1992.

San Luis Valley Rural Electric Cooperative. "4UR Guest Ranch—A Special Place." *The Newsboy* 19, no. 7 (July 1994): 1, 4, 5.

———. "The Depot at Wagon Wheel Gap." *The Newsboy* 39, no. 3 (March 2014): 3–5.

San Luis Valley Water Conservancy District, Alamosa. http://slvwcdco1.qwestoffice.net/3501.html.

Scamehorn, Lee. *A.E. Humphreys and Sons: Entrepreneurs of Western Resource Development.* Denver: Colorado Historical Society, 1984.

———. *Pioneer Steelmaker in the West: The Colorado Fuel and Iron Company, 1892–1903.* Boulder, CO: Pruett Publishing, 1976.

Seyfarth, Jill. *National Register of Historic Places for the Wagon Wheel Gap Fluorspar Mine.* United States Department of the Interior, listed September 26, 2019.

Shrake, Edwin. "Love Affair with a Loser." *Sports Illustrated*, March 29, 1965. si.com/vault.

Smith, Gene. "In Search of 'Black Jack' Pershing." *American Heritage* 63, no. 3 (Fall 2018).

Smithsonian Institution Global Volcanism Program. "Volcanoes of the World." https://volcano.si.edu/gvp_votw.cfm.

Steen, Pete, and Mildred Evaskovich, Mildred. *Transcription of a Diary kept by U.S. Forest Service Rangers Stationed at Wagon Wheel Gap, August 1908 through October 1909.* Original housed at the Rio Grande National Forest Supervisor's Office, Monte Vista, Colorado. 2018.

Steven, T.A. and P.W. Lipman. *Calderas of the San Juan Volcanic Field, Southwestern Colorado*. Washington D.C.: U.S. Geological Survey, 1976.

Stone, Wilbur Fiske. *History of Colorado.* Vol. 3. Chicago: S.J. Clarke Publishing, 1918.

Strochlic, Nina. "We Have a Painter to Thank for Yellowstone." *National Geographic.* nationalgeographic.com.

Thomas MacLaren School. "Who Was Thomas MacLaren?" maclarenschool.org.

Toll, Charles. "Letter from Wagon Wheel Gap, 1876." *Colorado Magazine* 33, no. 2 (April 1956).

———. Volcanic Hazards Program. https://volcanoes.usgs.gov/vsc/glossary/vei.html.

University of Denver Magazine. "The Phipps Legacy." March 1, 2011. magazine-archive.du.edu.

University of Virginia. "Early Research and Treatment of Tuberculosis in the 19th Century." Historical Collections at the Claude Moore Health Sciences Library, http://exhibits.hsl.virginia.edu/alav/tuberculosis.

U.S. Forest Service. "History and Culture of the San Luis Valley Area." www.fs.usda.gov.

U.S. Geological Survey. "Historical Topographic Map Explorer." historicalmaps.arcgis.com/usgs.

Vandiver, Steve. Letter to San Luis Valley Irrigation District Regarding Lost Lakes Priority. November 17, 1990.

Wagner, S.E., and C.A. Wetherill. *Hidden History of the Upper Rio Grande*. Charleston, SC: Arcadia Publishing, 2017.

Walsh, Elaine Colvin. *The Grande Dame of Quality Hill*. Denver: Volunteers of the Colorado Historical Society, 1991.

Walton, Izaak. *The Compleat Angler*. London: Richard Marriot, 1653.

Warmflash, David. "Could Small Amounts of Radiation Be Good for You? It's Complicated." *Discover*, April 6, 2015. discovermagazine.com

Wartman, Tom. Grandson of Tom Wartman. Personal communication, 2019.

Wason, Harriet L. *Rhymes of the Rockies, or What Poets have Found to Say of the Beautiful Scenery on the Denver and Rio Grande Railroad, the Scenic Line of the World.* Chicago: Poole Brothers, 1887.

WebMD. "Understanding Rheumatic Fever—the Basics." webmd.com.

Weiser, Kathy. "Chief Ouray—A Man of Peace." Legends of America, updated September 2018. legendsofamerica.com.

———. "Navajo Long Walk to the Bosque Redondo." Legends of America, updated June 2018. legendsofamerica.com.

Weisse, M. "Phipps La Garita Ranch." weisseguys.blogspot.com.

Wheeler, First Lieutenant George M. *Geographical and Geological Explorations and Surveys West of the One Hundredth Meridian*. Vol. 3, *Geology*. Washington, D.C.: Government Printing Office, 1875.

Whiteside, James. *Regulating Danger: The Struggle for Mine Safety in the Rocky Mountain Coal Industry.* Lincoln: University of Nebraska Press, 1990.

Wilkins, Thurman. *Thomas Moran: Artist of the Mountains*. Norman: University of Oklahoma Press, 1966.

Williams, F. and H. Chronic. *Roadside Geology of Colorado*. Missoula, MT: Mountain Press Publishing Company, 2014.

Wintz, Kim. Son of Ed Wintz. Personal communication, 2019.

Wright, John G. *Rocky Mountain Divide: Saving and Selling the West.* Austin: University of Texas Press, 1993.

Wyley, Kenneth. *CF&I Fluorspar Mill Tour with Gene Dooley and Ed Johnson.* Video recording, 2007.

———. Personal communication, Creede, Colorado, 2019.

Wyley, Nell. "Cottonwood Cove: From the Beginning, with Bibs and Nell Wyley." Wyley Family collection. 2010.

INDEX

D

E

F

G

H

I

J

K

L

M

N

P

R

S

T

W

Z